Screening Nature and Nation

Screening Nature and Nation

The Environmental Documentaries of the National Film Board, 1939–1974

MICHAEL D. CLEMENS

◊ AU PRESS

Copyright © 2022 Michael D. Clemens

Published by AU Press, Athabasca University
1 University Drive, Athabasca, AB T9S 3A3
https://doi.org/10.15215/aupress/9781771993357.01

Cover image: Still from *The Enduring Wilderness* (1963). Used with permission of
the National Film Board.
Cover design by Derek Thornton
Printed and bound in Canada

Library and Archives Canada Cataloguing in Publication

Title: Screening nature and nation: the environmental documentaries of the
National Film Board, 1939–1974 / Michael D. Clemens.
Names: Clemens, Michael D., author.
Description: Includes bibliographical references.
Identifiers: Canadiana (print) 20220156476 | Canadiana (ebook) 20220156603 |
        ISBN 9781771993357 (softcover) | ISBN 9781771993364 (PDF) |
        ISBN 9781771993371 (EPUB)
Subjects: LCSH: National Film Board of Canada—History—20th century. |
        LCSH: Nature films—Canada—History and criticism. | LCSH: Nature
        films—Production and direction—Canada—History—20th century. |
        LCSH: Nature films—Social aspects—Canada—History—20th century.
Classification: LCC PN1995.9.N38 C54 2022 | DDC 791.43/660971—dc23

This book has been published with the help of a grant from the Federation
for the Humanities and Social Sciences, through the Awards to Scholarly
Publications Program, using funds provided by the Social Sciences and
Humanities Research Council of Canada. We also acknowledge the financial
support of the Government of Canada through the Canada Book Fund (CBF)
for our publishing activities and the assistance provided by the Government of
Alberta through the Alberta Media Fund.

Canadä   Alberta
               Government

Contents

Acknowledgements

Writing can be a lonely endeavour. I am fortunate enough to have a community of people in my life who make the journey far less solitary.

This book began as my PhD dissertation in the Department of History at McMaster University. I would like to thank the members of my doctoral committee: Michael Egan, Ken Cruikshank, and Tracy McDonald. In particular, I want to acknowledge my supervisor, Michael, who provided me with the right dosage of intellectual insight and emotional encouragement throughout the process. I am very grateful for his support and friendship. And to the rest of the department, thank you for being such gracious colleagues.

I would also like to recognize the various institutions that permitted me to conduct my research. Thank you to the many archivists and librarians who helped me dig out obscure documents and other vital materials for the dissertation. In particular, I want to recognize André D'Ulisse, the head archivist at the National Film Board. André provided me with exemplary assistance. His tireless work and excitement about the project made this book possible. It has also been a pleasure working with Athabasca University Press. I would like to thank Connor Houlihan and the two anonymous reviewers for their insightful feedback.

These acknowledgements would be incomplete if I did not mention Caleb Wellum and Dave Szostak for their friendship and discerning eyes. Many of the ideas in this book were hashed out at the "Wallace" and other local haunts.

Finally, I could not have completed this project without the love and support of my family. Thank you, Mom and Dad. You have been a constant support in my life. Mathew and Melissa and Matt and Jackie also deserve credit for keeping me grounded. Titus's boundless energy was likewise a great source of joy and inspiration. I also have been blessed with wonderful in-laws. Rick, Karen, Laura, Grace, and Eric have been steadfastly patient and kind.

This book is dedicated to Jayne. When things seemed to be unbearable, she pierced the darkness. When things were chaotic, she brought peace. I love you.

Introduction

Established in 1939 by the federal government to be the "eyes of the country," the National Film Board of Canada (NFB) has become one of the most recognizable and decorated contributors to Canadian cinema.[1] Since its founding, the NFB has produced more than thirteen thousand documentaries, animated shorts, and feature films and won over five thousand awards, including several Academy Awards. Although its output has waned in recent years because of budgetary cutbacks and the rise of commercial filmmaking, the NFB remains a cherished cultural institution in Canada.

One of the most popular genres for the NFB has been the nature documentary. Viewers have loved these works for their educational value and meditative, almost wistful, style. For many Canadians who grew up in the twentieth century, NFB nature documentaries were an antidote to the grotesque commercialism of American cinema. When asked about the NFB's *Hinterland Who's Who* television spots that aired in the 1960s, wildlife painter Robert Bateman remarked that "this kind of programming [was] extremely important, especially for youth, because there [was] a dreadful trend towards 'being cool.'" NFB pictures, in contrast, were "uncool" in that they did not celebrate "consumerism, wastefulness, and destructiveness." Their real worth was that they helped "rekindle an interest in nature," Bateman observed.[2] Indeed, it was this unironic and elegiac aesthetic that appealed to domestic audiences. NFB nature documentaries quietly revealed a hidden world of beauty and complexity.

Screening Nature and Nation tells the story of how the NFB represented nature and how its depictions interacted with Canadian ideas
about the environment in the twentieth century. The films discussed
in this book span from 1939 to 1974 and represent a range of interpretations of nature. Nature films are investigated as they relate
to the Canadian government's nation-building project. Beginning
in 1939 and ending in the mid-1960s, NFB works classified nature in
ways that aligned with government values concerning national identity, progress, and the exploitation of natural resources. There are
striking continuities in these early films, but their discourses on the
environment also changed slightly over time, reflecting the shifting institutional, political, and cultural contexts in which they were
produced.

The 1960s was a pivotal decade for the NFB, as it was for most
cultural institutions. Even though NFB filmmakers were employed
by the government, many of them endeavoured to use their cameras
to engage with broader social concerns rather than merely propagate
government views. *Screening Nature and Nation* zooms in on cases of
ideological conflict in which NFB documentarians explored alternative visions of nature. A closer inspection of the environmental films
produced in the 1960s and 1970s reveals that NFB representations
of nature were sometimes radical texts that contradicted the state-
centred themes of the 1940s and 1950s.

Many young people growing up in Canada watched NFB pictures about
ecology, biology, conservation, natural resources, and geography as
part of their schooling.[3] General audiences, young and old, also gathered to watch NFB documentaries about nature in movie theatres,
town halls, and other local community venues. Sometimes they were
shown before the feature presentations; other times they were the
feature presentations. Canadian ambassadors even exhibited NFB
documentaries about the environment in other countries. Diplomats
believed that the evocative images and straightforward narration of

these moving pictures effectively advertised the natural bounty of Canada to foreigners looking for a place to put down roots.

It is easy to see why people regard NFB filmmaking as an artistic venture that pushed the boundaries of national cinema. Norman McLaren's vivid animated shorts, Alanis Obomsawin's stirring documentaries, and Zacharias Kunuk's sensational *Atanarjuat: The Fast Runner* are often cited by proud Canadians and movie critics as shining examples of the country's vibrant film culture. Nature films too are celebrated as extraordinary works of nonfiction cinema. Bill Mason's *Paddle to the Sea* (1966) and Peter Lynch's *Project Grizzly* (1996) are among the best and most thought-provoking films about nature ever produced in Canada.

These excellent movies, however, tended to be outliers. Most NFB documentaries, including those about the environment, were works of public information that supported the principles and political ambitions of the state. When the federal government established the NFB in 1939, it did so with the civic-minded aim of producing films in the "national interest" and "interpret[ing] Canada to Canadians and other nations."[4] The word *interpret* had a narrow meaning for the government, at least early on. Filmmaking was imagined by the state as a tool for national planning and instruction.[5] Burdened with the task of uniting a multicultural population stretched across a continent, the government hoped that the NFB would "bring coherence to a divided polity" by defining the parameters of citizenship and national identity.[6] Shifts in documentary filmmaking practices in the 1950s and institutional changes in the 1960s ushered in new and bolder forms of cinematic expression. Even so, the paternal voice of the government endured in NFB cinema. Regional viewpoints, oppositional voices, and avant-garde forms of moviemaking were incorporated into nation-building discourses on ideal citizenship and the establishment of the welfare state.[7]

As a government institution tasked with producing and distributing both entertaining and educational cinema, the NFB offers a fascinating look into state "interpretations" of nature. The documentaries reveal an official attempt to represent nature and govern Canadians' relationship with the land. NFB filmmakers can thus be seen as cinematic ambassadors of the state, encouraging audiences to "look here," "pay attention to this story," or "think about nature in this way."[8]

What did official representations of nature look like? What purposes did they serve? In general, NFB films cultivated *a sense of belonging* through cinematic images of nature. Canadians, the NFB proclaimed, were a people whose history and political culture were defined by their relationship with the country's vast geography. Whether it was a government-sponsored documentary about forestry or an ethnographic film on cod fishing in Gaspé, an NFB movie repeatedly proclaimed that nature was a dominant force in Canadian history and culture.

Journalist Bruce Hutchinson summarizes this vision in the introduction to the NFB's 1967 centennial book, *Canada: A Year of the Land*. If one is to "learn the meaning of the nation, all its hopes and fears," he writes, then that person must "look to the land and its secret cargo."[9] It is the land, "not the statute books and legal contracts," that binds the nation together.[10] Hutchinson reasserts a popular argument about Canadian national identity, one that has been championed by politicians, artists, writers, and nationalists since Confederation. To understand what it was to be Canadian, to know what Canada was really like, one had to acknowledge the role that northern nature played in its formation. The proposition that Canada was defined in relation to its geography was valuable for both the NFB and the state because it created what Benedict Anderson calls "imagined communities."[11] Images and stories of nature contributed to a cohesive definition of the nation as a strong and resilient people forged by the refining fire of geography. This brand of Canadian identity was preeminently Anglo and white and excluded alternative ways of thinking about nature, place, and homeland.

NFB cinema supported state attitudes toward nature in other ways too. On a practical level, the NFB instructed audiences about the utilities and constraints of nature and taught them how to exploit the natural world so that the nation could prosper.[12] According to the NFB, nature was an important public commodity, in fact the key to progress. It therefore needed to be safeguarded so that every citizen could enjoy its bounty. For this to happen, the government had to take an active role in managing its protection and development.[13] Canadians thus had to adhere to state instruction if the country was to flourish.

This government vision of nature was most evident in movies produced in the 1940s and 1950s. NFB documentaries in this period strongly endorsed the wise-use ethos of the government, conflating national progress and survival with the industrial exploitation of natural resources. In the early 1940s, for example, NFB pictures argued that timber, ore, wheat, and other raw materials were essential to winning the Second World War. Thus, it was necessary that the country (and its resource industries) embrace modern conservation methods established by the government to ensure the safekeeping of those vital resources.

In the postwar period, NFB films about nature were similarly utilitarian, extolling the virtues of the nation's natural abundance while encouraging its development. Documentaries about agriculture reasoned that for the country to emerge from the Second World War strong and healthy, farmers had to adopt state-authorized measures in their land practices. Doing so, NFB films claimed, would create a more efficient way of farming and increase yields.

Lurking beneath the surface of these state-sponsored documentaries in the 1940s and 1950s were strong undercurrents of high modernism, which James C. Scott defines as "a strong . . . muscle bound version of self-confidence about scientific and technical progress, the expansion of production, the growing satisfaction of humans' needs, the mastery of nature (including human nature), and, above all, the rational design of social order commensurate with the scientific understanding of natural laws."[14] Scott argues that states employ a high modern way of seeing that reduces complexity in

northern spaces. Specifically, ethnographic documentaries about the Inuit validated the government's efforts to modernize and develop the region as a part of mainstream Canada. Finally, depictions of a modern North epitomized state conceptions of the land as a source of scientific knowledge, national wealth, and material progress. Imagining Canadian landscapes as either modern or Indigenous reflected the government's view of faraway geographies. Paralleling the vision of state planners and engineers, NFB cinematography framed social and ecological spaces as static and fixed objects rather than fluid and historically contingent places.

NFB films did not always represent nature from a state perspective, however. The NFB also existed as a platform on which ideas about the definition and meaning of nature were *negotiated* between the government and the public. Indeed, alternative notions of the environment were intertwined with NFB documentaries produced in the 1960s and 1970s. The NFB's official mandate—"to interpret Canada to Canadians and other nations"—can therefore be historicized in a completely different way. Interpretation connotes complexity and subjectivity. Although the state influenced NFB productions, the NFB was more than just a mouthpiece for government values or ideas. In fact, the NFB was a site for dissent and opposition.

Emboldened by the endless possibilities of cinema, filmmakers "interpreted" Canada from a multitude of angles and vantage points. They questioned, ridiculed, or reformulated government attitudes toward the meaning of nature and the state's quest to control it. As a result, the NFB broadened the ecological imagination of Canadians and even inspired an activist environmental movement. Some documentarians asserted that nature was more than just a resource to be exploited; it was also a place of sublime beauty and intrinsic value. Other filmmakers decried the government's reliance on rational planning and science as means of improving nature. Certain directors further claimed that nature was a dynamic and interconnected web in constant flux. There was no such thing as "improving nature."

The first break from government discourses about the environment occurred in 1960 with the release of Larry Gosnell's *Poison, Pests, and People*. Gosnell challenged the belief that Canadians should manipulate the environment just to serve the short-term needs of the agricultural industry. A few years later, NFB documentarians began advocating for a noninstrumentalist appreciation of wilderness environments. Bill Mason, Ernest Reid, and Christopher Chapman used their cameras to exhibit the grandeur of creation and to stress to viewers the importance of protecting the country's last vestiges of wilderness from industrial exploitation.

Discourses on nature continued to evolve in the 1970s. As the NFB supported multicultural voices and diverse perspectives, new works about nature and humans' relationship with it emerged. The most famous was Boyce Richardson's *Cree Hunters of Mistassini* (1974), which recorded the hunting traditions of the James Bay Cree. The film celebrated Indigenous ways of thinking about human and nonhuman relations through Cree hunter Sam Blacksmith, who advocated an ecological way of living characterized by care and humility. *Cree Hunters of Mistassini* contrasted the environmental logic of the state with the dynamic and holistic worldview of the Cree. In doing so, it critiqued the environmentally ruinous James Bay hydroelectric project, a paragon of high modern achievement. The film argued that such efforts destabilized traditional patterns of existence and exposed local ecosystems and traditional cultures to catastrophic changes. More importantly, the film was one of the first works to show that racial inequity was closely tied to environmental destruction.

An investigation of NFB productions provides a new perspective on Canadian attitudes toward and ideas about the environment. Specifically, it contributes to our understanding of how the government tried to mediate Canadians' encounters with nature. Film is a powerful medium capable of shaping our hearts and minds, including our environmental habits. "Cinema," argues Adrian Ivakhiv, "is a machine that produces or discloses [the] world."[20] Through financial support and political clout, the government controlled both the medium and the message, expressing to Canadians in powerful, programmatic language how to engage with the land.

By examining the documentaries of the NFB, we can also glean insights into how other representations of nature were produced in twentieth-century Canada. Filmmakers used their cameras to disagree with and contest official definitions and narratives of nature, and they helped inspire an activist environmental movement. The state frequently used the NFB to define the limits and uses of nature in Canada. Environmentalists and Indigenous filmmakers, however, used the NFB as a platform on which to disparage these official policies and project alternative visions of Canadian ecological relationships.

Screening Nature and Nation takes a historical approach to understanding the relationship between filmmaking and nature.[21] Using formal, stylistic, and narrative elements specific to cinema, the NFB reflected on and helped produce various ways of seeing the natural world. *Screening Nature* also makes a larger point about the importance of film as both a recorder and a shaper of history. Cinema is a rich and diverse archive that reflects our historical attitudes toward the natural world. Its presence in our lives also means that it has a considerable influence on our environmental practices. The films that we watch have the power to shape how we interact with the physical world.[22] Moving pictures of flora, fauna, and terrestrial places contribute to our affective and cognitive relationship with nature. As the German film theorist Siegfried Kracauer once observed, cinema "has a definite bearing on the era into which it is born; that it meets our inmost needs precisely by exposing—for the first time, as it were—outer reality and thus deepening, in Gabriel Marcel's words, our relation to 'this Earth which is our habitat.'"[23]

1

Filming like a State

Canadians must . . . cooperate with the government, for it
is that which ensures there will be sufficient resources in
the future.

—*Water for Prairies*

On 14 September 1943, a small committee from the National Film
Board of Canada (NFB) gathered in downtown Ottawa to discuss
an unusual request made by the Department of Agriculture (DOA).
Earlier that year, the DOA had approached the NFB to make a series
of documentaries about "the relationship of the soil to plant, animal,
and human life."[1] The NFB was taken aback at first. It did not have a
lot of experience making educational movies on the virtues of soil.
Most of its productions up to that point were dramatic newsreels
about the Second World War. Still, it was difficult to ignore such an
invitation. The DOA was an important sponsor of the fledgling
agency, and it had deep pockets.

The committee debated the merits of the DOA's request in the
waning light of that September afternoon. Eventually, the members
resolved to establish an entire production unit devoted to investigating the "urgent phases of Canadian agriculture."[2] In a letter to

Minister of Agriculture James Gardiner, the committee explained that this new division would produce "information films" on a variety of farming subjects, including "rural health and sanitation, care of livestock, weed eradication, animal and plant diseases, farm electrification, horticulture, and farm beautification." Although the committee was confident that the DOA would accept the proposal, it was apprehensive that it might not pass muster with the NFB's governing body, the Ministry of National War (MNW). To avoid a setback (and a squandered funding opportunity), the members shrewdly justified that the agricultural films would be "of great importance to the war effort and to post-war planning."[3] A week later, the MNW permitted the NFB to proceed with the film project. The Agricultural Production Unit (APU) immediately went to work producing a series of vignettes about Canadian agriculture.

The APU yelled its final "cut!" in 1949, but its influence on the NFB reverberated long after that. The unit's popularity with viewers across Canada encouraged the NFB to produce and distribute more documentaries on the environment. In the ensuing years, the NFB made dozens of films about agriculture, wildlife conservation, natural resources, and geography. More importantly, the documentaries of the APU expressed the close bond between NFB filmmaking and government discourse about nature. The APU's resolution to "promote a direct facing of the present and future problems of Canadian agriculture" was informed by the state's desire to make films in the national interest.[4] The country was at war, and invigorating a healthy agricultural sector was a priority for the Liberal government. The relationship between government discourses and NFB production priorities would continue through the 1940s and 1950s. Documentaries about the environment were typically made at the behest of state sponsors that wanted to promote their various policies and initiatives regarding the uses and limits of the natural world. This relationship confined NFB filmmakers to a certain vision of the world, although it did have its benefits. Government patronage kept the lights on and the cameras rolling.

In general, NFB films made between 1940 and 1955 reinforced the state's utilitarian philosophy that nature should be used to strengthen and expand the economy. Films that instructed audiences on how to manage their farms and documentaries that promoted the benefits of a strong (and government-led) resource policy argued that the environment was a gift to be exploited vigorously but wisely.

The specific messages and aesthetic strategies of these works depended on the political and social contexts in which they were produced. During wartime, the NFB distributed a series of natural resource films that supported the government's total mobilization agenda. The documentaries used dramatic voice-over narration and newsreel footage to communicate to viewers the importance of conserving timber, minerals, wheat, and other strategic materials. In the postwar period, NFB documentaries about the environment tended to support the aspirations of the nascent welfare state. Agricultural films, for instance, endorsed government initiatives to improve the social, economic, and environmental conditions of Canadians across the country. The documentaries invited farmers to incorporate modern agricultural techniques, electric technologies, and conservation strategies advocated by government experts. Doing so would improve the lives of farmers and make their land use more efficient. Such improvements would strengthen the economic well-being of the nation. As the Advisory Committee on Post-War Reconstruction explained in its final report, agricultural development was essential for "a balanced and prosperous economy."[5]

NFB documentarians tackled a range of subjects in their films about the environment during this period. Despite their topical differences, the films collectively advanced a state way of seeing nature, in particular the ideology of high modernism. Filmmakers such as APU producer Evelyn Cherry praised the large-scale transformation of nature and the tidy arrangements of simplified resource landscapes. It was no fluke that depictions of a farmer tilling the land with his state-of-the-art tractor, a government officer calculating the circumference of a conifer, and wind passing through crops sprayed with pesticides were some of the most prominent features in NFB cinema during this period. The filmmakers accurately reflected the visions of their Canadian sponsors, who saw social and environmental spaces as things to be streamlined, managed, and exploited.

Wartime and Films about Natural Resources

The association between NFB production priorities and the government was forged from the beginning. Acting on the recommendations of Scottish documentarian John Grierson, the federal government established the NFB to function as an information service to "help Canadians everywhere understand the problems and way of life of Canadians in other parts of the country."[6] Under Grierson, the NFB operated as the voice of the government, teaching, encouraging, and persuading Canadians to comply with its wishes. Documentary filmmaking was a "hammer" that "mold[ed] and pattern[ed] men's actions," explained the film commissioner in an interview during his tenure.[7]

Government influence on NFB filmmaking was the most salient during the Second World War. In 1940, the infant organization was recruited by the MNW to support the war effort. The NFB's commitment to Prime Minister Mackenzie King's total mobilization strategy was further entrenched in October 1941 when an order-in-council designated the minister of national war services as the overseer of the NFB. Over the next five years, the NFB dutifully churned out propaganda films and newsreels series, such as *Canada Carries On* and *World in Action*, each work commanding members of the public to do their part in helping the Allies win the war. Nonmilitary documentaries about food, health, and labour were also drafted into service for their country. Domestic life—how a person cooked, farmed, or saved money—was linked to the overall war effort. To support the individuals fighting overseas, it was vital that all Canadians be mindful about how they lived.[8]

Stylistically, NFB wartime films, in the words of one critic, were "direct to the point of vulgarity."[9] Grierson did not argue the point. In fact, he liked to brag to his colleagues back in England that NFB documentaries were not encumbered by the indignant moralism or rank patriotism that characterized UK movies.[10] NFB films were straightforward, stripped of any cinematic splendour.[11] And that was the point. The films might have been "vulgar," but their simplicity made them perfect vehicles for conveying government ideas and values. NFB films spoke clearly and definitively for the state, telling Canadians what they "needed to know" and how to "do their best by Canada and themselves."[12]

John Grierson's belief that the NFB should broadcast government values shaped how it represented the environment. In wartime documentaries, nature was depicted primarily as an asset to be expropriated and used against the enemy.[13] *Coal Face Canada* (1944) is a perfect example of how the NFB linked the exploitation of the country's natural resources to the success of the war effort.[14] In the film, director Robert Edmonds shows the importance of coal (and the combustible energy it provides) through the eyes of Bruce Adams, an army veteran who has returned home after being honourably discharged from military service. Like his father before him, Adams finds work in a coal mine. "Once a miner, always a miner," he says glumly as he chips away in a dark tunnel.[15] At first, Adams is unhappy with the work. The subterranean environment is stifling, and mining seems to be trivial compared with soldiering on the European battlefield. Over the course of the documentary, however, Adams learns to appreciate the strategic importance of his vocation. Although coal mining is not glamorous, it is nonetheless essential to the military success of the Allies. Adams and others harvest resources used to develop important weapons, such as highly explosive bombs and medical supplies. In this sense, coal miners were presented as indispensable "combatants."

Coal Face Canada's description of the environment as a resource vital to the needs of the nation (domestically and abroad) is typical of NFB films during this period.[16] *The Strategy of Metals* (1941) and *Battle for Oil* (1942) similarly demonstrate how the exploitation of raw materials helps Canada fight overseas. In *Food—Weapons of Conquest* (1941), narrator Lorne Greene bellows that the western prairies are a vast resource that meets the "real food needs of fellow men."[17] Grain nourishes both the Canadian military and its allies, many of whom are experiencing food shortages. *Hands for the Harvest* (1943), a documentary produced for the APU, similarly contends that agrarian resources are crucial to winning the war. The film describes how farmers "of all ages persevere" during wartime. Despite wartime austerity measures, they plow their fields and harvest their crops without complaint because they know that the fruits of their labour will provide Canadian forces with the "energy" to keep fighting.[18]

Although the NFB supported the exploitation of the environment as part of the government's total war strategy, it also recognized that valuable commodities were finite. Indeed, conservation was a central theme in wartime documentaries about resource extraction. Echoing the government's new liberal mandate to actively manage social and environmental spaces, the NFB argued that state-led conservation tactics were essential to maintain a healthy surplus of the country's timber, ore, wildlife, and grain. Conservation films produced during the Second World War typically followed a specific narrative formula. At the start of the documentary, the narrator addresses a problem (a resource shortage). Then the film briefly describes the origin of the issue (either human mismanagement or natural catastrophe). Finally, it concludes with a solution (government intervention, conservation measures, and the application of scientific principles).

Timber Front (1940), one of the first conservation documentaries produced by the NFB, exemplifies this approach. Sponsored by the Lands, Parks and Forests Branch, the film explains that timber resources were "vital" in the "struggle against the enemy" and that managing this commodity was "critical to the war effort."[19] The film beseeches lumber companies to protect the country's forests by adhering to state conservation measures.

Timber Front begins with a folksy chronicle of logging in Canada. "So into the woods plunged the logger, the real North American pioneer, with a capacity for hard work . . . unsurpassed in history," the narrator remarks as men in woolen plaid shirts march across the screen. Logging was not a job for the faint of heart, but it was honest work. With their axes, these brave men "helped build a nation." But the days of the solitary bark skin are long gone, reports the narrator. New technologies and large-scale operations transformed the logging industry in substantial ways. Timber extraction in the middle of the twentieth century was easier and far more efficient than it had been in the nineteenth century. Loggers could clear massive strips of land in an astonishingly short period of time. In the past, the comparatively slower pace of timber extraction meant that the forest could still protect itself from harm. Young saplings were allowed to grow, and certain species were left alone. In this new era of logging, however, forests were cleared en masse. As a result, adjacent forests were more vulnerable to disease, fire, and abuse. By the 1940s, timber resources were rapidly disappearing. Although Canadians were the "owners of 800 million acres of forest land (one-third of the country's geography)," that number was rapidly declining, the film states ominously.[20]

Technology made it easier to cut down trees, but the real culprit behind the depletion of forestry resources was the individual operating the machinery. *Timber Front* declares that human negligence was ultimately to blame for Canada's exhausted timber stands. In a greedy attempt to maximize their yields, industrial logging operations "stripped" Canada's "virgin forests bare." The gendered language was intentional no doubt. Not only did it mirror the wartime propaganda of the government, but also it highlighted the so-called purity and vulnerability of feminine nature. This was rape on a national scale. On cue, the camera cuts to a hellish landscape of gnarled stumps and mud. The ravished countryside is reminiscent of the bombed-out front line in Central Europe. Timber men have left "a trail of scars—deserted mills, and houses, wasted logs, and stumps." In the wake of this "slash and . . . waste," devastating forest fires can erupt, destroying the remaining trees. "Over 46 million dollars are lost" in Porcupine, Ontario, alone, the narrator laments.[21]

The tone of *Timber Front* is melodramatic (and thus tonally consistent with most wartime pictures), but it accurately documents the problem of deforestation in early twentieth-century Canada. Advanced machinery, increased manpower, and a cut and get-out mentality in the forestry industry ravaged the country's woodlands. The situation was serious enough in the 1920s that provincial governments across the country introduced new restrictions on logging activities. Despite nationwide attempts to regulate the resource extraction, loggers continued to mow down Canadian forests at an alarming rate. Anxiety about the health of the country's timber resources peaked in the 1930s. The federal government tried to step in, but timber companies continued to chop down everything in sight.[22] Legislators were helpless in stopping big companies from taking what they wanted. A series of devastating forest fires in the late 1930s did not help the already grim situation. According to a report by the Lands, Parks and Forests Branch published in 1939, tree loss was "considerably above the average of the last ten years."[23] Timber shortage remained a major concern for Canada in the early 1940s. Not only did unrestrained logging activities threaten the health of the country's export economy, but also they imperilled its ability to support the growing needs of the military, which relied on the resource to build shelters, temporary bases, and other wartime infrastructure.

The situation is dire, *Timber Front* declares, but there is a way out of the mess. If Canadian forests are managed wisely, then they will recover. The narrator implores contemporary loggers to embrace a new land ethic of conservation and management and to adopt the sustainable logging methods prescribed by the Canadian government. Although this mindset might limit short-term profits, it will ensure the long-term viability of this national resource. The forests of Canada can be "an immense asset to the future" if they are harvested "scientifically and in a far-sighted manner," Donald Roy Cameron, chief of the Dominion Forest Service, tells a class of young foresters. If the timber industry heeds these words, then the log drive will no longer represent "a slaughter but a carefully managed harvest." There will be no more "scarred and desolate hillsides," just "reserves of beauty, a shelter for wildlife, and a great reservoir of timber sufficient for the needs of the entire world."[24]

Timber Front's proclamation that wise-use management is a panacea for resource exhaustion and environmental ruin is emphatically high modern. The documentary fixates on the conservation strategies and technological and scientific remedies endorsed by the government. Armed with state-of-the-art instruments, experts from the government reduce forests to a ledger of measurements and equations based on their carrying capacity and overall health. The language used in the documentary is telling. "Planes equipped with automatic cameras" record every timber stand within their lines of sight, the film brags. "Propeller[s] and cameras click" as the planes survey the land in a "fraction of time." It takes only a few minutes to capture and then simplify this vast and complex wilderness in black-and-white photographs. These images contain all the information that the foresters need. In the past, loggers and forestry men had to enter into the woods themselves to measure the girth and height of a tree. Not anymore. The photographs captured by the airplane are used to estimate board feet and dollars and cents. The narrator in *Timber Front* goes on to praise the "modern forester." This college-educated individual is a "mathematician in an office," and a pencil is his axe, the film informs viewers. Using trigonometry, he measures the "height of the tree's shadow" in the photograph. With this information, he tells loggers which trees yield the highest economic value and which still need to grow.[25]

The NFB produced many other films about the war effort and the interdependence of natural resources, government conservation strategies, and industry after *Timber Front* was released. Subsequent documentaries focused on the issue of stabilizing economic and natural resources during the war. According to Grierson, it was paramount that the NFB continue to make films that "stimulated greater public effort towards stabilization." In a letter to Donald Gordon, head of the Wartime Information Board (WIB), Grierson explained that the NFB would produce films that tackled the obstacles undermining government stabilization measures—namely, "the lack of cooperation from industry." The problem was not that "control programs were inadequate," Grierson explained. Quite the contrary—they were essential in ensuring that the country did not collapse economically or starve from resource shortages. But Grierson believed that industry compliance was key if economic and resource stabilization was to be achieved. Resource industries needed to observe government conservation measures and operate prudently with the well-being of the country in mind. The main purpose of such documentaries was to point out that "stabilization is the people's program" and that "without their full understanding and cooperation it cannot achieve its maximum."[26]

The most common NFB stabilization films were about agriculture and manufacturing. For many farmers trying to make a living in the 1940s, the Second World War created a number of challenges. The two most pressing problems that they faced during the war were labour shortages and equipment deficiencies. Young farmhands and able-bodied sons were shipped off to Europe to fight for the Allies. Help was not easy to find back on the farm. Hampered by a depleted workforce, farmers could ill afford to have their equipment break down. They needed their machines to replace the labour that they lost when their sons and hired hands left for the European battlefields. But breakdowns did occur. Unfortunately, manufacturers were preoccupied with supplying the military with weapons and other wartime equipment; they did not have the time or the resources to help local farmers fix their equipment. This was obviously bad news for the individual farmers and, more broadly, the entire agricultural industry. To make ends meet, farmers had to increase the price of their products. If prices continued to spike, however, many Canadians would be unable to afford goods like grain, beef, poultry, and dairy.

The Liberal government decided to step in to help alleviate some of the pressure and, more importantly, ward off inflation. Permitted to make unilateral decisions under the War Measures Act, the government began to institute wage-control measures, including controls that regulated the prices of certain agricultural products, such as grain and beef, as well as the costs of manufactured parts. The general idea was that these measures would grease the wheels of agricultural production and simultaneously limit inflation so Canadians could afford the price of food. For obvious reasons, price controls were not popular among rural folks. Most farmers needed top dollar for their goods if they were to survive the lean years of war.

Looking for an effective way to explain its price-control schemes, the federal government requested that the NFB create a series of educational films about how these measures functioned. The messages of the films were generally the same: although wage and price controls meant that farmers had to tighten their belts, the restrictions would stabilize Canadian agriculture and the economy in the long term. Farmers were therefore encouraged to do their part to help their country by sacrificing their immediate needs.

According to Need (1944) is a perfect example of the agricultural films that the NFB made during wartime. Sponsored by the WIB and the Wartime Prices and Trade Board (WPTB), the documentary introduces (and attempts to justify) the government's price-control policy.[27] The film begins by explaining that Canadian farmers rely on dependable equipment to harvest their crops on time. The problem is that war makes farming difficult. Farm machinery is expensive and time-consuming to fix or replace. Before the war, farmers could expect to have their equipment fixed or replaced in a reasonable amount of time and at a reasonable cost; this is not the case during wartime. Manufacturing plants are devoted to fashioning munitions and other military goods and thus unable to fulfill the demands of desperate farmers. According to the narrator, the WPTB has resolved this dilemma by establishing wage and price controls on the market.

To persuade farmers of the necessity of price controls, *According to Need* uses dramatic reenactments with stage actors. In the documentary's most notable sequence, a middle-aged farmer complains to an employee of a manufacturing plant that he is unable to cultivate his fields because something on his tractor is broken. He sent the damaged part to the plant "months ago" but still has not received a replacement part. The farmer is perturbed—he needs the tractor to function so that he can continue to provide "food for the Allied armies, . . . food for the liberated people of Europe, . . . food for civilians here at home who are working harder and eating more than ever before." A nationwide food shortage might well occur if that "part can't be replaced by morning," the farmer warns. The employee only shrugs his shoulders, irritating the farmer further. "That's a lot to expect. That's a moulded part, . . . practically made by hand, . . . [and] foundry help is scarce too. And many of those parts would require many such men," the worker says. "Unfortunately," he continues, the "men, materials, and machines needed for that part are also needed for war. . . . Don't count too much on getting your part this morning. War production comes first." The two men dig in their heels. "But food production is war production," the farmer rebuts. "Isn't anyone making sure of the machinery that makes food production possible?"[28]

Before the quarrel escalates, a government man from the Selective Service Committee saunters in. He is cool and confident, as in most NFB depictions of government officials in the 1940s and 1950s. Turning to the disgruntled farmer, he says calmly, "This year the production of farm implements and parts is going to be limited to exactly what farmers need and no more, and by needs the government means exactly the equipment they can't possibly get along without." In this new system, he explains, a farmer is required to give an inventory to the WPTB, which assesses his needs. Before the farmer can protest, the man explains that the government is committed to examining "every last pound of metal and man hour to see what it would take to meet [a] farmer's needs." The clarification seems to soothe the peeved farmer.[29]

The man from the Selective Service Committee then turns to the manufacturer and explains that the government has also implemented price ceilings on his machinery. Consequently, he cannot charge a farmer more for labour just because he requires a part right away. The worker responds gruffly, "I have heard damn near enough about these ceilings. Seems to me it's just another way of you guys keeping the wages down." The official reprimands the worker for his self-centredness: "Now look here. If we give you more money, through subsidies, to compensate for the ceiling, then we will have to give it to everyone else. Then our costs will go up, and we will have to charge the farmer more," he admonishes. The worker does not understand why this is an issue. "Okay. Okay. You've got to charge him more. What's the problem with that?" Patiently, the officer lectures the worker that without ceilings, "everybody else will be raising wages and prices." In other words, the farmer will have to charge the manufacturer and all other Canadians more for his products. At that moment, both the farmer and the worker nod. They understand that they need to make sacrifices to help each other and, more importantly, to help the entire country remain productive during the lean years of war. "The need of one is recognized as the problem of all, and local affairs that have been transformed by the urgency of war into national matters are being dealt with on a national scale," the narrator concludes.[30]

Fictional scenes like the one in *According to Need* were relatively unconventional for the NFB, which typically produced films that used stock footage, voice-of-God narration, and interviews with real subjects. The WIB was looking for a different way to reach its audience, however, and asked director Dallas Jones to use dramatic sequences to communicate its policies.[31] The WIB believed that these kinds of scenes were effective in demonstrating the necessity of government measures as well as the benevolence of state institutions.[32] The fictionalized moments in *According to Need* are hardly Oscarworthy, but they do succeed in presenting the government as both pleasant and discerning. From an educational standpoint, the reenactments also make the abstract concepts of scarcity, stabilization, and price controls intelligible to lay people. The logic of price controls and other wartime measures is plainly explained in these scenes—wage and price austerity in agriculture was necessary to stave off inflation and keep the war effort going.

The WIB was pleased with how *According to Need* turned out. In a memo to the NFB, the WIB requested that Jones use similar theatrical interludes in *Mrs. Consumer Goes Shopping* (1944) and *Money on the Farm* (1945). Grierson evidently saw some merit in letting his filmmakers use some creative licence to get the WIB's message across. For Grierson, form mattered only if it prohibited filmmakers from speaking on behalf of the state. Fictionalized sequences, if used properly, could actually help amplify government messages about the exploitation and conservation of natural resources.

Despite its unique style, *According to Need* was not that different thematically from other NFB wartime pictures about the environment. In the film, Jones promotes an instrumentalist view of nature. Indirectly, he frames the agrarian landscape of the prairies as a valuable resource that serves the immediate needs of Canada during the war. Furthermore, *According to Need* upholds a government vision of the management of human and natural resources. Much like in *Timber Front*, Jones declares that Canadians must submit to state policies and accept government intervention in their lives. Although the policies established by the state require personal sacrifice, they are necessary for the overall health of the nation. In *Timber Front*, Frank Badgley and Stanley Hawes contend that government conservation programs are essential to safeguard the material needs of the country during wartime. *According to Need* is less obviously tied to resource management, but it also typifies the NFB's loyalty to state-sponsored messages concerning the role of the government in regulating nature and society during wartime. In the latter documentary, state officials instruct farmers to comply with price controls and to maximize their agricultural productivity despite nationwide cutbacks.

"New Land of Promise!"

As the cinematic voice of the government, the NFB declared to viewers that conservation and economic stabilization were vital to the well-being of Canada's resource economy. The upshot of submitting to the state's resource management schemes was that Canada and its allies would survive the demanding Second World War without exhausting the natural reserves of the country. There was another benefit too. If Canadians adopted a wise-use approach to resource extraction, then nature would continue to be a wellspring of raw materials and commodities during peacetime. This cornucopia all but ensured that the nation would prosper in the postwar period.

Representations of Canada as a place of great natural wealth and therefore economic potential were evident in a number of NFB documentaries produced throughout the 1940s. Films about resource fecundity were still part of the NFB propaganda machine, yet their style was more ebullient than didactic. They did not dwell on issues of scarcity or price controls. Instead, they celebrated the nation's abundant geography and its latent possibilities. Sanguine depictions of a country brimming with mighty rivers, dense forests, and vast prairies were meant to rouse in viewers a sense of national pride and to provide hope for the future. "It would be a poor information service . . . which kept harping on war to the exclusion of everything else," John Grierson clarified in an interview with the Canadian Broadcasting Corporation. As the commissioner noted, the NFB also produced works "about the everyday things of life, the values, the ideals which make life worth living."[33]

Representations of natural abundance and national prosperity are particularly striking in Dallas Jones's *New Home in the West* (1943), a historical documentary about the first Ukrainian settlers in Canada. According to the narrator of the film, the nineteenth-century pioneers were attracted to the "unsettled, bush-covered land of the Canadian West" precisely because of its potential as rich farm-land. The "wilderness," with all its natural advantages, provided the brave immigrants with a unique economic "opportunity" and a "new freedom," the film proudly boasts.[34]

The lavishness of nature is a central motif in *New Home in the West*. Cinematographers R. Putnam and Brother Constantine photograph the western frontier with wide lenses and slow pans. The grasslands unfurl for miles into the horizon. The land is seemingly infinite. Megafauna, in contrast, are filmed in close-ups. Bison and elk lope across the screen, plump and seething with life. The lush cinema-tography in *New Home in the West* affirms that the land that the Ukrainian pioneers have selected as their home is a Garden of Eden.[35]

Although the NFB advertised *New Home in the West* as a historical film, its nation-building message was clearly aimed at contemporary audiences, especially new immigrants looking to establish themselves in a new country. The documentary asserted that Canadian nature gives settlers and newcomers a chance at the good life. Canada is a land of opportunity, the documentary unsubtly proclaims. Any-one willing to put in the work will be rewarded, for the land is replete with natural wealth. As the film testified, Ukrainian pioneers' success in creating a permanent home on the prairies was made possible because of the country's fecundity.

Canadian Wheat Story (1944) similarly presents Canada as a land of natural splendour and thus limitless possibilities. An introduction to wheat farming for high school students, the film describes Can-ada as a place "endowed by nature" and the prairies as "the world's greatest wheat-producing area." With the help of an animated map, the documentary depicts the geography of the western plains as a "gigantic bowl" of arable land stretching from central Manitoba to the foothills of Alberta and covering an area of 190,000 square miles. Millions of years of favourable environmental conditions have made Western Canada "one of the most productive regions in the world," the narrator explains.[36] Once again, the country's natural resources are framed as a kind of national birthright. Its bountiful natural features have bequeathed to Canada an economic opportunity that cannot be found anywhere else in the world.

The dual themes of labour and progress in early NFB films were closely tied to depictions of natural abundance. *New Home in the West*, for example, highlights the industry of the Ukrainian settlers and their ability to alter this teeming landscape. Although their task is difficult (taming the vast prairie wilderness is tough going), the pioneers slowly convert raw nature into productive space. Their persistence is admirable. Farmland needs to be cleared before winter arrives, so they work tirelessly morning to evening chopping down trees and clearing bushland. The assiduousness of the Ukrainians is eventually rewarded, and their crops flourish in the mineral-rich soil. With their fields in order, the immigrants are able to establish a permanent settlement on the prairies—"a new home in the West."[37]

Canadian Wheat Story likewise claims that natural abundance is only part of the equation of national progress. The bounty of the land has to be developed if it is to reach its potential. Indeed, the central conceit of the documentary is that the fertile prairies must be continuously exploited in order to keep up with the demands of a hungry (and growing) nation. Director J. Stanley Moore spends most of the documentary focusing on mechanized wheat-farming operations in the West and scientists working in labs to create new and better strains of wheat. The film also investigates modern innovations in grading and inspection practices. According to the narrator, these activities "ensure the maintenance of high export standards."[38]

The thesis that labour and technology are the keys to unlocking the nation's potential is also evident in the wartime picture *Battle of the Harvests* (1942). The documentary, written, directed, and produced by NFB veteran Stanley Jackson, explains that western farmers help establish "new standards of health for the future." Taking advantage of the land's rich topography, the farmers lay "the foundation of a nation permanently strong of body and will." Because of their hard work, Canada is a place "where the blessings of food, health, and space are the right of every man."[39]

Documentaries that represented Canada as a place of natural plenitude and untapped economic potential proffered a mechanistic view of the environment. Nature was portrayed as a passive object that could be controlled or overcome. (The language of ecology and dynamic ecosystems had not yet entered the vocabulary of NFB cinema.) *Battle of the Harvests* and other works emphasized the pliability of nature and the ability of Canadian industry to transform wild environments into resource landscapes. The films typically begin with a series of shots of untouched wilderness: forests, mountains, rivers, or prairies. Then they shift their attention to the people and institutions that wrestle with and inevitably conquer them. In *Look to the North* (1944), images of oil refineries, bulldozers, and airplanes are accompanied by jubilant commentary on the taming of raw nature. Even in the remotest parts of the Canadian North, nature has been dominated; its oil, minerals, and timber flow freely throughout the country because of the technological ingenuity of Canadian engineers, the film declares.[40]

The tropes of natural abundance, industrial exploitation, and national progress were also evident in NFB works produced after the Second World War. Documentaries such as *Red Runs the Fraser* (1949), *Land in Trust* (1949), *Look to the Forest* (1950), *Trees Are a Crop* (1950), and *Water for Prairies* (1950) continued to promote the government's belief that the development of Canada's frontier spaces was integral to propelling the nation to new economic and social heights. Representations of schools of salmon, golden wheat fields, and bustling timber yards declared to viewers that Canada, to quote a line from the 1949 documentary *Land in Trust*, was a "new land of promise!"[41]

These films, most of which were sponsored by government departments, reflect the optimism of the postwar age. Humans are depicted as powerful agents of change, first occupying and then modifying the natural world to suit their needs. Through state-sponsored science, technology, and expert knowledge, subjects in NFB documentaries reshape nature so that it can produce ample yields. *Red Runs the Fraser*, an exciting film about the salmon run in British Columbia, epitomizes NFB enthusiasm about resource development. In the film, the Fraser River is described as a "highway" that continuously supplies the country with protein-rich salmon. The fish are "quickly brought in, scaled, and cleaned (one every second), put in cans, sealed, and then sent to distributors," the narrator exclaims.[42] (It takes about two minutes to package the fish.) The Fraser River and the canning facilities dotting its shores exist as one continuous assembly line— nature and technology work together to feed Canadians.

Red Runs the Fraser goes on to show how industrial efficiency and innovative technology ensure that this productive relationship is maintained. The salmon run is fraught with danger, the film informs viewers. The desperate, gasping sockeye have a difficult time making it back to their spawning grounds and are therefore not able to reproduce at a sustainable rate. They head upstream, dodging anglers, predators, and Hell's Gate, a formidable gorge in the heart of the Fraser River. To protect the salmon from this deadly gauntlet, scientists and fishery experts from British Columbia and Washington investigate ways to make the passage through Hell's Gate easier. According to the narrator, the scientists develop "comprehensive plans," "tagging methods," and "experimental hatcheries" to solve the problem. After all the data has been compiled, engineers design a "state-of-the-art" system that will shield the sockeye from the jagged rocks and rushing water. They create fish ladders and elevators to lift the breeding salmon safely across the raging torrent of Hell's Gate. The engineering feat, the film declares, saves the salmon and, by extension, the lucrative fishing industry.[43]

Representations of Canada as a place of natural abundance "unleashed through Euro-Canadian technological expertise," to quote historian Carol Payne, are closely related to another theme of early NFB filmmaking: the celebration of territorial expansion.[44]

NFB documentaries about natural resources repeatedly suggest that frontier geographies are ready to be exploited. They celebrate the institutions that colonize remote environs and reshape them in ways that support the development of Canada as a whole. Territorial expansion was a key element of nation-building efforts, and those who participated in this endeavour embodied what it meant to be truly Canadian.

The discourses of territorial expansion and natural resource exploitation in Canada's frontiers usually suggest that anyone who resisted these projects were quaint, obsolete, or even primitive. Indeed, Indigenous peoples were depicted in early NFB documentaries as an incarnation of the wild and lusty frontier. Their presence, though fascinating in a kind of exotic way, reaffirmed to viewers that the Canadian interior was an unruly space. Ironically, the presence of Indigenous peoples in NFB films was also used to support the claim that much of the resource hinterland was empty and untapped. First Nations groups were represented as being parts of nature, and as a result, their existence did not dispute the declaration that the land in the North and the West were available for exploitation. This flawed depiction of Indigenous peoples was rooted in racist discourses about the social and political inferiority of nonwhites and obfuscated the reality that Indigenous peoples had used and sustained the resources of the lands that NFB filmmakers claimed were vacant. This portrayal was not necessarily intentional, for NFB documentarians were products of their times and the cultural narratives that informed their worldviews. Nevertheless, they were complicit in reproducing a colonizing discourse about white, Anglo-Canadian power. By misrepresenting the lives of Indigenous peoples as primeval and unsophisticated, the NFB brushed away the bloody history of colonization and created a sanitized depiction of national identity founded upon natural fecundity, technological prowess, and Anglo superiority.

Agricultural Documentaries, the Welfare
State, and the Remaking of Nature

During the Second World War, the NFB had three main objectives: to galvanize public support for the war, to boost Canadian morale during a period of economic retrenchment, and to provide audiences with timely information on both global and domestic events. Toward the end of the war, the NFB's usefulness as a government agency was less clear. What purpose did this propaganda machine serve during peacetime? What did films "in the national interest" mean for a country not under duress? For certain members of Parliament, the NFB's utility in postwar Canada was ambiguous. Some even went so far as to suggest that the NFB was a waste of taxpayers' dollars.

It appeared that the NFB was on the verge of collapse. Before matters could get worse, the indefatigable John Grierson came to the defence of the NFB by reestablishing its role as the voice of the Canadian government. The commissioner outlined his vision for the NFB after the war. According to Grierson, the NFB would transition from producing wartime propaganda to "providing [the country with] a supplementary system of national education."[45] Reaction to his proposal was mixed at first. Disapproval from the Conservative Party and budget cuts dampened the Liberal Party's enthusiasm for the postwar success of the NFB. Although opposition to it persisted through the early 1950s, Grierson's concept gained traction within the government. The commissioner's mission to support government educational initiatives conveniently aligned with the aims of the emerging welfare state. In the mid-1940s, the Liberal government had introduced a range of social policy measures related to Indigenous affairs, housing, personal hygiene, and unemployment. What better way to support (and in some cases expand) these initiatives than through a government-operated cinema? Under the governance of the Ministry of Reconstruction and Supply (and later the Ministry of Natural Resources), the NFB redirected its filmmaking to promote government programs and social policies in the post-war period.

NFB films about the environment were part of this larger strategy. Like other sponsored works produced during this period, documentaries about the natural world supported the government's vision to reform social and environmental spaces through education and legislation. Agricultural films in particular documented the state's efforts to support local farmers and help them make the land more productive. According to these films, social and agricultural spaces would improve considerably if farmers accepted the wisdom of state expertise. They would no longer be exposed to the vagaries of climate, markets, or bad luck. A boost in efficiency and economic productivity would not only benefit individual farmers but also strengthen the nation.

The filmmaker most responsible for this representation of Canadian agriculture was Evelyn Cherry, head of the APU and one of the first female filmmakers in NFB history. Throughout her career, Cherry urged farmers to revolutionize how they managed the land. According to the young director, a vibrant agricultural industry could be achieved only if farmers transitioned from their old methods of farming to new, state-authorized techniques and conservation schemes.

Cherry was the perfect ambassador in many ways for the government's welfare state initiatives on farming. Born in Yorkton, Saskatchewan, in 1906, she grew up in the heart of farm country. Most of the townsfolk in Yorkton were immigrant farmers who had settled in the area in the 1880s. As a child, she watched her neighbours slog it out trying to make a living on the prairies. In the spring of 1929, Cherry graduated from the University of Missouri with a degree in journalism. She returned to Saskatchewan to work as a journalist for the Regina *Leader-Post* just before the stock market crashed. The farmers whom she knew as a child were still labouring against weeds and hungry pests. But now they were also up against a devastating recession and one of the worst droughts in Canadian history.[46] Some persevered, but many did not. The Great Depression and subsequent "dust bowl" hit the prairies hard and left a mark on Cherry, influencing both her filmmaking interests and her belief in the necessity of environmental and social reforms.

In the spring of 1931, Cherry left the prairies and went to England to work as a documentary filmmaker with John Grierson at the General Post Office (GPO). She quickly learned nonfictional filmmaking and, as one colleague noted admiringly, could dismantle and repair movie cameras "as well as any mechanic."[47] Before the Second World War broke out, Cherry quit the GPO and headed back to Saskatchewan to work as an independent filmmaker. Evelyn and her husband, Lawrence Cherry, established a small production company in the province, mostly making films about life on the prairies. In 1940, she produced two short documentaries for the Saskatchewan Wheat Pool: *By Their Own Strength*, which traces the history of wheat farming in the West, and *New Horizons*, a silent film that documents immigrant farmers and their struggles to make a living on the prairies. The films were seen by only a handful of individuals, farmers mostly, but they were remarkable works of nonfictional cinema. Without relying on narration, *New Horizons* presented the vivid story of environmental change in the Canadian West. Using simple but evocative cinematography, Cherry showed how nature shaped human settlement. She also demonstrated to viewers how centralized organizations such as the Saskatchewan Wheat Pool helped farmers overcome ecological problems such as drought.

In 1941, the young filmmaker accepted an invitation from Grierson to work for the NFB. Her first year at the NFB was busy. Cherry wrote, directed, and produced several films about the relationship between ordinary citizens and geography. As she immersed herself in the work, she began to think more about the social role of documentary filmmaking. Influenced by her mentor, Grierson, Cherry saw her documentaries as a way to make Canada a better place to live. "I have only seen cinema for what it can do to cause more excitement in education . . . [and] to inspire people to greater efforts to make the country a better place," she explained in an interview in 1975.[48] Her faith in the social potential of cinema meshed perfectly with the NFB's larger goal to support the welfare state through the filmmaking that educated and unified the country.

After Cherry wrote and produced two films for the *World in Action* series, *The Main Dish* (1943) and *Coupon Value* (1943), Grierson approached her to see if she would supervise the APU. She accepted the position and immediately began developing films that "reveal[ed] the unique problems confronting farmers in the modern world."[49] With the support of the DOA, Cherry made a series of films that taught farmers how to implement government solutions into their agricultural practices. It is not hard to imagine farmers scoffing at this young, confident woman with her modern answers to their age-old problems. But Cherry slowly won her viewers over by speaking their language and by acknowledging their unique concerns. Her films eventually became some of the most loved and widely viewed works in NFB history.

Cherry's first film with the APU was *Windbreaks on the Prairies* (1943). The documentary encapsulates the welfare state ethos of NFB works in this period. Vividly shot in colour, *Windbreaks on the Prairies* examines the problem of soil sterility, an issue especially germane to western farmers in the 1940s.[50] In the film, Cherry investigates the history of drought on the prairies and provides a remedial solution to damaged landscapes and lives. The message is simple: Canadian farmers need to work alongside government experts if they want to restore the land to fertility.

Cherry chose to make a film about soil aridity because it was one of the biggest factors in the collapse of farming communities in the West. Canadian agriculturalists were still reeling from the impact of the Great Depression. Confronted with a sharp drop in commodity prices and environmental calamities such as drought and soil erosion, farmers were hit hard in the 1930s. At first, they could not sell their products. Then they were unable to grow them. Many farmers defaulted on their loans and went bankrupt. Cherry believed that agriculture on the prairies could be restored if people understood the human origins of the issue and learned about how government intervention could help them recover.

Windbreaks on the Prairies begins with an idyllic montage of farmers harvesting grain. As the images flicker by, the narrator, Thomas Tweed, waxes nostalgic about Western Canada at the turn of the century: "On wheat, the West was built; on wheat, the East flourished."[51] However, as cultivation technology improved and farmers applied more effective ways to clear the land, the rich soil of the prairies became exposed to harsh wind and relentless sunlight. The film cuts to a sequence of environmental ruin. Dust whirls across cracked earth. Wind rips through abandoned shanties. Because of their recklessness, the film declares, Canadian farmers are vulnerable to the full wrath of nature.

The investigation of soil aridity in *Windbreaks on the Prairies* was exceptional for its time. Most commentators claimed that soil erosion was merely the result of aberrant weather. But Cherry had a different view: desiccation of the soil had a human origin. Overzealous farmers and their steel plows laid waste to this once fertile environment.[52] In their vigorous efforts to break the ground, farmers unwittingly destroyed its buffer against the strong prairie wind, and the farmland became helpless to protect itself.

The documentary does not linger on the mistakes of the past, however, but encourages farmers to adopt new practices. With some hard work and a little bit of help from the state, farmers could restore the land to its original glory. In his baritone voice, Tweed exclaims that scientists and agricultural experts employed by the federal government assist farmers by "correct[ing] some of the man-made mistakes of the past."[53] A shot of farmers digging irrigation channels alongside government employees underscores the importance of cooperation between the individual and the state. (It is a picture of national harmony that by today's standards is overly earnest.) Together they reorder the environment and lay the foundation for a healthier agricultural industry.

The role of the government in the lives of farmers is critical to understanding environmental films such as *Windbreaks on the Prairies*. The documentary was born from a larger welfare state initiative to clarify the role of the government in the lives of ordinary Canadians. Although the onus is on farmers to change their practices, the government is a central character in the restoration of the environment. The film explains that agricultural improvement is heavily financed by government initiatives such as the Prairie Farm Rehabilitation Act. The film also describes how the DOA's experimental arboreal station at Indian Head, Saskatchewan, assists farmers by supplying them with thousands of trees at very little cost. According to the scientists at Indian Head, these trees create a barrier against wind and thus protect the rich topsoil from eroding. "The government station is an inspiration to many farm people," the narrator claims.[54]

Although *Windbreaks on the Prairies* brims with iconic images and poetic landscapes, its primary aim was to educate viewers. On this ground, it was successful. Upon its release (and subsequent circulation in rural circuits and film councils), a number of people praised its presentation of how the government was working to improve the lives of farmers. Allan Beaven, an officer with the Canadian Forestry Association, for example, proclaimed in a letter to John Grierson that the documentary would "most certainly" assist farmers "trying to get back on their feet." "At no time in the past has the need been greater for Western farm stability and improvement in farm living conditions, so the advent of such a film will indeed be timely," he wrote. Beaven had big plans for the film. "*Windbreaks* will play a big part in our educational campaign, and will be shown to around 65,000 prairie people each year and as it takes us some five years to cover every point on the plains, over 300,000 people will have the opportunity of seeing it during this period on the tree planting lecture car," he reported.[55]

Cherry continued to make documentaries that supported government intervention in Canadian agricultural practices through the middle part of the 1940s. In addition to promoting state-directed conservation strategies, she made sponsored films that instructed farmers on how to implement modern husbandry techniques and business strategies.[56] In *Five Steps to Better Farm Living* (1945), for instance, Cherry convinces farmers that their fields would become more profitable if they "studied the information put out by both provincial and dominion Departments of Agriculture."[57]

Five Steps was part of a larger government program to improve agricultural conditions across the country. Just before the film was released, the federal government established the Agricultural Prices Support Board and the Farm Improvement Loans Act to revive agriculture in Canada. In fact, Cherry's documentary was an adaptation of a comprehensive government study authored by H. R. Hare, an agricultural economist working for the Dominion Department of Labour. A year before the film was released, he wrote a short pamphlet titled *Little Chats on Farm Management* for the Economics Division of the Dominion Department of Agriculture. Hare observed that Canadian farmers across the country made uninformed financial decisions that "resulted in the accumulation of indebtedness."[58] He argued that this "failure" occurred because farmers did not grasp basic economic principles and were "prejudiced against modern agricultural methods."[59] If agriculture was to improve, then "the old mental plan" of farm operators "must be superseded by one more carefully thought out and written," Hare concluded.[60]

His technocratic solution to farming figures prominently in Cherry's documentary. Elaborating the recommendations that Hare makes in *Little Chats*, *Five Steps* explains that Canadian farmers can avoid loan defaults and miserable crop yields if they improve their capital investments, purchase victory bonds, and replace outdated machinery. The last point was especially important. Using modern equipment and electrical technology was essential if farmers wanted to enhance their productivity and improve their quality of life. To illustrate this point, Cherry shows the benefits of owning a gas-powered tractor. The results are impressive; large acres are plowed in hours, not days.

The tractor is the central motif throughout the documentary. It not only connects farmers with the recommendations of the government but also represents a modern and productive farming life. In the margins of the script for *Five Steps*, Cherry wrote that the tractor was a key element of the film because it was "symbolic of freedom from drudgery, symbolic of plenty, and symbolic of a happy life." The machine "can be used to free man instead of enslave him."[61] Cherry's awareness of the symbolic power of the tractor was astute. Advances in mechanized farming in the 1930s and 1940s had a tremendous effect on agriculture in Canada. No other piece of technology reshaped the Canadian agricultural landscape more than the tractor. It led to increases in productivity and reduced the need for itinerant labourers. With little help, a farmer could quickly convert crops into revenues. Furthermore, the speed with which the tractor operated allowed agriculturalists to devote more time to planting and growing new crops.[62] As Cherry summarizes in *Five Steps*, tractors save farmers time, energy, and money because of their speed advantage over horse-drawn plows. Proponents of the tractor saw this type of technology as a way to "spawn ecological harmony, economic prosperity, and freedom from nature's constraints," to borrow historian Joshua Nygren's words.[63] In short, technology ensured not only agricultural success but also humanity's victory over an adverse landscape, which for Cherry had hitherto prohibited rural Canadians from experiencing the good life.

Five Steps was a departure in style and form for Cherry. Her pre-NFB documentaries about rural Canada were notable for their visual creativity and political complexity. Even *Windbreaks on the Prairies* is remembered for its poetic cinematography and artistic editing techniques, which abridged the history of the dust bowl in a span of seconds. *Five Steps* is simpler and more straightforward. It looks more like an industry training video than a documentary film for a general audience. After she completed it, Cherry admitted to her husband, Lawrence, that she was tired of the DOA's impetus to produce "educational and not sociological films."[64]

Figure 1. A farmer plows his field with the help of a tractor in Evelyn Cherry's *Windbreaks on the Prairies* (1943). Used with permission of the National Film Board.

Although the cinematic possibilities of making APU documentaries such as *Five Steps* were limited, Cherry committed herself to using films to help farmers across the country. If that meant making dry educational works, then so be it. A retired Cherry conceded in 1975 that the NFB's government-sponsored filmmaking program was the best way to reach far-flung populations and draw them into mainstream Canadian culture. "The work I was doing was valuable and precious in helping to strengthen unity across the land," she explained.[65] In an industry that often catered to urban elites, her films were iconoclastic—she went to the towns and villages of middle-of-nowhere Canada to help farmers participate in the larger discourse of nationhood.

While *Five Steps* is primarily didactic, Cherry's proficiency as a documentary filmmaker still shines through. In the film, Cherry employs a variety of advanced narrative and aesthetic strategies to persuade audiences of the benefits of agricultural modernization. A Cherry film is instantly recognizable—each of her works contains what the filmmaker liked to call "nameless archetypes." According to her, she used nonspecific subjects, plain in both appearance and social standing, because doing so helped audiences identify with the characters and situations. Cherry was intentional about this particular strategy. If the story rang true, then spectators were more likely to embrace the government ideas presented in the film.

Cherry went to great lengths to ensure that her subjects were ordinary (and thus relatable) in *Five Steps*. During production, she visited farms in Manitoba, Saskatchewan, and Alberta to find an "unexceptional" subject. She eventually settled on a middle-aged cultivator from rural Alberta. He is "very typical," Cherry wrote to her cinematographer, "about 40 to 50, an intelligent man with character in his face." "His wife," she continued, "is a nice looking woman, tall and well-built with an attractive smile and nice eyes." Their children were also handsome in that bland way. "The son is almost nineteen, a tall boy . . . who intends to stay on the farm and is intelligent," and the daughter was "17 or 18, tall and pretty, and she can really cook."[66] For Cherry, they were the ideal subjects for her film. They could have been plucked from anywhere in Canada. They were wholly unremarkable and therefore perfect for projecting her ideas about the role of the individual in the larger nation.

Cherry's use of nameless archetypes to connect audiences with the core themes of the film was effective. According to sentiments recorded in film council evaluations, audiences liked her documentaries precisely because they saw themselves in the scenarios projected onscreen. Viewers of *Farm Electrification* (1946), for example, lauded the director's ability to capture "the essence of rural life in Canada." *Land in Trust* (1949), a documentary about soil erosion, also "received very positive comment[s]" for its depiction of agricultural society.[67] F. F. Morwick, a professor in the Soils Department at the University of Guelph, exclaimed that the film was "timely and important" and a "competent presentation of a *national* topic."[68] Local audiences in

New Brunswick were similarly enamoured with Cherry's realistic portrayal of a father and son struggling on the family farm.[69]

Partly, audiences saw themselves in the documentaries that Cherry made because of their generic backgrounds. Like the characters, the settings of her films were indistinct and thus remarkably prosaic. Her agricultural landscapes often look like matte paintings or composites of ordinary farms stitched together into a single frame. Cherry used certain compositional techniques and visual tropes favoured by contemporary agricultural photographers to create a kind of mythical Canadian homestead. The farming landscapes in *Windbreaks on the Prairies*, *Five Steps*, and *Soils for Tomorrow* (1945) are curiously uniform in their presentation. There are no distinguishing features or topographical landmarks within the frame to divulge the location of the scene or the figures toiling in the distance. The image is always the same: a small farm (silo, house, and barn) positioned against a flat horizon of corn, wheat, or other monocrops. If it were not for the clouds drifting across the frame, the viewer would think the image to be a photograph.

The simple and lonely arrangement of Cherry's agricultural landscapes conveys two major ideas: first, that rural Canada is truly isolated and therefore vulnerable to the capriciousness of nature, and second, that Canada's agricultural frontier is more or less the same across the country. Cherry limned the diversity of regionalization, subsuming local environments within an ecologically reductive "national" farming landscape. Her representation of agriculture as unexceptional also reflected a state way of seeing farming environments in midcentury Canada. By obscuring specific references to place, Cherry represented farming geographies as a detached space whose primary purpose was to produce food and generate wealth. In this sense, all agricultural landscapes were essentially the same. They are conspicuously absent of ecological diversity or social variety. Imagining Canadian farms in this way mirrors the vision of state planners, who used grids and charts to foreground the lucrative aspects of an otherwise complex and messy reality in Western Canada.

The decision to use nonspecific locales in her films served a more direct political function as well. By ignoring variations in soil quality, climate, and a farm's distance from market, Cherry suggested that Canadian agriculture was homogeneous and therefore equally ripe for large-scale transformation. Because farms were more or less the same across the country, government solutions to agricultural problems could be administered everywhere.

Furthermore, since there were very few references to specific locations, Cherry's documentaries could be viewed virtually anywhere in the country. Audiences did not need to stretch their imaginations. As far as the audience knew, the film could have been shot in their own town. The universal aesthetic of Cherry's cinematography made these NFB films especially valuable to state branches that planned on showing the films across the country, such as the DOA. Distribution was essential to the government's national educational strategy, for it helped integrate rural populations into mainstream Canada.[70] Film circuits and councils provided a means by which the state could talk to citizens and teach them about the role of the government in their lives.

The NFB circulated its educational films in a variety of ways. Between 1942 and 1946, it ran citizenship film forums in rural schools, churches, community centres, and factories. Projectionists, known as field men, drove around the country with film equipment and electric generators. Along the way, they would set up shop and show the NFB film reels to the locals. After the war, the itinerant field operatives were replaced with newly formed local film councils, which showed NFB films on a more constant basis and in a variety of public spaces. These viewings were welcomed by local communities who were eager to see what was happening in the rest of the nation. Donald Buchanan, an art historian and the founder of the National Film Society of Canada, observed in a contemporary article about the significance of these film councils that audiences "turned out in crowds for the showings." The rural circuits and film councils were "a gadfly to social discussion" and helped rural populations "feel connected" to the rest of the country.[71]

This "mobile cinema" practice aided the government's nation-building efforts and welfare state goals to unite the country by disseminating its agriculturally modern message to rural parts of the country. To help stimulate audience support, government officials directly monitored public reception at local screenings and in some cases even gave talks after the films were shown. In film forums in which Cherry's documentaries were exhibited, officials from the DOA facilitated conversations with the audiences about the importance of incorporating modern solutions to their agricultural problems. After a film concluded, the officials would stand up and talk practically about how to implement farm electrification and apply modern husbandry strategies.

Evelyn Cherry was thus a kind of proxy for state values and education. She promoted the ecological imagination of the welfare state by presenting the government as a benevolent institution that helped Canadians maximize the efficiency of nature. Ironically, Cherry left the NFB because of accusations that she was a communist and that her depiction of ordinary farmers was subversive. Her depictions of working-class Canadians apparently did not sit well with many in Parliament, and she went back to making documentaries under her own production company in the early 1950s.

Science and Agricultural Improvement

There was a striking thematic continuity in nature documentaries produced from 1939 to 1949. *Timber Front*, *Windbreaks on the Prairies*, and *Five Steps* represented nature from a state perspective in which the environment was figured as a passive object to be exploited, controlled, and managed by government experts. This way of seeing the environment persisted into the middle of the century. In the 1950s, NFB documentaries were similarly characterized by their high modern ideology, specifically the notion that nature could be made to serve the needs of the growing nation through technology and resource management practices. Documentaries in the 1950s, however, introduced a slightly different twist to this narrative: nature could be improved through the discipline of state-sponsored science.[72] *Let's Look at Water* (1947) shows scientists in lab coats purifying contaminated rivers in rural and urban communities across the country, saving lives in the process. Other documentaries—such as *Trees Are a Crop* (1950), *Look to the Forest* (1950), *The World at Your Feet* (1953), and *Chemical Conquest* (1956)—contend that laboratory research and the formulation of chemical pesticides are essential for maximizing yields and maintaining healthy and productive agricultural activities. Equipped with scientific knowledge and technologies developed by university-educated men, the Canadian farmer can expect to reorder his farm in a way that supports long-term agricultural success.

The NFB's confidence in the miracles of agricultural science in the 1950s paralleled the Canadian government's "blind faith in science's ability to solve the world's problems."[73] As Clinton Evans observes, science was conceived by the state as a powerful tool to help industry convert the postwar Canadian environment into a veritable breadbasket of staple commodities. The DOA was especially enthusiastic that scientific solutions would help farmers overcome common problems of inefficiency and waste.

One of the most vocal proponents of state-sponsored science in agriculture at the NFB was Larry Gosnell, a graduate of the Ontario Agricultural College at the University of Guelph. In his first film, *The World at Your Feet*, the narrator explains that "there is a world within a world in the earth at our feet, a world of living things where the surge of life wrought by nature's silent magic brings forth the fruit that sustains our life." In order to unlock the full potential of this "silent magic," Canadian farmers need to learn the "intimate and sympathetic knowledge of the ways of nature." Only then can they "reap its continuing abundance."[74]

The World at Your Feet was intended for two kinds of viewers: high school students and cultivators interested in learning more about the science behind agriculture. The film shows how healthy soils maintain the "harmonious balance" of photosynthesis and germination in plants.[75] Despite its educational goals, it was one of the more innovative films developed by the NFB in the 1950s. Gosnell used an assortment of cinematic techniques to present the earth as a thriving community of microscopic organisms. Using highly magnifying cameras in a process that he termed *cinephotomicrography*, Gosnell takes audiences below ground on "an intimate tour of the circulatory systems of root hairs and leaves, and into the mysteries of the microscopic world in the soil where millions of minute living things scurry continuously."[76] Tiny organisms flit across the screen as they decompose organic matter, thus revealing their secret purpose to audiences for the first time. According to the narrator, the process unfolding onscreen helps the soil maintain a healthy supply of calcium, magnesium, and potassium. The topsoil is now primed to support life, including the seeds planted by the farmer. To illustrate the result of this process, Gosnell uses time-lapse photography of roots shooting up through the fertile earth and growing to maturity in a matter of seconds.

Like Cherry's films, *The World at Your Feet* was produced as part of a larger government strategy to shape agricultural attitudes and, more specifically, modernize farming landscapes in Canada. Sponsored by the DOA, the documentary urges farmers to familiarize themselves with the latest trends in the science of cultivation. The DOA did not just fund the project; it also actively participated in the production and distribution of the film. Dr. P. O. Ripley, chief of the Field Husbandry Division, Experimental Farms Branch, advised Gosnell on the set of the documentary, thus ensuring that it supported the scientific opinions of the DOA. After the film was completed, the department promoted it to the Canadian public. In a memo to his staff, Deputy Minister James Gordon Taggart explained that every employee "must see and promote the film" because it "tells a story that should be told as widely as possible . . . the story of organic soil, of soil care and structure and how man by knowing and co-operating with the laws of nature, can make soil produce abundantly."[77] He also advised his employees to help distributors and theatre managers promote the film by handing out pamphlets to members of the public.

Gosnell's next documentary, *Chemical Conquest*, elaborated an idea first explored in *The World at Your Feet*: the importance of science in improving Canadian agriculture. Like its predecessor, *Chemical Conquest* exhibits an unwavering confidence in high modern solutions to improve nature. As the narrator states, "Nature to be commanded must be obeyed, and to be obeyed she must be understood." Once a farmer understands the environment, he will be able to "work closer in harmony with those natural forces which provide him with his sustenance."[78] Gosnell suggests that good farming begins not in the soil but in a laboratory. It is in these chemical labs, far away from a planter's field, where the most important developments in horticulture occur. Scientists in laboratories such as the DOA's Science Service Laboratory (located at the University of Western Ontario) devise newer and more effective pesticides and herbicides to help farmers combat the scourge of insects, diseases, and weeds that threaten crops across the country.

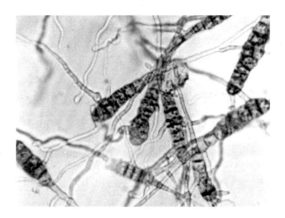

Figure 2. Nature under the microscope in *Chemical Conquest* (1956). Used with permission of the National Film Board.

Gosnell first became interested in the subject of pesticides when he read a *Fortune* article entitled "Farming's Chemical Age." In the article, chemical engineer Eric Hodgins asserted that chemicals were more important to the "future of American agriculture than the shift from horses and mules to tractor power."[79] Hodgins argued that new technology allowed farmers to produce and harvest crops on an unprecedented scale. Yet there was a price to pay for this efficiency: adopting modern techniques and intensifying crop production created the perfect environment for pests.[80] He claimed that pesticides allowed farmers to maintain monoculture crops by eradicating pests. As a result, a farmer could harvest greater yields per acre, decrease his man-hours, and cut production costs. Gosnell was intrigued by Hodgins's thesis.

In the film, Gosnell frames insects and fungi as menaces that need to be exterminated. In a style suggestive of wartime propaganda, which frequently vilified the Germans and Japanese as subhuman "insects," *Chemical Conquest* demonizes pests as "foreign invaders" bent on destroying Canadian productivity.[81] The development of pesticides, Gosnell asserts, is the necessary weapon in this "war" against "intruders." Ominous music plays as a fat worm munches on a tobacco plant in what the narrator describes as "an orgy of leaf feasting." In a style similar to that of the Canada in Action wartime newsreels, the narrator demands that farmers "take back" their crops from these killer pests. The agricultural health of the nation is at stake. Armed with chemicals such as 2,4-D, described as weapons that "shift the balance back in the farmer's favour," farmers can reclaim their soil.[82]

Although *Chemical Conquest* vaunts the capacity of science and technology to improve nature, an examination of the production history of the documentary reveals that Gosnell was more ambivalent about pesticides than the film lets on. In his production notes, he admitted that the issues that farmers faced (soil erosion, pestilence, etc.) were the symptoms of a larger problem. "Nature hasn't made any special arrangement to take the ways of man into account," he wrote.[83] Like Hodgins, Gosnell believed that the agricultural sector's shift toward specialized monoculture crops disrupted "the inherent balance in nature." He believed that modifying the environment to accommodate these changes was a dangerous game indeed. The filmmaker was also unconvinced that pesticides would restore the balance of nature. As he pointed out in his research, scientists had not adequately solved the problem of insect immunity. Although DDT, made available commercially in 1945, was successful at first, insects eventually developed resistance to it.[84] Gosnell also suggested that pesticides such as DDT killed organisms vital to the health of local ecosystems. Science had yet to create a pesticide that left bees and butterflies unharmed, the filmmaker lamented in his notes for the film.[85]

Furthermore, Gosnell was troubled about the state of agricultural research and development in Canada, which he described as a "complex and expensive race." Although he supported what he saw as the noble efforts of the chemical industry to solve the troubles of the farmer, he was skeptical of the rapidity with which it introduced new pesticides. "Little is known of the mechanism of their action," Gosnell admitted privately. The problem for him was that chemical companies were releasing potent compounds whose "mode of actions is not fully understood," he wrote. "As long as the federal laws with respect to toxicity, effectiveness, [and] residual character are complied with, no one will stop the distribution of a given chemical."[86]

Chemical Conquest makes only passing reference to some of his misgivings about pesticide use, likely because Gosnell did not want to antagonize the sponsor of the documentary, the DOA. The narrator does warn that "with the application of pesticides to insects, soil, and plants, we are bringing some of the most powerful chemicals produced by modern technology in contact with biological forces which we do not fully understand. The results could well be disastrous." This is the only cautious remark in an otherwise enthusiastic and positive film about agricultural science. The narrator quickly assures viewers after this statement that state-funded research is working hard to learn about the effects of pesticides.[87]

Although the documentary does not investigate the relationship between pesticide use and ecological collapse, Gosnell's personal ambivalence about this scientific solution demonstrated the gap that sometimes existed between individual views and state narratives. Not every filmmaker uniformly supported the high modern views of the state or its technological solutions to agricultural problems. As we will see in chapter 3, Gosnell would challenge more directly the hegemony of high modern agricultural solutions by examining the hazards to human health arising from pesticide residues on food products.

The NFB was tasked with presenting a vision of Canada that aligned with state ideology. This mandate inflected the kinds of films that it made about nature. Canadian audiences were exposed early on in NFB cinema to a progressive narrative about humans remaking their environment. Concomitantly, nature was presented as a productive and state-managed space—an essential component of the country's economic future. In the early 1940s, NFB wartime films claimed that natural resources were essential for Allied victory. As such, they needed to be conserved and monitored by state institutions. The documentaries produced during the Second World War were also utilitarian in their representations of nature. They suggested that Canada's abundant resources would sustain the nation during reconstruction. Depictions of healthy crops, ripe fruit, and robust forest stands affirmed the nation-building myth that the country had plenty of raw commodities and that this plenitude would stimulate economic growth. NFB filmmakers continued to perpetuate state discourses about the environment in the postwar period. Documentarians Evelyn Cherry and Larry Gosnell focused on the role of the government in the lives of Canadian farmers. They instructed farmers to modernize their equipment, purchase chemical fertilizers and pesticides, and incorporate state-sponsored recommendations into their agricultural practices.

NFB documentaries about agriculture not only taught farmers to adopt methods prescribed by the government but also introduced audiences to a high modern way of seeing nature. Filmmakers such as Cherry presented a homogenized vision of the Canadian landscape in which the value of nature was measured in terms of carrying capacity and acreage. Narrative devices such as those that Cherry used simplified agricultural spaces into a standardized and national landscape. Other filmmakers, such as Gosnell, developed new cinematic technologies to make the landscape more comprehensible. His cinephotomicrography technique allowed the filmmaker to show audiences a more "scientific" view of the natural world. The camera went below the soil to discover a substratum of microbes and chemical reactions. The shift from iconic farming landscapes to the invisible world of soil extended in many ways Cherry's picture of the universal farm to its logical conclusion: the Canadian environment was fundamentally the same above and below the earth. Nature was essentially malleable; it could be manipulated, reshaped, and improved.

2

Visions of the North

Never ask the explorer, still shrouded in distant solitudes,
to tell his fondest memories. You would not understand,
perhaps, if he said: "It's the wind blowing through the
valley, the moon perched between two spruce trees,
the waterfall hissing, the gurgle of the brook, the shrill
cry of the hawk to the cliff above its nest, the nostalgic
singing of the finch, the lapping of the wave on the boat,
the small Eskimo who smiled at his mother in the hood
of the anorak, the find of a pebble on the beach that tells
the story of the land or, on the slope, a plant that nobody
has ever seen, an insignificant, unnamed grass which adds
a link to human knowledge." These are great adventures.

—Jacques Rousseau, "Toundra"

The National Film Board of Canada (NFB) filmmakers defined the
limits, uses, and value of the environment for Canadian viewers
throughout the twentieth century. Their works reflected dominant
attitudes toward nature, especially those advocated by the state. In
early NFB cinema, in the 1940s and 1950s, nature was depicted as
a homogeneous space that could be simplified and exploited. Local

environments were smudged together into an archetypal national landscape characterized by its efficiency, utility, and economic potential.

On a more fundamental level, documentaries about nature were integral to the NFB's presentation of Canada as well as its nation-building mandate. The NFB imagined Canada as a wilderness nation whose past, present, and future were inextricably tied to its fecund (albeit fragile) geography. Images of well-managed resource environments encouraged viewers to link Canadian identity to the transformation of the natural world into a productive and lucrative space. Certainly, the splendour of Canada's geography evoked a nostalgic yearning for the land as it appeared to early settlers, but it also signalled to viewers that theirs was a land of improvement and infinite horizons. Progress necessitated that Canadians keep marching westward or northward to conquer these robust geographies.

Discourses about the relationship between nature and nation were palpable in the cinematic landscapes of NFB documentaries. As film scholar Martin Lefebvre explains, cinematic landscapes "connect films both to the world and to the various traditions and reasons for representing it."[1] The settings in NFB films are therefore ripe for analysis. In their immediate filmic contexts, cinematic landscapes help establish a sense of time, atmosphere, and texture. When examined in the larger historical and cultural milieu in which they were produced, cinematic landscapes also reveal how the NFB and indeed Canadian society imagined the natural world. By disentangling the tropes and motifs that recur in NFB depictions of the land, we can understand more fully how this government agency participated in the construction of nature and how cinema contributed to Canada's literal and imagined relationship with its geography.

To explain how and why the NFB visualized landscapes the way that it did, in this chapter, I examine NFB representations of the North, a place that scholar Sherrill Grace calls "one of the most long-lived nationalist markers in Canadian culture."[2] The NFB made dozens of nonfictional films about the North, including films about industrial development, geology, science, and the Inuit. In all these works, the North looms large. Despite the supposed objectivity of the documentary camera, however, representations of northern spaces were never impartial. As NFB filmmakers trudged through the snow and composed shots with frostbitten fingers, they framed the landscape from a certain point of view. Through the lens of the filmmaker, the North was more than just a geographic feature or an ethnographic fact; it was also a place of national significance layered with colonial ideologies about racial superiority, progress, and modernism.

Beginning in the 1940s and moving through to the 1970s, the NFB represented the North in three major ways: as a wilderness sublime, as an exotic "other," and as a modern space governed by the state. Although these representations appear to be incompatible (images of a desolate North seemingly contradict later depictions of a developed hinterland), jointly they expressed a southern and specifically federal vision. These ideological framings further cemented the North as an emblem of national identity. This unforgiving yet poetic landscape reminded southerners of their rugged (and mythical) Nordic past as well as their profitable future. Through a combination of nostalgic images and modern narratives, NFB filmmakers integrated distant lands and exotic peoples into the larger story of a nation coming into being.

Idea(s) of the North

The word *North* in the Canadian lexicon is a complicated one. It denotes different things to different people. Its definition also seems to change constantly. Although geographers and government surveyors have staked their professional reputations on where this region begins and ends, the North is best understood as a landscape of "shifting boundaries"—that is, fluid and evolving.[3] In physical terms, the word *North* has been used to describe the backcountry directly above Georgian Bay as well as the territory that stretches from sixty degrees latitude all the way to the Arctic Circle. But the idea of the North is also located deep inside the national imagination. As humorist Stephen Leacock mused in 1936, the "vast unknown country of the North, reaching . . . to the polar seas, supplies a peculiar mental background" for Canadians.[4] The North is therefore more than a point on a map; it is also a place of dreams, myths, and desires.

Leacock's description of a landscape of the mind anticipates the theories of geographers and historians who argue that place is historically and socially contingent.[5] Landscapes are imaginative environments as much as they are physical objects. (The term *landscape* was first employed in the seventeenth century by painters to describe what they were painting, not actual environments but their facsimiles.) Thus, Louis-Edmond Hamelin asserts that "mental structures . . . constitute the most powerful determinants of the North." People's expectations of what the region should look like "surpass that of the most easily identifiable physical realities such as freezing."[6] The Inuit and the Dene, for example, regard the broad sweeps of the North as their homeland, whereas Canadian artists and storytellers from the South figure the North as a mythological place of death, despair, or enlightenment. Some Canadians even see this geography as the source of the nation's vitality. Despite the variety of interpretations and renderings of the North, a number of scholars have noted that the dominant view of the North is based on a southern perspective. As an institution created by the federal government, the NFB contributed to the social production of northern landscapes from a southern perspective.

The various "mental structures" that Canadians from the South have used to conceptualize the North are complex indeed. Pierre Berton, the popular Canadian historian, once observed that this region is as "elusive as the wolf howling just beyond the rim of the hills."[7] It shifts and plays tricks on the mind. Nonetheless, there are a few enduring ideas about this piece of geography relevant to the NFB's presentation of it. One of the most popular southern beliefs about the landscape featured in NFB documentaries is that the North is a forbidding and primeval wilderness, "majestic in its grandeur," to quote Shelagh Grant.[8]

The first people to imagine the North as terra incognita were seventeenth-century European explorers. When these bold travellers first anchored in the cold waters off present-day Ellesmere Island, they imported, among other things, a puritanical fear of the unknown. For the sailors, ice shelves, broken and splintered by wind and wave, were proof positive that the northern wilderness was indeed Hell on Earth. Who knew what demons lurked in the melancholy shadows of a midnight sun? Ideas about a wild and malevolent North endured through the nineteenth century. The mysterious fate of John Franklin's expedition (1845–48) and rumours of cannibalism, insanity, and icebergs that reduced mighty bulkheads to mere splinters excited the Victorian imagination about the Arctic.[9]

Whereas newspapermen and penny dreadful writers regaled their audiences with frightening tales of shipwrecks and hypothermia, a group of nineteenth-century artists proffered a slightly different outlook. Painters Frederick William Beechey, Caspar David Friedrich, and Edwin Landseer saw the Arctic as a kind of wilderness sublime, beautiful, rapturous, and spiritually transcendent. The emptiness of the North and its unfathomably large glaciers were heady reminders of the eternality of raw nature and the transitoriness of humans.

Images of an Arctic sublime became a central feature of Canadian culture.[10] In 1930, Group of Seven painter Lawren Harris boarded the SS *Beothic* and headed north on a government-sponsored expedition. During his two-month tour of the Arctic, he encountered the same haunting landscape that arrested the imaginations of Victorian painters. Harris was moved by this resplendent world of ice and snow. The anemic shorelines and isolated peaks stirred in him a kind of spiritual and patriotic ecstasy. "No man can roam . . . the Canadian North without it affecting him," Harris mused. The "coolness" and "clarity" of the landscape, the "feel of the soil," and the "rhythms of its hills" melt a man's "personal barriers," intensify "his awareness," and project "his vision through appearances to an underlying hidden reality."[11]

Harris and his colleagues in the Group of Seven were captivated by the Arctic as well as the austere landscape of the near North, which extended across northern Ontario and Québec. With broad strokes and rich colours, the painters created a kind of mythological geography that reduced northern spaces to abstract depictions of ice, snow, pines, and splintered topography. Over time, their paintings of the North helped establish "a new aesthetic" in Canadian art that "grew and flowered from the land."[12] Middle-class consumers and tastemakers loved these representations because in their view, they expressed the "spirituality and essential Canadian-ness of untouched northern land-scapes."[13] The North was Canada, and Canada was the North.

The NFB and the Northern Wilderness

The construction of the North as a wilderness bereft of civilization was one of the most popular tropes in NFB cinema. Documentarians working in the 1940s and 1950s frequently depicted the North as a rugged and vacant landscape of Precambrian rock and crystal-clear water. Like the Group of Seven, NFB filmmakers consciously and unconsciously filled this wild void with nationalist sentiment about its intrinsic Canadianness.

The first film to frame the North as an antimodern wilderness was Radford Crawley's *Canadian Landscape* (1941). The documentary follows Group of Seven painter A. Y. Jackson as he traverses the wilds of northern Québec looking for a subject to paint. The film describes the Canadian Shield country that Jackson travels into as a "vast and unsentimental land" marked by "harsh ribs of rock," "jag-ged spruce," and "spongy muskeg."[14] Crawley's camera foregrounds the ruggedness of the environment by panning over knotted bushes and twisted brambles clinging to the sides of ancient moss-covered rock faces. This wild landscape is the same unforgiving country that frontiersmen had to contend with in the early years of settlement, the film reports. Whereas other areas of Canada have been tamed by the plow and axe, the northern wilderness remains an uncultivated and therefore pure space.

As a documentary, the film makes an implicit claim about the truthfulness of what is shown. But we must remember that "cinema is never pure vision; it is a coproduction between material practices and human imagination."[15] What appears onscreen (the North as a wild and empty landscape) has been carefully constructed. In the film, Crawley consciously avoids revealing aspects of human culture, preferring to linger on the uninhabited forests of the region. This representational strategy is common throughout *Canadian Landscape*. In the same way that Jackson "clears away the bric-a-brac" to get at "nature's basic design," Crawley employs filmmaking techniques to remove the ecological and cultural "bric-a-brac" to create a mythological portrait of the North. The edge of the camera lens and the scissors of the film editor deliberately cut out images of civilization. This filmic prestidigitation is evident in a sequence near the beginning of the documentary. Crawley sets his camera on the ledge of a cliff. Instead of framing the shot to include Jackson and his easel, Crawley films over the shoulder of the artist. As a result, the subject of the film is not present in the frame—just the wilderness. By excluding Jackson from the screen, Crawley provides spectators with an unobstructed view of the immense and seemingly vacant North. The perspective encourages the viewer to contemplate what geographer Bruce Braun refers to as the "yawning gap between culture and nature, city and country, modernity and its pre-modern antecedents."[16] If Jackson were foregrounded, then the viewer might be distracted from his version of the North and be reminded that humans travel through this geography and sometimes even stop to paint it.

Crawley's representation of the North as a wild frontier was intended to be an imitation of the works of Jackson. According to his biographer, Barbara Wade Rose, Crawley used protracted shots of rocks, trees, and rivers to emulate the sombre aesthetic of the Group of Seven. His style was "unhurried and at home," notes Rose, "much in the way a painting by the Group of Seven might dwell on the Canadian Shield."[17] In *Canadian Landscape*, Crawley wanted the cinematography to emulate the style of Jackson's paintings so that audiences could appreciate the vitality of his work on a whole new level. As a result, Crawley made the documentary in 16 mm Kodachrome (expensive at the time) and used mostly wide-angle lenses to parrot the landscape perspective of Jackson's images.

Rendering the landscape as an uninhabited space meant, however, that certain ecological and social realities were ignored. Romantic depictions of "wilderness" are often characterized by their "amnesia and erasure," explains W. J. T. Mitchell. In the case of *Canadian Landscape*, the film's iconography, though visually arresting, ignores the past and trades history for natural beauty.[18] Crawley's depiction of an unoccupied wilderness censors from the historical record acts of violence, colonization, and environmental destruction. The film's setting of northern Québec and Ontario is home to local Indigenous populations, including the Algonquian and Iroquoian peoples forcibly removed from their homelands in the eighteenth century by French and English settlers and then again in the nineteenth century by the lumber industry. Crawley's documentary also ignores the anthropocentric changes that transpired (and continue to transpire) there. Pulp industries, mining companies, dam operators, and eventually cottagers have altered the landscape in profound and permanent ways.

Crawley's depiction of the North was not historical, then, but a product of the NFB's nation-building agenda, which sought to use iconic Canadian landscapes as symbols of nationhood. In *Canadian Landscape*, the narrator states that the North is representative of "the spirit of Canada" and "the essence of the nation." Later he describes the "silent barren that lies beyond the fringe of settled Canada" as the "birthplace" of Canada.[19] To operate on this figurative level, it was imperative that the image of the North remain abstract, almost mythological, in its adaptation. In presenting the North as a near-allegorical wilderness symbolic of national identity, the filmmaker tapped into a rich visual and rhetorical tradition in Canadian culture. Since Confederation, political ideologues have used images of the wilderness North to promote a certain brand of national identity. Throughout the nineteenth and twentieth centuries, boosters, statesmen, and writers likewise suggested that the North was expressive of Canadian personality. The people of Canada are a resilient lot because presumably they had to overcome the obstacles of the hostile North in order to survive. In an address to the Montréal Literary Club in March 1869, lawyer and nationalist R. G. Haliburton argued that Canada was defined by its harsh climate and challenging topography. One only needed to "glance at a map of the continent" to understand that this was "a northern country inhabited by a northern race," he pronounced.[20] The nineteenth-century Canadian imperialist and educator George R. Parkin similarly argues in his widely distributed book *Imperial Federalism: The Problem of National Unity* that Canada's national identity was specially formed in a northern atmosphere. The chilled environment invigorated Anglo-Saxon institutions, encouraging progress and a mighty and resilient form of civilization.[21]

Canadian Landscape expresses a theme central to NFB cinema: geography matters. Several years later, film commissioner Arthur Irwin declared in an article written for *Maclean's* magazine that Canadians were "molded by a stern and difficult land."[22] In the introduction to the NFB's 1967 centennial book, *Canada: A Year of the Land*, journalist Bruce Hutchinson similarly opined that, if one is to "learn the meaning of the nation, all its hopes and fears," that person must "look to the land and its secret cargo."[23] His words neatly captured the sentiments of many photographers and filmmakers working at the NFB in the middle part of the century. The myriad NFB films and photographs proclaimed that northern wilderness was the quintessential feature of the nation and contained within its imagery the secret to understanding what it meant to be Canadian.

The assertion that both the character and the political economy of the country have been shaped by nature is not new to Canadian historiography. In the 1930s, Harold Innis and Donald Creighton famously posited that "staple commodities" and terrestrial super-highways such as the St. Lawrence River and the Great Lakes supported the growth of a burgeoning empire.[24] Canada was indeed abundant with natural resources, but its unruly topography also constrained settlement patterns and commercial expansion. One could not simply plow a field in the middle of the Canadian Shield. Even the most daring of entrepreneurs had to take what the land gave them. Whether they liked it or not, the North dictated the development of the nation. The thesis that northern nature moulded Canada's unique cultural, political, and economic identity persisted well into the 1970s.

The geographic determinism of Innis and Creighton is further evident in the works of literary critic Northrop Frye. In his evocatively titled *The Bush Garden*, Frye declared that Canadian culture was characterized by a "garrison mentality." The "huge, unthinking, menacing, and formidable physical setting" in which Canadians find themselves inspires an existential dread, a "deep terror."[25] Although the North in *Canadian Landscape* does not conjure up "terror," its unfathomable size and density certainly leave an indelible mark on the imagination. Crawley claims in the film that the North dominates our imagination and has a specific bearing both on how Canada has developed and on how its people have evolved.

As a young organization tasked with defining the nation for Canadian viewers, the NFB, not surprisingly, represented the North in this way. *Canadian Landscape* supported its nation-building mandate to unite the country by visualizing iconic landmarks such as the North. Claire Campbell writes that a sense of belonging "requires visual and intellectual engagement with a place that we can see or imagine, and a story that we associate with it."[26] For Canadians, that place was the wild country found (or, as Campbell argues, constructed) in national parks, abstracted in Group of Seven paintings, and depicted in NFB documentaries. The NFB declared that Canada was a wilderness nation characterized by a sublime northern geography.

John Grierson was conscious of the importance that landscapes play in fostering what Benedict Anderson calls "imagined communities."[27] The commissioner specifically hired the film's director, Radford Crawley, because of his experience promoting Canada to international audiences and recent immigrants. In the 1930s, Crawley had produced a series of short promotional films for Canadian Pacific Railway that marketed the natural splendour of the country to tourists and immigrants heading west. In Grierson's mind, there was no one better suited than Crawley to create a positive and marketable vision of nationhood.[28] The filmmaker's skill in commodifying landscapes through cinematography meshed perfectly with the NFB's mission to define and then project a certain brand of Canadianness.

Crawley's construction of the North as an idealized wilderness illustrates how NFB filmmakers produced (and projected) landscapes of national significance. To imagine the North as a marker of Canadian identity is an imposition of the mind. A jack pine does not literally contain within its bark an invisible force that binds Canadians to their homeland. Neither is there anything intrinsically "Canuck" about snow or ice, as Crawley's film suggests. It is only through a complex system of signification and reproduction that limestone rocks or icebergs floating aimlessly in the Arctic Ocean symbolize the nation. Culture and all its racialized assumptions about nationhood are at the forefront of these depictions, guiding the artist's brush strokes, the writer's keystrokes, and in the case of Crawley, the filmmaker's eye.

Ethnographic Films and the Exotic North

Not all NFB documentaries visualized the North as an empty wilderness. In fact, between 1944 and 1970, the NFB produced over thirty ethnographic films about the people who lived in the North, including films about Inuit art, traditional hunting and fishing practices, and community development. "There was a kind of cult of photographing the Eskimos," remarked Lorraine Monk, an executive producer with the NFB's Still Photography Division.[29] Filmmakers, photographers, and other visual artists working for the NFB were inspired by Inuit people's creativity and their ability to live off the land without the help of modern technology. For these NFB employees, northern people represented a world wholly alien and therefore fascinating. Although these works challenged the notion that the North was physically "empty," their depiction of Inuit culture as "simple" and "primitive" nevertheless reinforced a colonial vision of the region as antimodern, temporally and spatially distinct from the rest of Canada. Ethnographic documentaries fixated on the exotic features of the North and revelled in its otherness. Like *Canadian Landscape*, documentaries about Indigenous people in the North satisfied the desires of middle-class audiences who yearned for glimpses of the atavistic and wild.[30]

Laura Boulton, an amateur musicologist and documentary filmmaker from Ohio, was one of the first to represent the North as a primitive wilderness inhabited by strange peoples in NFB cinema. In 1943, Grierson contacted Boulton to see if she wanted to contribute to the NFB's *Peoples of Canada* series. Boulton accepted the invitation, boarded the RMS *Nascopie* in Montréal, and sailed to Baffin Island with cinematographer Ross McLean. After she landed on Baffin, Boulton hired an "Eskimo schooner" and travelled throughout the neighbouring islands, recording walrus hunts and other Inuit activities for six weeks.[31] The footage that she captured was eventually used to create two films, *Arctic Hunters* (1944) and *Eskimo Arts and Crafts* (1943).

Although Boulton's assignment was to "capture an accurate record" of the life of the Inuit, her films reduced their culture to "an endless struggle for existence."[32] In both *Arctic Hunters* and *Eskimo Arts and Crafts*, Boulton presents the Inuit as a primeval group living among wild animals and extreme weather. Her preoccupation with their ostensibly bizarre rites and customs and their crude technology exemplifies what E. Ann Kaplan describes as an "imperial gaze," a way of seeing geographic otherness by emphasizing Indigenous people's closeness to nature.[33] In Boulton's films, the Inuit are practically indistinguishable from their environment. "Like the animals, the Eskimo survives by following the seasons," the narrator in *Eskimo Arts and Crafts* explains.[34] The North is an alien wilderness where even its inhabitants live like beasts, Boulton's documentaries appear to say.

The presentation of the North as an exotic landscape inhabited by "primitive Eskimos" was later repeated in the documentary films of Doug Wilkinson. His films were more popular than Boulton's and helped establish a template for northern iconography in the mid-twentieth century. His career at the NFB began in the spring of 1945 after Wilkinson was discharged from the Canadian Army. His first NFB project was a short documentary about "Operation Muskox," an ostentatious display of sovereignty in the North in which a cavalcade of Bombardier snowmobiles and Canadian soldiers marched across the Eastern Arctic. The film shoot was difficult, but it also proved to be transformative for the filmmaker, who worked on set as a camera operator alongside cinematographer and veteran of northern filmmaking Roger Racine. Wilkinson fondly recalled those bone-chilling days in the "very bleak, very barren, and very stormy North."[35] For him, they sparked an artistic curiosity that burned for the rest of his career. It was the extremity of the North and its inhospitable climes that inspired the filmmaker to go back. In an interview with the *Whig Standard* many years later, he elaborated that "I hated the land, but I wanted to find out how the Eskimo came to live there."[36]

After Wilkinson finished working on *Exercise Muskox* (1946), he convinced the NFB to send him back to the North so that he could make his own film about the Inuit. With the blessing and financial backing of the NFB, he took a train to Churchill, Manitoba, in the winter of 1948 and made the now famous documentary *How to Build an Igloo* (1949), a short film that celebrates the architectural ingenuity of the Inuit. The following year, Wilkinson returned to the Arctic, this time with his wife, Vivian Wilkinson, who worked as a location manager, and Jean Roy, an eighteen-year-old cinematographer. For the next fifteen months, Wilkinson and his small crew lived with the Tununermiut at Pond Inlet. They filmed *Angotee: Story of an Eskimo Boy* (1953), a fictional account of a young Inuk growing up in the High Arctic, and *Land of the Long Day* (1952), a documentary about Inuk hunter Joseph Idlout. The latter film became one of the most popular works in the history of the NFB. Critics and audiences from around the globe praised *Land of the Long Day* for its "remarkable beauty" and "absorbing exposition of Eskimo life." The film even won the prestigious Golden Reel Award in 1953 as the most outstanding documentary released that year.[37]

Shot on location in the northern part of Baffin Island, *Land of the Long Day* presents the Arctic landscape as an ominous and otherworldly space, cold and dark. Roy keeps the frame wide and uncluttered to accentuate the enormity of this alien environment. His arrangement of polar landscapes recalls the paintings of Edwin Landseer and Lawren Harris. The camera pans slowly over the peaks and valleys, creating extended moments of gothic excess in which viewers are confronted with their own frailty and limitation. The visual power of this wild landscape is further enhanced through the use of light and dark. Abstract shadows slash through the blank environment, making the North in *Land of the Long Day* appear supernatural and expressionistic. Intercut throughout the film are telephoto shots of wildlife and close-ups of Inuit peering from their anoraks. These powerful images declare to the viewer that this is a place that time forgot.

Wilkinson establishes the North as a prehistoric landscape in the opening scene of the film, a wide shot of three igloos clustered against a purple horizon. As the camera tilts down to the camp, John Drainie, a radio actor impersonating the Inuk hunter Joseph Idlout in what one Toronto film critic panned as a "mawkish and infantile voiceover," describes life in the Arctic.[38] "All winter long it is night in my land," he says. "In winter only the moon shines over my land. Between November and February, the sun has gone away. We live out our winter lives hunting and trapping by the light of our winter friend, the moon."[39] The chorus of howling wind and baying huskies punctuates the dramatic narration with mystical affect, confirming that this is a strange world indeed.

Although the cinematography is central to Wilkinson's presentation of the North, the lives of the Inuit people are the most important feature in this tableau of racial and geographic otherness. In *Land of the Long Day*, Wilkinson focuses on details of Inuit life vastly different from those of people who dwell in the urban South. According to the film, Idlout and his family abide on the thin edge between survival and annihilation, relying on innovative ways to capture, clean, and preserve their food. The climate dominates their livelihood in ways that most viewers cannot fathom. The Inuit must build their homes out of the raw elements. Despite the crude materials, they develop an intricate system of cutting out blocks of ice that fit together to keep the heat inside.

The last scene of *Land of the Long Day* further illustrates how Wilkinson uses the Inuit's closeness to nature to amplify the exoticness of the North. The sequence begins when Idlout's father, the family patriarch, spots a pod of migrating narwhals in the bay. They have returned to the shallows to breed and are therefore vulnerable. Idlout and his friend Kadloo set out for the mammals in their sealskin kayaks. Across the dark sea, the men paddle their crafts—like two needles stitching across woolen fabric. The cetaceans notice the hunters and try to escape, but Idlout and Kadloo are veterans. They corner the frantic whales in the shoals. Idlout grabs his harpoon and hurls it at one of the narwhals, aiming just behind the blowhole. His aim is true. A cauldron of blood and sea foam gurgles around the kayak. Before the leviathan sinks, the men drag it ashore. The scene is filled with blood and gore. But Wilkinson plays it straight, suggesting to the viewer that this violent struggle is a natural part of Inuit life in the extreme North. The ferocious acts of the two hunters mean that their families can eat enough muktuk (narwhal blubber) to last the long and dark winter months.

The narwhal hunt is a perfect example of how Wilkinson fabricated moments in *Land of the Long Day* to create a portrait of antimodernism. The thrashing flippers of the whale, the steely concentration of Idlout, and the unsteadiness of Wilkinson's camera all contribute to the film's verisimilitude. Nevertheless, a deeper look into the production of the film reveals that this record of primitiveness was not as genuine as Wilkinson leads viewers to believe. Certain scenes were created for emotional affects. The filmmaker explained in his production notes that the bloody spectacle of the whale hunt was specifically designed to provoke shock in the audience. In a letter to his cowriter, Leslie McFarlane (author of the famous *Hardy Boys* series), Wilkinson professed that he needed the climactic moment of the documentary to feel "primitive and elemental."[40] To achieve this feeling, he had McFarlane rewrite the scene so that Idlout hunted with his harpoon instead of his rifle. This amendment would make the film "appear more authentic," he explained to his cowriter.[41] As minor as this change might seem, it had larger implications for the Inuit in particular and the North in general. By using racial stereotypes of the Inuit as primitives, Wilkinson actively contributed to a larger twentieth-century cultural discourse that imagined the North as a wild frontier inhabited by the other.[42]

As the narwhal hunt reveals, Wilkinson used formal, stylistic, and narrative elements specific to ethnographic cinema to recreate an ahistorical (but popular) image of the North. It is easy to criticize him now for his deeply flawed representation of the North and the people who lived there. Yet *Land of the Long Day* was also one of the first NFB documentaries to exhibit a liberal sensitivity toward Indigenous peoples. In private, the filmmaker considered Idlout a "dear friend," and he repeatedly commended the Inuk for his ability to thrive in the inhospitable environment, which Wilkinson admitted that he was unable to do himself.[43] His admiration for Idlout and the Inuit in general is plain in both the film version and the book version of *Land of the Long Day*. In his account of his time on Baffin Island, Wilkinson characterizes the Inuit as a discerning, patient, and self-reliant people—masters of their own destinies. Likewise, in the documentary, he clearly venerates Idlout and his ability to navigate the tempestuous Arctic Ocean in a handmade kayak to hunt a 940 kg animal with nothing but a harpoon. During production of the film, Wilkinson also commented on how witty the Inuk hunter was. Idlout liked to make fun of Wilkinson and laughed at the absurdity of having a blundering white man follow him around on packs of ice. But Idlout was also a gracious host and took time to teach the filmmaker how to live off the land, Wilkinson was quick to point out in interviews. Over time, the two developed a deep bond. Wilkinson became well versed in Inuit culture, and Idlout developed a keen passion for photography.

Still, it must be acknowledged that Wilkinson's representation of Idlout in *Land of the Long Day* was refracted through a colonial prism, which presented people who lived close to nature as primitive and therefore inferior. Ironically, it was also this proximity to the natural environment that Western culture tended to celebrate and mythologize. According to scholar Shari Huhndorf, twentieth-century North American culture was fascinated with "Eskimos" because they represented the "most intense Darwinian struggle."[44] With the rise of social Darwinism as a way to explain racial superiority and the evolution of culture, the Inuit represented two very different things to white people from the South. On the one hand, their crude habits and tools exhibited their lowly place on the social ladder (and, as we will see, the need for modernization). On the other, their ability to survive in extreme environments despite these limitations reflected the human ideal of being completely self-sufficient. The Inuit were products of a world where only the strongest and cleverest survived. In *Land of the Long Day*, Wilkinson focuses on Idlout's strength and his exceptional hunting acumen, honed—according to the narrator—over years of living close to and respecting the rhythms of nature.

The film's idealized representation of the Inuit thus promotes what Shepard Krech III describes as the myth of "the ecological Indian,"[45] which asserts that Indigenous peoples embodied a romanticized lifestyle founded on a harmonious relationship with nature. As philosopher and ecocritic Neil Evernden explains, "Anyone seeking . . . the eternal standards by which humans ought to live . . . would have to inquire which standards are given by nature. Hence, the widespread interest in primitives, who are often presumed to be living by those primitive standards."[46] In the NFB documentary, Idlout and his family are presented as caretakers of the land, never taking more from it than their needs require. They are innocent, uncorrupted by greed or lust. For Wilkinson, the Inuit were not just artifacts of a dim and ancient world but also icons of ecological bliss and moral purity.

Wilkinson's motivations for documenting the North and its people were complex. The filmmaker was clearly fascinated by the intense northern environment and the alluring charisma of his subject. But

Figure 3. An Inuit man preparing to throw a harpoon at a sinking seal, October 1951. Doug Wilkinson, Library and Archives Canada / National Film Board of Canada fonds/e010692610.

he also firmly believed that documentary filmmaking was a social tool that helped bridge the gap between the urban South and the remote North, a world that he believed was on the verge of disappearing. In an article written for the Canadian magazine *The Beaver*, Wilkinson lamented that "the Eskimo was on his way out" and that southerners were "slated to be the interested spectators of his demise."[47] His films, he argued, preserved an image of a noble people about whom most Canadians knew very little. If documentarians did not undertake the challenging task of heading north to document its people, then the public would not have any "knowledge of the Eskimo . . . and his daily life on the land."[48]

For Wilkinson, such ignorance was a tragedy. Southerners had much to learn from individuals such as Idlout. The filmmaker viewed Canada as a multicultural mosaic; to understand the nation in the middle of the twentieth century, one had to acknowledge the country's diversity and Indigenous past. Wilkinson, and the NFB more generally, used documentaries as a way to record Indigenous culture before it disappeared or was assimilated into mainstream Canada's historical record. And yet this humanist impulse to document cultural difference justified his use of certain filmmaking liberties, such as eliminating the use of the rifle during the narwhal hunt. The irony was that this commitment to cultural preservation was a colonial project of southerners. Such depictions were mostly nostalgic and therefore ahistorical.

Wilkinson's melancholic representation of the Inuit can be seen as a cinematic form of salvage ethnography, a paradigm for observing and recording Indigenous cultures. As a documentary filmmaker, Wilkinson tried to apprehend the reality and history of the Inuit on celluloid as a way to archive their culture. In the early twentieth century, anthropologist Franz Boas similarly implored others in his field to photograph Indigenous peoples and their communities before they evaporated from human history. Boas argued that these visual accounts created an archive of distant cultures, preserving their rites and passages for the rest of time. Through the act of photography, contemporary viewers could understand, even inhabit, the worlds of these primeval peoples in ways that writing could never fully capture.

As numerous scholars have pointed out, salvage ethnography is deeply flawed and steeped in colonial notions of the other. Specifically, it renders Indigenous peoples as icons of the past and confines them to fixed spatial and temporal environments. Film scholar Adrian Ivakhiv likens salvage ethnography to the wilderness preservation movement that emerged in the 1960s, which endeavoured to preserve a romantic image of prelapsarian nature. Wilderness and the Indigenous person were wholly blameless entities, living in an Edenic world of ecological and social harmony—until the modern world corrupted it. Like the idea of wilderness, salvage ethnography placed Indigenous peoples within a stable landscape, a "static diorama" that can be "scrutinized through the colonial eye of science, power, and romantic nostalgia."[49] "The point in both cases is to recreate something presumed to be authentic, whole, and essentially static in nature, the product of evolutionary processes perhaps, but no longer evolving," writes Ivakhiv.[50]

Wilkinson's ethnographic work with the NFB reaffirmed the popular view that the North was an antimodern wilderness landscape, motionless in time. Wilkinson never explored the contemporary effects of modernism on Inuit culture or acknowledged their agency in adopting or resisting government initiatives, despite working as a field officer for the Department of Northern Affairs and National Resources. Instead, he used a pastiche of exotic locales, dramatic narration, and images of supposedly primitive peoples to suggest that the real Arctic was temporally and spatially distinct from modern Canada.

Consequently, Wilkinson's films concealed the historical reality of the landscape, which in fact was undergoing radical changes. Most Eastern Arctic communities in the twentieth century were not isolated from the rest of Canadian society, as films such as *Land of the Long Day* suggested; they were adapting to external forces that brought with them new economic and social conditions. In the early part of the century, political visionaries exclaimed that the North was "Canada's last frontier." By the end of the 1930s, the federal government had asserted its sovereignty in the Arctic in the form of military exercises and scientific expeditions. At first, federal authority in the North was characterized by a policy of benign neglect. Although the state was legally responsible for the welfare of the Inuit as per *Re Eskimo* (1939), the details of northern administration were vague and often contradictory.[51]

This era of inattention, however, was eventually replaced by a more active and interventionist period of administration after the Second World War. In the 1950s, when *Land of the Long Day* was filmed, the social programs of the welfare state ballooned. One of the state's objectives for northern peoples was to integrate them into mainstream society. Government officials argued that the Inuit were suffering from a host of issues, including starvation, disease, and alcoholism. According to federal employees, these challenges were a consequence of living in extreme isolation in a harsh environment.

The solution was simple for the state: northern communities needed to embrace the core values and securities of the modern world. To help the Inuit and the Dene achieve this stability, the government provided them with low-rent housing and increased social services. The state also tried to overcome the perceived environmental handicaps of living in the Far North by integrating remote communities into the wage economy and the political process.[52] In more isolated regions, the government forced communities to relocate to more agreeable environments.

But the development strategy of the state faltered in unanticipated ways. The permanent settlements established by the federal government conflicted with the old authority patterns and kin-based sharing relationships characteristic of Inuit culture. Furthermore, the Inuit who had to move to communities far away from their traditional hunting and trapping grounds felt confused and displaced.

Despite this complicated history of northern peoples, NFB filmmakers such as Laura Boulton and Doug Wilkinson persisted in

depicting the North as a primeval wilderness—exotic and dangerous but ultimately quaint. This benign representation obfuscated
the tremendous effects of the modernization schemes of the state
on Inuit people. It also overlooked the agency of northern peoples
struggling to reclaim their dignity and traditional cultures in this
period of transition.[53] It could be hypothesized that Wilkinson's nostalgic records satisfied southern unease about their role in colonial
domination and the forced absorption of Indigenous peoples into
the Canadian political system.

The NFB's depiction of northern communities changed in the
1960s to more directly reflect the values of the welfare state, which
sought to draw the Inuit into mainstream society. To address
the current plight of the Inuit, several NFB filmmakers went to the
North to investigate the subject of northern development. In
these films, the Arctic was still framed as a hostile environment.
Unlike the sentimental films of Wilkinson, however, these pictures
argued that the Inuit were miserable living there and that they
needed to accept government assistance in order to overcome this
difficult geography.

The film that embodied this welfare state vision of the North the
most was *The Annanacks* (1964). Directed by René Bonnière and written by Don Snowden, an information officer for the Department of
Northern Affairs tasked with solving poverty and unemployment in
the North, the film documents the relationship between government
officers and the George River Inuit. According to the narrator, the
Annanack family and other members of the village are on the "verge
of starvation because of the decline in the herds of Caribou."[54]

Desperate to survive, the Inuit travel to Fort Chimo to seek help
from the federal government, representatives of which are camped
there. After they arrive, the George River residents are advised by
a sympathetic Snowden to trade their ample supplies of timber (a
rarity in the Arctic) for food. With the "guidance and assistance of
the Department of Northern Affairs and National Resources," the
narrator exclaims, the residents form "the first Eskimo cooperative."

Later in the film, Bonnière shows how the federal government has helped the rural community by teaching its members the "democratic process of elections." Under the mentorship of the state, the newly elected president, George Annanack, begins integrating the George River settlement into a regional economy by establishing fishing and logging operations.[55]

The portrayal of the Inuit as a backward people in need of financial and educational help from the government was a product of the progressive, social democratic values of the welfare state in the 1960s.[56] The film stereotypes the Inuit as a people besieged by a barren environment. State officers, in contrast, are presented as compassionate experts who can help the Inuit escape their difficult situation. (This depiction of the Inuit diverges from Wilkinson's representation, which frames the Inuk hunter as self-reliant, resourceful, and happy.) In *The Annanacks*, the federal government is actively involved in helping the Inuit resolve issues "of distance, climate, lack of communication, and lack of technical training and business techniques." After being taught how to transition from a hunting economy to a modern wage economy, they can "maximize their use of natural resources." In doing so, the state helps facilitate a "measure of security."[57]

Despite their different agendas, documentaries about social and environmental reform in the North, such as *The Annanacks*, were thematically consistent with Boulton's and Wilkinson's representations. Both types of film constructed cinematic landscapes defined by their extremity. Furthermore, they visualized the North as an object of southern desire, conveniently sewn into the mythological and political fabric of the nation.

Landscapes of Discovery

NFB filmmakers projected their own visions of the North onto the physical environment and in the process defined the meaning of the landscape for Canadian viewers. Radford Crawley imagined the North as an empty wilderness emblematic of national identity. Doug Wilkinson and Laura Boulton represented the North as a pristine world that titillated southern audiences with images of the exotic and the primeval. In the more progressive documentary *The Annanacks*, Bonnière claimed that the Arctic was inimical to the well-being of the people who lived there on account of its extremity and inhospitable weather. For Bonnière, the North was a landscape in desperate need of modernization and state governance.

Whether the landscape was conceptualized as a platonic ideal that existed somewhere outside time or a space requiring government intervention, the North was ultimately framed as something that served the interests of those in the South. This was also true of NFB documentaries about Arctic exploration, which promoted the intellectual and physical colonization of northern spaces. Films such as *Across Arctic Ungava* (1949), *The Last Voyage of Henry Hudson* (1964), *Alexander Mackenzie: Lord of the North* (1964), and *Stefansson: The Arctic Prophet* (1965) documented the "opening up" of the North to the political and economic interests of the South. In these rousing tales of northern adventure, the landscape was reconfigured as an object of imperial desire—somewhere to plant a flag, a region brimming with resource potential.

This representation of the North is most conspicuous in *Across Arctic Ungava*.[58] The documentary fits neatly into the history of northern exploration in Canada: both the circumstances of its production and the film itself are rooted in a larger discourse about the allure of the North, the landscape's suitability for displays of courage and masculinity, and more generally southern mastery over northern nature. The film documents francophone botanist Jacques Rousseau as he travels to "the unmapped wilderness" of the Ungava Peninsula.[59] He is joined by geologist Edgar de Aubert de la Rue, geographer Pierre Gadbois of the Geographical Bureau of the Department of Mines and Resources, and Jean Michéa, an ethnologist and amateur filmmaker who recorded the expedition with his stout 16 mm camera.[60]

Rousseau's expedition, financed by the Arctic Institute and the National Museum, never intended that the footage captured be made into a documentary. The images of Ungava were an appendix to the scientific notes and charts of "the least known regions in the Eastern Arctic."[61] After some of the footage was shown to the voyage's patrons, however, it took on a life of its own. Michael Spencer, executive producer of the NFB's *Arctic Notebook* series, was one of the first to see the footage. He was astounded by Michéa's camerawork, which contained the most "fantastic and thrilling images of northern life" that he had ever seen.[62] Spencer requested that P. J. Alcock, head curator of the National Museum, send the material to the NFB immediately.[63] Alcock agreed, and Spencer began working on a documentary about Rousseau's expedition and the "keen excitement of . . . Canadian exploration."[64] To get the project off the ground, Spencer turned to Doug Wilkinson for help. After Wilkinson watched the reels himself, he began to stitch the hours of footage into an exciting, albeit abbreviated, yarn about northern exploration and, as I argue, southern mastery over northern spaces.

The mise en scène of *Across Arctic Ungava* is vital to the film's ideological position, for it is where the theme of terrestrial conquest eventually unfolds. Using Michéa's panoramic images of the Ungava landscape, Wilkinson presents the North as a desolate wilderness that tests the limits of modernity. The baroque soundtrack, composed by Louis Applebaum, blares over wide shots of spongy tundra, which "stretches for thousands of treeless miles."[65] The landscape dominates the frame. For Rousseau and the rest of the team, the environment is both a primary shaper of destiny and a formidable foe.

The landscape is perhaps best understood as a character in the film; it serves as a foil to the protagonists who labour to travel through it in order to gain valuable insight into the region's economic potential. To dramatize this conflict between humans and northern nature, Wilkinson portrays Rousseau and the other men as blundering novices in the art of frontiersmanship. It appears that most of their lives have been spent in sterile laboratories or comfortable university classrooms. The inexperience of Rousseau's team and their feebleness in this vast wilderness are depicted early in the film when two of the explorers battle the turbulent Kogaluk River. The men paddle vigorously in their canoes, but the water is too powerful, and they yield to its powerful current, drifting downstream. Sisyphus in the North.

If the first half of the film establishes the landscape as a source of conflict—an impediment to rationality and order—and the men as feeble southerners, the second half shows how the expedition members eventually subdue the unruly environment and turn it into a place of knowledge, familiarity, and passivity. By the middle of the documentary, the North takes on a far less menacing quality as the explorers adapt to the northern environment. The scientists haul Arctic char into their canoes with ease. They paddle effortlessly in the same tributaries that overwhelmed them earlier in their journey. They march over the jagged terrain with confident determination. In the documentary's most iconic moment, they portage up a rocky slope with the nimble expertise of veteran outdoorsmen. After they arrive at the summit, the men pause dramatically, like wool-clad conquistadors, and survey the vast Arctic terrain. The latter image is clearly staged for the camera. Shot from a low angle, the frame visually establishes that Rousseau and company have finally mastered the mysterious Ungava landscape and that everything before them is theirs for the taking. Significantly, their mental and physical energies can now be devoted to searching the terrain for geological and biological data. As the scientists noted in their findings and in their logbooks, the North shrank in size and lost some of its mystery.[66] It no longer held the same power that it did at the beginning of their voyage.

Interestingly, *Across Arctic Ungava*'s jubilant record of southern superiority over (and conquest of) northern nature diverges from Michéa's written account of the journey. In the film, the expedition is narrated as a series of triumphs, each discovery greater than the previous one. Michéa's observations, recorded in a journal, were less celebratory of and more ambivalent about conquering Ungava than Wilkinson's film or Rousseau's personal account of the mission. Comparing the two different accounts of the expedition, we can understand more fully how NFB filmmakers constructed a view of the North that aligned with dominant and specifically state ways of seeing the Arctic environment (as virgin territory, a place where masculinity is performed, a wild landscape brought to heel by southern daring).

According to Michéa, a Canso "flying boat" dropped the party off at Povungnituk, a small trading post on the eastern shore of Hudson Bay. The men headed inland on the Kogaluk River, paddling for three days with their Montagnais guides until they landed at Tassiat Lake. Michéa wrote in his journal that though the explorers were actually experienced outdoorsmen, the first leg of the trip left them "nearly dead" from fatigue.[67] But they pushed on. The next morning, they packed their belongings and began a twenty-mile portage across the countryside, a journey, he notes, that would have been impossible without the help of the four Montagnais (a significant fact mostly ignored in the documentary, likely because it distracted from the romance of men from the South wrestling with nature in the North).

On 2 August 1949, the explorers arrived at their supplies cache on the pebbled shores of Payne Lake, worn out and aching from their portage. After spending the night on the beach, the party lurched on, crossing Payne Lake at dawn. From the shorelines of Payne, they headed east into the uncharted territories of Nunavik, Québec, "the first white men to go there." But "we were not in paradise," Michéa observed bleakly in his journal. The landscape was "nothing but rocks," and there was "nothing worthwhile, even for [the] geologist or botanist." Worse, the explorers discovered that they were lost. The men wandered aimlessly in the rocky wilderness, disoriented by the monotonous horizon and dejected by the rough terrain that continued to unfurl before them. As Michéa wrote, "In such a land,

there is no definite boundary between the west part of Ungava peninsula (water flowing to Hudson Bay) and the east part (water flowing
to Ungava Bay)." Even the "native guides did not know the easiest
route." The befuddled party had to watch "when one small lake was
emptying in[to] another" to see if they were still heading in the right
direction.[68] Finally, on 12 August, the explorers passed into more
familiar country and reached their destination: a small trading post
overlooking the immense Ungava Bay. They spent a week at the
post collecting samples of Arctic flora and rocks, charting fluctua-
tions in the weather, gauging soil readings, and battling a plague of
mosquitoes and blackflies.[69]

The difference between Michéa's chronicle of the Ungava expedition and the euphoric tale of northern exploration (and conquest)
narrated in Across Arctic Ungava is revealing. On the one hand, Michéa
wrote dismally about how the explorers were overwhelmed by nature.
And though they learned a little about the resource potential of the
region, they could not get out of there fast enough. (Rousseau, it
should be noted, was far more enthusiastic about the territory, in
particular its potential for the introduction of reindeer herds and
as "an important reservoir of game for an extensive native population."[70]) On the other hand, Wilkinson reinterpreted "actuality,"
creating an exultant record of their journey to promote a more
celebratory and patriotic vision of northern exploration and development.[71] In Across Arctic Ungava, nature is rendered as a dangerous
obstacle that eventually is vanquished. As the men travel through the
land, the North becomes understandable. By the end of the film,
the region is represented as a "friendly" place overflowing with economic potential. When the narrator boasts about the vast resources
beneath the surface of the tundra, the audience cannot help but
speculate about a future in Ungava that includes bulldozers, airstrips,
oil rigs, and maybe even hotels.

Science Films and Southern Authority in Northern Spaces

Arctic expeditions were an important part of Canadian public memory and national myth making. Stories of brave men who endured inhospitable weather and rough terrain to map the unknown were dramatic reminders of Canadians' identity as a gritty people and their destiny in the North. *Across Arctic Ungava* contributed to this popular rhetoric of northern conquest, and in the process, it reimagined the North as an empty but ultimately knowable space primed for development.

Science films, a variation of the northern exploration genre, similarly configured the North as a rationalized landscape defined by its economic value and accessibility. Documentaries about Arctic biology and geology were touted as educational works that examined the North from a scientific point of view. The region was not a barren world of ice and snow, they claimed. Quite the contrary. It was alive with organisms and sparkling with valuable minerals such as iron ore, copper, zinc, and nickel. By emphasizing the region's fecundity, however, the NFB also supported the government's ambitions in the North, in particular the remaking of the landscape into a resource hinterland.

Dalton Muir's *High Arctic: Life on the Land* (1958) is a perfect example of how science films endorsed a southern vision of the North as a site of resource development and industrialization. Its emphasis on the economically viable properties of the North announced to viewers that the region was suitable for industrialization. Even extreme environments shrouded in myth and mystery could be brought into the economic order of Canada. In this sense, Muir's documentary paralleled the efforts of the South to transform the North into an object of knowledge and rationality in the middle of the twentieth century.

The film's link to larger discourses on northern science and territorial colonization is not immediately evident, however, for the documentary purports to be an objective record of geography. In his statement of intent, Muir described *High Arctic* to the NFB as "a factual film" "in good taste."[72] Strowan Robertson, the writer of the documentary, likewise pronounced the film an "impartial" investigation of Arctic geography: "No film has reached the public which gives an accurate picture of the geological, geographical and biological conditions of this immense area." "Consequently," explained Robertson, "the average citizens know of the Arctic only in terms of polar bears, Eskimo[s] and extreme cold." Through its investigation of the flora, fauna, and geological history of the Arctic, the documentary seeks to demystify "the last of the relatively unknown areas of Canada."[73]

Produced by Unit B's Science Program, *High Arctic* was intended to be used by schoolteachers.[74] The NFB encouraged teachers to pin up reviews of the documentary "to arouse interest" and "to stimulate follow-up activities" with their students.[75] Film distributors even provided educators with worksheets for learners to fill out while they watched the documentary.[76] The quizzes were compatible with contemporary biology and geography textbooks and thus could be incorporated easily into the Canadian public school curriculum.

High Arctic begins by dispelling the notion that the North is an alien world, hostile and inimical to life—a common misperception. After a long shot of a seemingly barren landscape, the narrator explains that there is more to this place than meets the eye; the North is not an unfriendly world of "rocks, scars, and sterile earth" but an abundant landscape where "ecological systems thrive and work."[77] The narrator goes on to describe how organisms have adapted to this environment. The camera zooms in for a close-up of some moss clinging to rocks. A simple organic structure allows the nonvascular plant to prosper despite a lack of water and exposure to the elements, the narrator reports. Even in the most inhospitable regions of the globe, nature endures.[78]

For Muir, the camera was an instrument used to reveal scientific phenomena that static means of representation (maps, charts, and photographs) could not. The cinematography in the film captures

Arctic ecology in "vivid detail," supplying audiences with "exciting evidence of plant and animal life and their constant struggle for survival in the harsh environment."[79] Long, medium, and close-up shots "support the ecological thesis" of the film and create "a sequence of pictorial beauty" supported by "the most telling statistics."[80] Muir presents a macroview of the Arctic landscape with the help of high-powered lenses and aerial cinematography. Editing also helped in this regard. A time-lapse sequence of receding ice in the spring shows audiences how geology and climate work together to form the Arctic landscape.

Although *High Arctic* seems to be apolitical, its declaration that the North is both abundant and knowable is noteworthy. Why the emphasis on value and viability? Examined in the larger context of northern development and northern science in the twentieth century, the film evidently supports the political and economic ambitions of the state in the Arctic. As historian Stephen Bocking has shown, science was a critical component of the federal government's postwar schemes in the Arctic.[81] Funded by the state, biologists, meteorologists, and geologists in the 1940s and 1950s gathered useful bits of intelligence on northern geographies to make a case for the North as a site for development and national wealth. Muir similarly used the superficial objectivity of documentary cinema and science to remove the shroud of mystery surrounding the North and to show that this landscape is in fact a region of untapped prosperity.

High Arctic is closely linked to state ways of seeing northern landscapes in other ways too. The filming of Muir's documentary was made possible because of the Canadian government's presence in the High Arctic. To make production easier, the crew worked out of the Eureka weather station, a scientific research base funded by the federal government. Such outposts, however, were never purely about science. Besides its contribution to meteorology, the station was an act of occupation during the Cold War.[82] Eureka and other installations like it were bastions against Soviet encroachment;

their very presence declared to the outside world that Canada was there first.

Muir also collaborated with scientists who worked for the Arctic Institute (1944) and other state-financed programs, such as the Geological Survey of Canada's Operation Franklin (1955), in making the documentary. Such relationships, to quote historian Edward Jones-Imhotep, "embodied wider struggles to bring a certain understanding of the nation into being."[83] Through their efforts to observe, collect, and test the North, scientists slowly marked the terrain as knowable. Muir's documentary affirmed the federal government's sovereignty in northern spaces and, through the act of filming the region, acknowledged the state's claim to the natural resources of the Arctic.

The close relationship among the NFB, science, and state power in the North appears again in James de B. Domville's *Arctic IV* (1974). The film, which follows biologist Dr. Joseph MacInnis as he explores the Arctic Ocean near Resolute Bay, suggests that scientific research and national sovereignty are inextricably linked. The documentary begins theatrically with MacInnis hovering a couple of hundred metres above the North Pole in a helicopter. In a voice-over, the scientist reports to Prime Minister Pierre Trudeau that his subaquatic expedition in the Arctic Ocean is about to begin. Trudeau responds by calling the scientific voyage a "great achievement for Canada."[84] The scene is emblematic of the film's larger assertion that scientific discovery is as much about proclaiming Canadian sovereignty as it is about knowledge of the physical world.

The association between state authority and science is repeated later in the film. In an interview with the director, MacInnis explains that he is "trying to change the consciousness of the Canadian people and awaken them that almost half of *their* country is under water and that it needs exploration, management, and understanding." He continues that "I do dramatic things to draw attention to the fact we need this kind of exploration, . . . and what better way to do that than pick the pinnacle of diving—that is, the North Pole?"[85] This was more than just science; it was about revealing the heights and depths of Canadian boundaries. MacInnis, who showboats throughout the film, jumps into the ocean and scuttles below the surface to plant a flag under the ice. The scene surpasses the first sequence in the documentary, which visualizes how scientific discovery and state ownership are linked: the government financed research institutes and expeditions in the North, and scientists helped establish a government presence in northern spaces.

NFB filmmakers themselves helped lay the groundwork for the colonization of the North by providing visual proof of the economic potential of the landscape. As part of the filmmaking process, documentarians such as Doug Wilkinson, Dalton Muir, and James de B. Domville amassed cinematographic information on the environment. The camera surveys Arctic geography, providing viewers with a seemingly detached perspective on the North and its features. The images acquired through this kind of filmic surveillance indirectly contributed to southern knowledge of northern spaces. As Jacques Rousseau explained in his report on the Ungava expedition, cinematic images like the ones captured by his companion Jean Michéa "add materially to [Canada's] scanty knowledge on sub-soil" and thus "contribute to the development of the mining industry."[86] In the botanist's estimation, filmic proof clearly proved that the North was a "vital strategic area of Canada" that contained "great mineral wealth."[87]

Bruno Latour's theory of the production of scientific knowledge helps explain how NFB cinema contributed to the formation of the North as an object of imperial knowledge. In *Science in Action*, Latour argues that "knowledge" cannot be *defined* without understanding how it is *gained*.[88] Knowledge, he explains, is an active "cycle of accumulation" in which information and material objects are discovered and then brought back to a central location to be collated. Those in the centre thus have the capacity to acquaint themselves with people, things, and events from the comfort of their labs or offices.[89] With each discovery, scientific institutions amass the financial wherewithal and the political power to send out more expeditions into the dark corners of the map. These voyages supply even more information about the external world. The cycle is repeated until the last "unknown" regions are rendered known. This comprehensive knowledge then helps establish imperial or central authority over far-flung and disparate geographies.

The parallels between the accumulation of scientific knowledge and the role of state-sponsored films are worth noting. How is knowledge about the periphery brought back to the centre for assessment? First, Latour explains, information is rendered mobile. Second, data collected by field scientists are stabilized so that they can be transported back intact. And third, the information is aggregated and organized into practical knowledge.[90] Early scientific expeditions used carracks and other vessels to transport detailed sketches, maps, and samples of flora and fauna back to scientific institutions so that they could be observed more easily. Today information is collected via newer and more adaptable communication technologies, such as the internet, GPS, and the film camera.

NFB movies were vessels that carted seemingly neutral scientific information from the North back to the centre in the South. Images of the landscape were stabilized by archiving the information onto celluloid and then made combinable through film prints and distribution services. An airborne NFB camera could glide above the landscape and record everything within the scope of its lens. Back south at the NFB headquarters in Montréal, the footage could then be edited into a coherent narrative so that the landscape could be better understood, approximated, and in the end rationalized. No matter how far away or overwhelmingly large the North was, the landscape ended up on a scale that Canadian observers could dominate by sight.[91] Films provided an easily interpreted visual record of the North by reducing it to an aspect ratio of 1:66.1 and transmitting that image into theatres, classrooms, or government offices. It was what film scholar Bill Nichols describes as "an economy predicated on distance and control, centred around a single, all-seeing vantage point."[92] Although NFB documentary filmmaking's primary intention was not to claim space for the government, its mission to be the "eyes of Canada" unwittingly supported state objectives in the North by making it visible and thus controllable.

A Developed Northern Landscape

A number of NFB documentaries explicitly presented the North as a modern landscape by depicting the region as a resource-rich environment essential to the economic development of the nation. In the 1940s, wartime films such as *Northwest Frontier* (1942), *Highways North* (1944), *Northwest by Air* (1944), and *Land of Pioneers* (1944) proclaimed the "awakening of a new land."[93] Industrial projects such as the Alaska Military Highway and the Canol pipeline are vaunted for connecting the resource-rich but remote North to the rest of Canada. "Yes, the country is wild and rough in places, but the isolation of the Canadian northwest is gone forever," the narrator of *Northwest by Air* boasts as a survey plane flies over the Mackenzie River delta, its wings glinting in the sun. New transportation arteries and superior aerial technologies herald "the grandeur and the future promise of Canada's great northwest."[94] These networks will allow for the extraction and distribution of raw materials to the rest of Canada. *Northwest Frontier*, a film about the pioneers who "go north," similarly describes the landscape as a site in transition. The "old, isolated North" is being replaced by the "new, pulsing currents of modern business and social life moving in." The documentary goes on to argue that advances in technology make the full transformation of the North into a developed hinterland all but inevitable. "The bush plane," the narrator extols, is "drawing this huge territory into the mainstream of Canadian life."[95]

The colonization of the North by the South is evocatively captured in NFB cinema through depictions of what David Nye terms the *technological sublime*.[96] In the script for *Northwest Frontier*, James

Beveridge describes the arrival of southern technology in the North as an ecstatic experience. "A shadow swept down the river, a new noise split the silence, the roar of aircraft down the Mackenzie, over Great Bear Lake, . . . up to the Arctic Islands," effuses the screenwriter.[97] The plane, with its sleek lines, raw power, and ability to conquer space and time, arouses a feeling of transcendence, of godlike power over geography. Like the tractor in Evelyn Cherry's agricultural documentaries, the aircraft is a powerful motif in a number of films about northern development and progress. The plane symbolizes a nation coming into being as well as the power of technology over the environment.

The NFB continued to produce films that celebrated the North as a modern landscape, vital to the national economy. Documentaries such as *Beyond the Frontier* (1952), *Our Northern Citizen* (1956), *Down North* (1958), *The Accessible North* (1967), *North* (1969), and *A Northern Challenge* (1973) extol the abundance of natural resources concealed beneath the Arctic and sub-Arctic terrain and then commend the efforts of the individuals and institutions that transform this raw geography into useful territory. The North is "bountiful," "raw," and "plentiful," the narrator of *A Northern Challenge* rhapsodizes.[98]

Many of these northern development films also called attention to the social benefits of a modernized North. In *Down North*, Hector Lemieux describes the Mackenzie River delta as a "fertile sub-Arctic valley" undergoing environmental as well as social transformations.[99] The delta region, in Lemieux's estimation, is a utopian landscape where Indigenous and white people work together, plundering the region's natural wealth for the benefit of all. Through a combination of Indigenous labour and "white man's technology," the land supports the economy of "Canada and the world."[100]

Despite their proclamations of social equality and welfare, depictions of a modern and industrial North in NFB documentaries are often distinguishable by their colonizing discourses. Aerial shots of the "virgin" landscape flash across the screen as the narrator in *Down North* talks about the region's availability for "exploitation." Later, images of fecundity are juxtaposed with industrial technologies such as excavators as they clear the once pristine land. These depictions are more than just neutral records of events in the North; they assert, with great pomp, that the white enterprise has conquered the crude northern landscape and harnessed its natural resources. Films like *Down North* even go so far as to suggest that southern colonization of the northern landscape benefits the "primitive" Indigenous people who live there. For the South has brought churches, missions, and new jobs to the Inuit and the Dene.

Cinematography played a crucial role in presenting the North as a modern, productive, and colonized environment. According to the production notes for *The Accessible North*, the documentary employed aerial cinematography to show the "limitless space" of the sub-Arctic and its "abundant resources [, which] promise . . . a secure future."[101] Panoramic shots of industrial mining and bird's-eye perspectives on transportation infrastructure illustrate the enormous scale of northern development. "A ten-year, one hundred million–dollar program of highway construction is under way in the Yukon," the narrator boasts as the camera pans slowly over the modernized landscape. Over nine thousand tons of "payload" can move in fifteen hours from the "sub-Arctic down through the flat farmlands of the Peace River district."[102] The denuded landscape is not intended to shock or disgust the viewer; rather, it is meant to inspire awe at the ability of humans to alter this geography. Such representations vividly illustrate the South's total mastery over this once untamed (and therefore unproductive) wilderness.

The use of cinematography as a way to advertise the South's control of this landscape is most apparent in *North*, a fifteen-minute documentary coproduced by the Department of Indian Affairs and Northern Development (DIAND) and directed by Josef Reeve. The promotional poster for *North* emphasizes that the film's cinematography employs evocative imagery to highlight "the vastness, the variety, and the welcome of the North."[103] The film was first conceived in 1967 when Vic Adams, chief of the Liaison Division of DIAND, sent a letter to the NFB requesting a short documentary that would encourage "tourists," "sportsmen," and "business entrepreneurs" to visit the "captivating" Northwest Territories.[104] The NFB assigned Bill Canning, a young producer, to work on the project immediately. Canning was, in many ways, the perfect man for the job. He had just finished work on *Blades and Brass* (1967), a short film about the grace and beauty of hockey set to Tijuana Brass. The documentary did not contain any narration, only images of NHL players dancing around the ice. Without the help of voice-overs, Canning was able to effectively convey the poetic and simultaneously bloody spectacle that is hockey. Canning wanted to do something similar in the sponsored documentary for DIAND. Rather than "telling" audiences, he endeavoured to show them the plenitude awaiting them in the North. In a proposal for the film sent to Jon Evans, chief of the Industrial Division at DIAND, Canning explained that he was going to use "the pulling power of a film" to capture the North "as it really is."[105] For him, the North was the central character of the film. The natural lushness of the landscape, wrote the producer, "reaches down to our smog bound skies and whispers, 'Come, come and see me, come and fish my waters, come and see my mountains, my open spaces—Come North for I am the last frontier on my continent.'"[106] In an earlier meeting with Adams, Canning had suggested that the film be shot on 70 mm film stock but for financial reasons eventually settled for 35 mm. Canning stated emphatically that 16 mm "was out of the question for a film that would live or die on the scope and magic of its colour."[107] The officers at DIAND were initially reluctant to approve the original budget ($63,095) for the documentary but eventually acquiesced when Canning described how "wide panoramas" and "breathtaking aerial photography" would publicize "the vast difference in terrain" and show "that the land is virtually man free."[108]

North was released on 19 June 1969 at Hyland Theatre in Toronto in front of *First Time* (1969), a comedy helmed by Hollywood journeyman James Neilson and starring Jacqueline Bisset.[109] For the most part, moviegoers were more impressed with Canning's documentary. *North*, as one critic wrote, was "an eloquent introduction to our anticipated future activities in that part of Canada." "The truly fine photography stirred strong sentiments about Canada's North," he remarked. "We never got tired of seeing it," explained another film-goer.[110] Through its imagery, mostly mediated through slow pans and magisterial perspectives, *North* documents the "many-sided" views of the landscape, including both its exotic and its modern features. "The film captures the allure of it all," a promotional poster claimed.[111]

NFB pictures about the transformation and exploitation of this abundant hinterland, like *Down North* and *North*, reflected a twentieth-century Canadian exuberance about industrializing northern spaces. The discovery of oil at Norman Wells in 1920, the launch of the first Eastern Arctic Patrol under the command of Captain Bernier in 1922, and the arrival of the bush plane sig-nalled new economic possibility in the North. In his book *The Friendly Arctic*, famous explorer Vilhjalmur Stefansson described the North as "alive," "friendly," and "fruitful." It was only "the mental attitude of the Southerner that [made] the North hostile."[112] This antiquated view prevented the landscape from becoming, to quote Stefansson, "a country to be used and lived in just like the rest of the world."[113] Stefansson and others questioned the notion of an inhospitable North and argued that its difficult conditions could be overcome through technology, determination, and state sponsorship. The explorer's knack for storytelling and his compelling argument that the Arctic was in fact neither "lifeless" nor "silent" impelled politicians such as Prime Minister Robert L. Borden to examine the economic potential in the polar region more closely.[114]

After the Second World War, the Canadian government spent considerable time and money developing the North into an indus-trial landscape. Fearing a Soviet attack in the Arctic, the government established a military presence.[115] It also initiated widespread economic programs in the region to help stimulate northern development and encourage private investment. The development of the North received another boost from Lester B. Pearson in 1946. The diplomat and future prime minister wrote in an article that "Go North" had officially replaced "Go West as the call to adventure."[116] Echoing Stefansson, Pearson argued that "a whole new region has been brought out of the blurred and shadowy realm of Northern folklore and shown to be an important and accessible part of our modern world."[117] With aid from the government in the form of more capital and political labour power, the "snowy wastes of the Canadian North" would yield "many more mineral secrets."[118] A year later, in 1947, the Department of Mines and Resources produced a lengthy report entitled *Canada's New Northwest*. Its authors argued that the region was vital to the health of the national economy in the post-war period. The Department of Mines and Resources' report on the economic potential of the Arctic was an adumbration of things to come. As John Sandlos and Arn Keeling show, Cold War demands for industrial minerals such as nickel, cobalt, zinc, lead, copper, asbestos, and uranium in the early 1950s helped precipitate a concerted effort to industrialize the region.[119]

Government interest in the North reached its zenith in 1958 when Prime Minister John Diefenbaker and the Conservatives turned their "Northern Vision" into a successful federal election platform. In his campaign, Diefenbaker proclaimed that the future of Canada lay in the North, where rich mineral deposits and untapped raw materials would usher in a new era of growth and prosperity.[120] After he was elected, Diefenbaker followed through on his promise to exploit this abundant region and created the Roads to Resources program, which strengthened the nation and cultivated new avenues of commerce in the North. The development of the North did not end with Diefenbaker, of course. Under the leadership of Prime Ministers Lester B. Pearson and Pierre Trudeau, the Canadian state continued to reshape the North in its image.

Despite the concerns of a growing number of environmentalists and Indigenous rights activists about the exploitation of the landscape and the mistreatment of the people who live there, NFB documentaries were remarkably consistent in their appraisal of the North as an economic and political utopia through the 1970s. Films such as *A Northern Challenge* (1973) continued to support the industrialization of the North. Like other documentaries in the genre, it describes the Arctic barrens as, "until recently, a forgotten wasteland" but now a landscape of "oil, mineral, and gas resources." "As our need for these resources grows, they become increasingly important to Canada's future," the narrator explains in a formal, baritone voice. The film highlights how industrialization and new transportation infrastructure "demolish the effects of space and time."[121] Highways, railways, and most importantly, aircraft connect the North to the mainstream economic activities of the rest of Canada.

A Northern Challenge examines the federal government's decision to construct ten airfields in the remote Arctic. The Department of National Defence agreed to participate in the $5 million project and built six air bases with military personnel. According to the film, the airfields will "integrate a network of existing airstrips" and help "establish further links of northern communit[ies] and new resource areas." In addition to providing important connections to the rest of Canada, the airstrips will facilitate the conveyance of fundamental goods to the Inuit, who had been relocated. The Inuit at Whale Cove shudder at the mention of returning to "the hardship and insecurities of following caribou."[122]

Nonfictional filmmaking is a particularly effective way of envisioning the physical world. Audiences can view the world as the camera sees it: unmoored from the physical restraints of the human body. The camera pans, zooms, and tracks its way through a range of geographies, recording visual information about places near and far. But the camera is not as neutral or objective as it appears. There is always someone behind the camera manoeuvring its line of sight and therefore steering ours. Just as a cartographer foregrounds certain topographical features on a map and diminishes others, so too a filmmaker decides which aspects of the landscape to show and which to conceal.

Distinguishing between what is *found* and what is *constructed* in nonfictional cinema is difficult. "Documentaries," film scholar William Guynn explains, "tend to produce an image whose power of analogy is prodigious and capable of mimicking the chronology of real events by representing the movement of persons and objects through time."[123] To discern how individual filmmakers or larger institutions such as the NFB constructed Canadian landscapes, we must pay attention to the process of filmmaking as well as the larger context in which the images were produced.

In the case of the North, one of Canada's most enduring and potent symbols of national identity, the NFB envisioned a certain kind of landscape. Filmmakers such as Radford Crawley, Doug Wilkinson, and Dalton Muir used a combination of filmmaking techniques and narrative tropes to construct the North as a place of national significance—cultural, economic, political, scientific, et cetera. Their constructions reflected southern, and specifically federal government, sensibilities concerning the landscape. Normative representations of the primitiveness or economic potential of the region said more about the desires and expectations of the South than they did about the ecological and social realities in Resolute or Inuvik.

The NFB's representations of the landscape legitimized and clarified the state's ambitions in the North. Through depictions of both the exotic and the modern, NFB filmmakers reaffirmed the official vision of the landscape as a new frontier for state authority. NFB cinema stitched together a celebratory history of nation building in which the development of the North was presented as both necessary and inevitable.

In a way, filmmaking in the North was analogous to the Arctic expeditions of the eighteenth and nineteenth centuries. Like those intrepid explorers who built cairns and planted flags as acts of occupation, NFB documentarians claimed geographic, intellectual, and cultural spaces for the federal government in the North.[124] As NFB film crews marched through the North in search of images, they marked the region as "explored" and henceforth under the jurisdiction of the state.

The NFB's construction of the North was also inspired by its institutional mandate to integrate disparate geographies and populations into mainstream Canada. In some respects, the NFB responded to Harold Innis's famous concern about problems of communication infrastructure in the North. For Innis, communication was necessary to conquer space and time. Unreliable radio in the North threatened "Canadian National Life," he lamented.[125] NFB cinema helped unify the North and provided a reliable network of shared Canadian stories and governance in the North. In a 1962 annual report, executives of the NFB urged its members to "improve and expand its film distribution" in the North.[126] According to board members, it was paramount that the NFB work "effectively [to] bring the Canadian story to the peoples of the north" and to supply the "stories of the north to the rest of Canada and its world neighbors."[127] The NFB saw itself as a government-authorized cultural moderator tasked with linking peripheral regions to the rest of the country through a shared set of stories and cinematic images. At the official opening of the NFB head office in Montréal, Vincent Massey remarked that the agency would "play a vital part in making Canadians conscious of their country." Canada was "vast and complex," but through "the eyes of [NFB] cameras," Canadians could "know every nook and cranny." Massey lauded the "imagination" and "skill" of NFB filmmakers who brought Canada's "people more closely together" and gave "an awareness of [the country] and [its] identity."[128] To draw the North into mainstream Canada, the NFB ignored the paradoxes and differences of the landscape, framing it simply as either exotic or modern. Consequently, the NFB participated in what geographer Louis-Edmond Hamelin calls "Homogeneous Canadianization," a discursive process in which the North is made into a region similar to all other parts of Canada.[129] The image of an exotic North, or a North primed for development, was much easier to comprehend as a nationally significant space than a fragmented, complex, and even contradictory place.[130]

3

Cry of the Wild

I am going to leave my friends in the city,
I am going to leave my family,
I am going to leave my friends in the country,
I am going to look for what is free.
I am going to look for what is free—temporarily,
What is free? What is free?
There is many a trail to the wilderness, and many a tale
    out there,
where the wolves move through with the caribou,
where the breezes do not care, where the breezes do not care.
I have looked across the Northland as far as I can see,
and I have seen the creatures where they live in harmony,
and I am learning what that means.
All of us are runners, caught in the river's rays,
some of us are hunters, and some of us are chased,
and sometimes we change place.
When I am tired of the life I lead,
wonder where it leads,
when I am tired of the life I lead,
I wonder what I need, I wonder what I need.

                    —Bruce MacKay, "Theme Song"

The National Film Board of Canada (NFB) documentaries generally reflected a state way of seeing nature. The filmmakers framed the environment as a static object that could be first controlled and then exploited. There were several reasons that the NFB envisioned nature in this way. Doing so was practical: NFB filmmakers were merely producing what their sponsors wished them to produce. Documentarians were quick to recite the lofty ambitions of the agency ("to declare the excellence of Canada to Canadians and to the rest of the world") when they explained their motivations, but in reality, creative decisions were made for pragmatic reasons, such as funding.[1] The NFB relied on the federal government for financial support, and sponsored filmmaking was lucrative. As a result, most documentaries were information films commissioned by government departments and used in educational contexts.[2] The NFB fulfilled these requests and as a result defined the environment in ways that a government would. The quid pro quo relationship between the NFB and the government provided the NFB with financial stability, but it also shackled filmmakers to an "official" vision of nature.

The NFB did not adhere to government definitions of the environment, however, just because it required a dependable source of revenue. Filmmakers were also encouraged to make films that contributed to the nation-building mandate of the NFB to produce an informed and unified citizenry. Documentaries about nature thus tended to promote dominant, indeed official, discourses concerning the environment's utility as a resource and as a powerful national symbol of Canada's past, present, and future.

The NFB's representations of nature and the environment evolved in the ensuing decades. The government was still actively involved in NFB filmmaking in the 1960s, but the agency also began to produce documentaries that questioned the utilitarian ethos of the state so prevalent in early NFB cinema. Influenced by the nascent environmental movement and liberated to explore other avenues of inquiry because of institutional changes within the NFB, certain filmmakers argued that nature was not static, a resource to be exploited without consequence. Instead, they claimed, the natural world was a dynamic and interconnected ecosystem vital to the health of human and nonhuman organisms. Changes to the environment (especially disruptions caused by resource extraction technologies) produced unintentional consequences that affected entire ecologies. These environmentalist filmmakers helped initiate a wider and more holistic view of the natural world that included a nonutilitarian appreciation of the beauty of the wild and support for ecological diversity.

Alternative discourses about nature did not appear overnight, however. They developed over time. Nor did these perspectives completely replace traditional state ways of representing nature in NFB cinema. Indeed, the shift from "conservationist" to "environmentalist" narratives was complex, contested, and sometimes conflicted. Consider the documentaries of Larry Gosnell and David Bairstow. Both filmmakers proposed new ways of thinking about nature through their works. Unlike in the celebratory films of the 1940s and 1950s, Gosnell and Bairstow contended that humans inadvertently disturb the environment when they try to control it. But they fundamentally disagreed on how Canadians should respond to this problem. In his later NFB films, Gosnell warned that the agricultural industry's use of toxic pesticides to manage and improve crops destroyed local ecosystems and poisoned human bodies.[3] The only way to protect nature from harm was to stop using pesticides altogether. Bairstow, an accomplished producer with NFB, had a different solution to the problem of pollution, one more in sync with the technocratic solutions advocated by the provincial and federal governments. In *River with a Problem* (1961), Bairstow and director Graham Parker argued that state experts and scientists could (and in fact should) troubleshoot the environmental mistakes of the past. Government funding, specialist knowledge, and modern waste management were in fact vital to restoring "the balance of nature."[4] Thus, Bairstow proposed that sustainable economic growth was not incompatible with environmental protection.

The uneven development of environmental narratives in NFB cinema of the 1960s was also evident in its documentaries about wilderness protection. Like those of the preservationist movement in the late nineteenth century, NFB filmmakers such as Ernest Reid, Christopher Chapman, and Bill Mason believed that they could help Canadians reestablish a physical and emotional connection to nature through visual depictions of wilderness. Together they advocated for the protection of sublime nature in its original state. As modern urbanized civilization chewed up more tracts of land to satisfy the hunger for living space, it was important that humanity preserve the remnants of these wild sanctuaries. Its salvation in a sense depended on it.

Despite their radical critiques of industrial society, however, the filmmakers were unable to break away fully from the entrenched belief that humans should actively control nature in order to improve it. Sometimes the only way to save wilderness was through regulation and management, they argued. *The Enduring Wilderness* (1963), for example, occupied a fuzzy middle ground where contemporary discourses about preserving wilderness overlapped with traditional state attitudes toward scientific management.[5] For Ernest Reid, the film's director, wilderness preservation was a *technical* problem to be solved by park administrators and regulatory sophistication.

This view was in contrast to the more radical environmental ethos of Bill Mason, who was critical of the government's capacity to manage the wilderness. In his films *Death of a Legend* (1971) and *Cry of the Wild* (1972), Mason rebuked the retrograde government conservation policy on wolves. He argued that its schemes were based on the deep-rooted but misguided opinion that the predators were "wanton killers."[6] Exterminating wolves because their voracious appetites for blood threatened valuable resources was antiquated and, worse, pointed to humankind's dissolving relationship with the natural world. Mason claimed that the only way to protect the wild and thus mend humanity's connection to the natural was to appreciate its fierce beauty without intervening in its affairs.

In the two documentaries, Mason showed audiences that wolves were not inherently evil but rather magnificent and surprisingly tender creatures. More importantly, he suggested that their essence as roving predators was symbolic of the freedom and beauty of the wild. By understanding the wolf's true nature, Canadians could recapture a sense of the wild in themselves. Nevertheless, Mason also realized that the filmmaking process itself was an act of intrusion on nature. In his effort to document the wildness of wolves, he unwittingly manipulated them so that they would perform for his camera. In this sense, he was no different from representatives of the Canadian Wildlife Service (CWS), who also used sophisticated technologies and biological research to preserve wolf populations.

The NFB and the 1960s

To understand the evolution of environmental narratives in NFB cinema, it is important that we take a step back and explore the larger historical context in which they were produced. Two major factors influenced NFB filmmakers' progressive representations of nature in the 1960s and 1970s. The first factor was a shift in the NFB's philosophy on documentary filmmaking. In the 1940s and 1950s, documentaries were seen as objective—accurate and unbiased depictions of reality. How filmmakers presented that reality, or "truth," was relatively consistent. A voice-of-God narrator made sense of what was happening onscreen. The narrator, usually with a sonorous and authoritative voice, declared that what appeared onscreen was factual. Sometimes the images were filmed to fit the narrator's claims; at other times, the filmmaker used preexisting stock footage and cobbled it together to support the thesis of the film. In both instances, the content of the film (images, facts, figures, expert testimonies, etc.) provided a clear picture of the world as it really was.

At the beginning of the 1950s, however, belief in the supposed objectivity of documentary cinema began to erode. Filmmakers increasingly acknowledged and even embraced the idea that nonfictional cinema was actually subjective. The NFB released several innovative and well-regarded documentaries in this period of upheaval, such as *Neighbours* (1952), *Corral* (1953), *Paul Tomkowicz: Street-Railway Switchman* (1953), and *Les raquetteuers* (1958). In its own way, each film subverted the notion that there was a single truth about the world that could be expressed through the lens of the camera.

NFB directors continued to push the envelope of documentary filmmaking practices. Jean Rouch, a French filmmaker and one of the founders of cinéma-vérité in France, identified Pierre Perrault and Michel Brault's *Pour la suite du monde* (1963) in the influential publication *Cahiers du cinéma* as an important moment in nonfictional moviemaking. He remarked in an interview with Éric Rohmer and Louis Marcorelles about direct cinema that the NFB documentary was especially noteworthy because it provided a glimpse of this fragmented and sometimes contradictory world.[7]

The most radical NFB films in this period were produced by the much-celebrated Unit B. As a whole, they were some of the first documentaries in the history of cinema to interrogate the relationship between image and reality. Unit B sought to make high-quality and aesthetically engaging films that did not adhere to one viewpoint or official discourse on Canada or the world. Under executive producer Tom Daly, the unit produced groundbreaking works by Norman McLaren, Colin Low, Wolf Koenig, Don Owen, Roman Kroitor, and Arthur Lipsett. Influenced by the candid work of French photographer Henri Cartier-Bresson, Unit B filmmakers challenged authority and expertise by making films about everyday people and ordinary life. They followed their subjects around their environments, thus providing audiences the chance to see the world through their eyes. To aid their mobility on set, the crew developed lightweight equipment and synchronous sound so that the director could shoot the subject from a variety of angles and in spaces hitherto inaccessible.[8]

Over time, Unit B filmmakers developed a cinematic technique that they called "candid eye." Unlike the expository documentaries of the 1940s, candid eye films did not have a preexisting argument or script. The filmmaker seemingly just followed a story wherever it led them. The spontaneity of the candid eye process made it difficult to organize the narrative structure of the film. Editing helped with the storytelling, certainly, but filmmakers were comfortable with loose structures; they were more concerned with letting subjects speak for themselves. If their work bordered on incoherence, well, that was just a reflection of the messy world in which we live.

Unit B filmmakers famously resisted certain documentary techniques. They opposed voice-of-God narration, believing it to be passé and politically oppressive. Subjects should speak for themselves, they argued. Rather than using the booming voice of a narrator to impose an external order on the people or events onscreen, Unit B directors encouraged their subjects to narrate their own thoughts, even if they challenged the filmmakers' own beliefs. Sometimes there was no commentary at all. Finally, Unit B filmmakers avoided tidy endings in their documentaries. Film scholar Peter Harcourt argues that Unit B films were characterized by a "quality of suspended judgment, of something left open at the end, of something left undecided."[9]

The importance of candid eye filmmaking, as scholars Jim Leach and Jeannette Sloniowski observe, "lies less in the specific techniques" than in their critique of "some of the basic assumptions of documentary film theory and practice."[10] Candid eye and cinéma-vérité techniques raised questions about authorship and subjectivity, issues that the filmic dogma of John Grierson could not or would not answer. Unmoored from the restraints of old technologies and antiquated ideas about truth, authority, and cinema, NFB filmmakers were even comfortable including themselves in their films. They acknowledged the influence of their authorship on the films, including how a subject interacts with the camera.

As an institution, the NFB acknowledged the importance of making more complicated films, even if they defied the status quo. In the *Annual Report* for 1965–66, the NFB conceded that Canadians had come to expect a more complex type of film. "Audiences were becoming increasingly sophisticated, knowledgeable and organized," interested in the "intensive study of specific subjects, rather than in general information," the report noted.[11] Canadian viewers wanted films that "challenged and stimulated" rather than those that "didactically informed."[12]

These new currents in film theory had a tremendous impact on how nature was represented in NFB cinema. Although sponsored works were still prolific in the 1960s, filmmakers such as Larry Gosnell, David Bairstow, and Graham Parker went off script, investigating the root causes of environmental destruction without the blessing of government departments. They showed that the planet was a complicated place and that the meanings (and utilities) of nature were different depending on the individual or the community. Sometimes their films directly condemned the notion of state discipline and authority. From a technical standpoint, interviews about the effects of pollution were filmed on the fly, and cinematographers equipped with lightweight gear could record instances of ecological destruction at a moment's notice. In some cases, the camera mimicked the perspective of wildlife. Environmental cinema still had a long way to go, but NFB filmmakers helped develop a more sophisticated and journalistic way of representing nature.

The second factor that influenced NFB representations of nature in the 1960s was the advent of environmentalism as a popular social movement. Environmentalism developed out of two nineteenth-century intellectual trends: conservationism and the wilderness preservation movement. Conservationists argued that land practices should be guided by the principles of "wise use." This strategy ensured the sustainable exploitation of valuable natural resources in perpetuity.

Preservationists had different, more quixotic ideas about the protection of nature. Unlike conservationists, they advocated the safeguarding of large tracts of wilderness areas to be maintained in their supposed original states. John Muir, Henry David Thoreau, and Ralph Waldo Emerson argued that wild spaces needed to be protected from industrialization—that way people who travelled into the wild could experience the salubrious properties of nature and reinvigorate their spiritual and physical health.

Twentieth-century environmentalism was influenced by these two movements, but it also diverged from them in important ways. Conservationists, writes Samuel P. Hays, praised the "efforts of managerial and technical leaders to use physical resources more efficiently."[13] It was a practical movement devoted to the rational management of natural resources. Wilderness preservation was noninstrumentalist in that it was committed to protecting nature for its own sake. Nature was believed to be in its ideal form when it was undisturbed by humans. In contrast, environmentalism concentrated on humans and their surroundings. It sought to improve the quality of air, water, and land through both individual and collective activism.[14]

Environmentalism was particularly concerned about the effects of radioactive fallout and chemical poisoning on human and nonhuman environments. At the end of the 1950s, a cadre of young, educated citizens concerned about toxic substances and other Cold War–era dangers demanded greater transparency from private corporations and government bodies.[15] Activists also insisted on having a role in decision-making processes alongside scientists and policy-makers.[16] Indeed, it was not enough to warn the public; industry needed to be restricted from dumping wastes or emitting toxic fumes through regulation.

Rachel Carson's *Silent Spring* was one of the first books to warn the public about the dangers of environmental carelessness. Her book, writes historian Mark Dowie, engendered "a brand-new constituency of middle-class activists."[17] By the 1960s, it became nearly impossible for citizens to ignore the effects of industrial growth on the natural environment or on human health. The emergence of ecology as a scientific discipline in this period further confirmed the notion that postwar economic growth had an identifiable impact on ecosystems and human bodies. Over time, the public became more conscious of humanity's interconnectedness with the natural world.

Silent Spring was a major catalyst for the environmental movement in Canada, but it was not the only one. Modern environmentalism in New Brunswick was sparked by protests against the province's controversial spruce budworm spraying program in the 1950s. Sportsmen and scientists decried New Brunswick's war against the budworm, claiming that DDT was killing salmon and harming other game species.[18] In an attempt to save the province's forests, public protests challenged the government's use of pesticides.

Environmental attitudes in Ontario shifted in the mid-1960s when government institutions failed to curb the dumping of phosphate-based detergents into local watercourses.[19] Grassroots organizations responded to this public health problem by demanding changes in government regulations. They used the press and television to hold the polluters accountable and to mobilize public support for the banning of phosphate-based detergents. Pollution Probe was partially responsible for inspiring the environmental movement in Ontario. Inspired by Larry Gosnell's Canadian Broadcasting Corporation (CBC) documentary The Air of Death (1967), students from the University of Toronto formed the organization to generate support for their environmental cause.[20] Pollution Probe quickly grew, and by the end of the 1960s, the group had successfully campaigned against the institutions responsible for polluting the Great Lakes and other environmentally destructive projects.

Around this time, NFB filmmakers also began to investigate the relationship between humans and their local ecosystems. In fact, NFB documentarians were some of the first Canadians to sound the alarm on the unseen threats of pollution and their impacts on the natural world, inhabited by human and nonhuman organisms.

In the process, they helped change public attitudes toward the environment and its meaning. Significantly, NFB films about bio-diversity, ecological ruin, and pollution predated protests against nonsoluble detergents in Ontario's waterways or even Carson's *Silent Spring*. This suggests that there was an important link between NFB filmmaking and the birth of environmentalism in Canada.

The Problem with Pesticides

One of the first NFB documentaries to examine the harm to nature caused by industrial society was Larry Gosnell's *Poison, Pests, and People* (1960). The film explores the widespread use of pesticides in contemporary agriculture. DDT and other chemical compounds are key components of modern farming. Despite their apparent utility, however, there is a significant downside. Viewed by many as a mod-ern panacea against blight and pests, pesticides in fact distress local ecosystems and cause illness in people.

Poison, Pests, and People stands as one of the NFB's most intrigu-ing environmental documentaries. For one thing, it clearly diverged from the typical NFB representation of Canadian agriculture by advocating a more complex view of nature and by criticizing certain modern agricultural practices, which had been lauded as essential to farming. In the 1940s and 1950s, filmmakers such as Evelyn Cherry encouraged farmers to improve the land with science and technology. No matter the physical context, nature could be made to serve the needs of the farmer. Gosnell himself celebrated government strat-egies to transform the agricultural landscape into a more productive and homogeneous space in documentaries such as *The World at Your Feet* and *Chemical Conquest*. In *Poison, Pests, and People*, however, the filmmaker renounced his position and condemned society's constant tinkering with nature. Gosnell asserted that the modern agricultural impulse to modify the natural world (monocrops, new strains of grain, etc.) and then to control that hybrid space with pesticides created unanticipated ecological problems, including wildlife destruction and human sickness. Unlike most of his peers at the NFB and in the agricultural sector, Gosnell recognized that humans were inexorably part of the land beneath their feet. The things that people introduced into their environments in the name of profit and productivity had significant impacts.

It is easy to view Gosnell's work in *Poison, Pests, and People* in isolation, as a bold shift in environmental filmmaking. His documentaries about nature developed gradually, however. As a student at the Ontario Agricultural College at Guelph University, Gosnell learned that technology and science—organic chemistry and biology—were tools that allowed agriculturalists to transform the natural world. After he graduated in 1949, Gosnell began to make short documentaries about the heroic exploits of laboratory scientists who helped Canadian farmers protect their crops from ravenous pests by developing state-of-the-art pesticides and new, resilient strains of produce.

The filmmaker continued to applaud scientists' contributions to farming when he was hired by the NFB in 1951. Both *The World at Your Feet* (1953) and *Chemical Conquest* (1956) argue that agricultural science solves issues of productivity. Chemicals can make the soil more fertile. Pesticides also reduced the harms caused by insects and other pests, thereby allowing crops to flourish unmolested. During the production of *Chemical Conquest*, however, Gosnell encountered startling information about the country's dependence on pesticides to solve the problem of pests.

Gosnell began questioning whether insecticides were as helpful as they initially appeared. While he was conducting research for another film about agriculture and pesticides, he discovered that insects were becoming resistant to even the most potent chemicals on the market. This growing immunity forced the chemical industry to create even deadlier poisons to exterminate these "super pests."[21] But what did people know about these new toxins? What impacts might they have on other organisms?

The history of parathion, one of the most lethal insecticides in Canadian history, was a perfect example of the lengths to which agriculturalists were willing to go (and the risks that they were willing to take) to destroy pests. The pesticide was used by growers primarily to kill red mites, which feasted on apples. At first, the toxin was quite effective in exterminating the pesky bugs. Over time, however, the insects developed resistance to the substance. The tenacious adaptability of the mites inspired the chemical industry to introduce "400 or so new organic pesticides . . . that were just as lethal, if not more so, to the natural enemies of a given pest as to the pest itself."[22]

Good for science, perhaps, but this chemical arms race was not sustainable, Gosnell realized. Poisons more harmful than parathion threatened the health of other organisms, mammals even. Gosnell suggested that in its effort to destroy all pests, the agricultural industry had inadvertently compromised local ecosystems. The chemical compounds obliterated the pernicious bugs, but they also killed other organisms in the process. Gosnell concluded that once people use pesticides, "nature ceases to be on their side."[23] It is a kind of Pandora's box: this supposed cure-all gets away from them and wreaks havoc on the rich web of life thriving in the soil.

The agricultural industry's chemical war on insects troubled the young filmmaker. If birds and mammals were dying from insecticide poisoning, what did that mean for humans? After all, people were the ones who ate the produce sprayed with pesticides. A report from a Food and Drug Directorate lab in Ottawa told a sobering story. Gosnell learned that every person whom the lab had tested had traces of DDT in her or his body tissues and that the authorities were "very concerned about this situation."[24] They suspected that pesticides used in crop farming were to blame for a host of human illnesses, including cancer.

Despite the apprehensions, the Food and Drug lab could not do anything about the problem: it did not have the funds to conduct further research, and the scientists were skeptical that they could challenge the hegemony of the agricultural sector, which had a vested interest in the use of pesticides.[25] "Why do we use these chemicals so extensively if they are known to be dangerous to human life?" Gosnell mused after he read the report from the Food and Drug lab.[26] He hypothesized that society was unable to stop using them because the food industry "depends on them so exclusively that if we were to suddenly stop . . . there would be no crops."[27] In other words, pesticides were too ingrained in Canadian farming practices. Poisonous as they were, they were extremely effective in protecting crops from pests. And a crop sprayed with toxic chemicals was more likely to have a high yield. To cease using them was no longer an option. A pamphlet published by the technical staff at Cyanamid of Canada summarized the technological determinism that Gosnell was up against: "Insects and weeds are man's biggest competition for food. Millions of dollars' worth of food production are lost annually by infestations." The pamphlet claimed that if Canadians were to reap the benefits of "healthier livestock and more profitable crops," then pesticides were essential.[28]

Disturbed by the profligate use of dangerous chemicals in Canadian society and angered by the agricultural industry's indifference to their dangerous effects, Gosnell decided to expose the hidden dangers of this technology in his next film, *Poison, Pests, and People* (1960). The NFB was mostly on board with the project, but because of Gosnell's provocative claims, the agency closely monitored its production.[29] Don Mulholland, one of the producers on the documentary, cautioned the filmmaker that his "editorial viewpoint" was "highly partial." Mulholland explained that the film's premise that "we are all being murdered in our beds" was sure to rankle a few industry heads and potentially sour the relationship between the NFB and key government sponsors such as the Department of Agriculture (DOA). "If we're going to take that point of view, we have to be able to prove we're right—and we'll have to prove it in court," Mulholland advised.[30] Gosnell agreed that his claims were contentious. That was the point. "This is a very controversial subject," he wrote in a letter to Mulholland. "We will no doubt be vilified by chemical companies and pest control experts. Just the same, I think we should do it."[31]

Gosnell took the counsel of Mulholland seriously. He sent letters to a number of experts asking them if he could interview them about why pesticide residues were showing up on produce in grocery stores across the country. As he canvassed health-care professionals and agricultural experts, Gosnell came across a damning story about pesticide use, in which a "dangerous situation resulted from a lack of information." When the filmmaker visited several fruit and vegetable growers who supplied the big Campbell and Heinz plants in the Leamington district of southern Ontario, he was told by a farmer that he sprayed his crop with DDT very close to harvest and well after the legal time limit of twenty-five days. Gosnell asked a manager at Heinz about this, but the manager assured the filmmaker that it was not a problem because the chemicals "only concentrated in the skin of the crop."[32] The manager also promised Gosnell that canning factories tested their produce and would not can any food that had any residue. A representative from the canning facility in Leamington, which supplied 85 percent of the baby food consumed in Canada, confirmed "that they made a careful check of representative samples of baby food cans."[33] Gosnell sent a letter to the DOA for reassurance that this was the case. An official in the department replied two weeks later that Heinz did not have any facilities or procedures for carrying out these checks. Gosnell was flummoxed. Why would Heinz lie about this? The answer, of course, was money. Food producers believed that there were sufficient checks and balances within the agricultural industry to keep poisoned fruits and vegetables from appearing in grocery stores. There was no reason to cause alarm and certainly no need to recall any products.

The problem of pesticide use extended to other areas of the industry, Gosnell discovered. Farm owners represented a stable market for chemical producers, which advertised their pesticides to farmers as "miracles of modern science," Gosnell wrote. They showed a "single-minded dedication to the business of selling more chemicals, more powerful chemicals, to an ever-widening agricultural market."[34] Pesticide manufacturers benefited enormously from farmers' reliance on their products. If it was shown that these products were harmful to people and that their traces were ending up in grocery stores, then the companies would be ruined financially.

Gosnell's research on the agricultural industry formed the basis of *Poison, Pests, and People*. The film takes a journalistic approach. Gosnell interviews experts and visits labs across the continent to ascertain the threat of pesticide use to human health. The film begins innocuously enough. A quick survey of how pesticides are used in contemporary society introduces the viewer to the world of modern-day farming. Toxic chemicals such as DDT are sprayed around the world, the film informs the viewer. The substance protects monocrops from mites and fungi and stops outbreaks of malaria in India.

Despite all the good that pesticides have done for society in the twentieth century, there is clearly a hidden cost to their use, the film argues. DDT and other pesticides have disrupted wildlife and even entire ecosystems. Fish, birds, and mammals have been "poisoned in the destructive war man wages against pests," the narrator states ominously.[35] The film cuts to a close-up of a dying salmon. It has been unwittingly poisoned by DDT, the narrator reports. The chemical compound is breaking down the nervous system of the fish, and it can no longer take in oxygen through its gills.

Yet the problem of pesticides does not end with dead fish. The film argues that these poisons destroy local ecosystems and thus inevitably enter human bodies. Dr. W. C. Martin, a specialist in geriatrics in New York, and Dr. L. W. Hazelton, the president of Hazelton Laboratories in Falls Church, Virginia, confirm that pesticide use presents "a serious risk" to human health because of the process known as bioaccumulation. Martin explains that toxins amass up the food chain until they enter humans' digestive tracts. Dr. R. A. Chapman of the Food and Drug Division of the Department of National Health and Welfare suggests that people are also being poisoned from foods still wet with the toxic compounds. Pesticides discovered on fruits and vegetables at local grocery stores "can cause serious harm," Chapman says. Sometimes these toxins enter the body without people ever setting foot in a grocery store. In another interview, Dr. Malcolm Hargraves, a blood specialist at the Mayo Clinic, recounts with dispassionate authority several instances of people dying from chemical exposure merely because they lived close to crops sprayed with pesticides. When it rains, the chemicals filter into local reservoirs. People drink the water and are thus poisoned.[36]

The documentary's explanation of how pesticides invade and then poison human bodies was significant. Mirroring the work of contemporary ecologists, *Poison, Pests, and People* was one of the first NFB films to argue that people are connected to the larger environment and that even the smallest disturbance in the ecosystem has consequences for the whole web. Perhaps the clearest example in the film of the biological link between people and their surrounding environments is in a scene shot but deleted from the final cut.[37] It is a wide shot of a small park in some nondescript suburban neighbourhood. (Again, we see the use of typification as a filmmaking strategy in NFB films to communicate the universality of the message.) The camera then tilts down to a group of children playing in a pool. A passing truck sprays a thick fog of DDT along the quiet boulevard as the kids splash around. The billowing cloud obscures the children as it floats past the camera.

The documentary then cuts to a nearby forest, where the same poisonous cloud seen in the previous frame descends lightly on the trees. Pushing through the branches, the camera finally settles on a small stream where a fish killed by DDT bobs up and down in an eddy. The motif of water connects the image of the poisoned fish to that of the children swimming in the pool. The message is clear: people are unknowingly breathing in the same deadly fumes that kill smaller organisms.

Just as Mulholland predicted, the caustic *Poison, Pests, and People* infuriated a number of people within the agricultural industry. When a shorter version of the documentary, called *Deadly Dilemma*, was shown at the Resources for Tomorrow conference in Montréal, representatives from the Canadian agricultural sector criticized it. One member barked that the documentary "over-stressed the deadly effect of chemical sprays on wildlife."[38] Other viewers balked at the filmmaker's claim that DDT sprayed on the forests of New Brunswick to kill spruce budworms inadvertently destroyed the salmon population in the Miramichi River—even though the government's own scientists had been monitoring the issue since the mid-1950s.

Scientists employed by federal and provincial pest control programs also chastised Gosnell for his work. Dr. Beverley Smallman, director of entomology and plant pathology for the DOA, for example, complained that the filmmaker had "pulled the rug out from under them."[39] Smallman had expected a film about the "degree of control and highly developed sense of responsibility of the government" in monitoring toxic levels, not "fear mongering."[40] Unhappy with the depiction of the government, and in particular his department, Smallman demanded that the NFB pull the film from distribution, which it eventually did.

Larry Gosnell left the NFB shortly after *Deadly Dilemma* was blacklisted from distribution. He continued to make radical environmental films. Six years after *Poison, Pests, and People* was released, he directed one of his most famous and incisive documentaries, *The Air of Death* (1967). The film, made for the CBC, examined cancer and respiratory diseases related to air pollution. According to a CBC study, 1.5 million Canadians tuned in to the television broadcast, an astounding number for an in-house production. The film was a watershed moment in the history of Canadian environmentalism.[41] Gosnell's assertions that the Electric Reduction Company in Dunnville, Ontario, was responsible for illness in residents made a lasting impression on audiences who, until that point, had little knowledge of the relationship among pollution, air quality, and human health. Upon seeing the movie, concerned citizens urged the Ontario government to investigate the matter of air pollution more closely.

Like *Poison, Pests, and People*, the television program sparked a firestorm of controversy. A government report in 1968 confirmed Gosnell's suspicions that industrial pollution affected animal and plant health, but it also stated that people were not in danger.[42] The investigation committee concluded its report by reprimanding the CBC for airing an "irresponsible and alarmist" piece of journalism.[43] The CBC subsequently appeared in 1969 before the Canadian Radio-Television and Telecommunications Commission, which held public hearings on whether the national broadcaster should make political documentaries. Despite the backlash, Gosnell's films continued to inspire environmental activism in Ontario. Indeed, *The Air of Death* was a catalyst for Pollution Probe, the environmental organization founded by students and faculty from the University of Toronto.

Gosnell's environmental films are an important chapter in the story of NFB cinema. *Poison, Pests, and People* was one of the first NFB documentaries to argue that efforts to control nature (in this case, maximizing agricultural productivity by introducing inorganic compounds) affect the health of ecosystems and therefore the lives of Canadians. As the promotional piece for the film's premiere on the CBC's *Documentary 60* program noted, people were "part-losers in the battle of extermination."[44] In this sense, Gosnell introduced a necessary reclassification of the human/nonhuman divide asserted by twentieth-century conservationists and preservationists. Unlike his contemporaries, he based his understanding of the environment on the emerging ecological idea that people are part of a natural continuum and therefore susceptible to changes within it.

The visual motifs and environmental themes that Gosnell cultivated at the NFB leached into other arenas, including the CBC and then Pollution Probe. More broadly, the ideas that he wrestled with were early examples of popular environmentalism in Canada. His polemic against chemical insecticides in *Poison, Pests, and People* even predated Carson's seminal critique of pesticides, *Silent Spring*, by two years. Carson claimed that human efforts to manipulate nature were "conceived in arrogance, born of the Neanderthal age of biology and philosophy when it was supposed that nature existed for the convenience of mankind."[45] Gosnell likewise castigated the belief that people could modify the environment without consequence. The impulse to control nature without an awareness of the delicacy of local environments had devastating consequences for both nonhuman and human ecologies. This new perspective marked an important transition in both popular and NFB discourses on nature. Whereas state-sponsored films denounced the wasteful destruction of the environment because it threatened a valuable economic resource, Gosnell denounced postwar society's dependence on science and technology to improve the natural world because it destabilized an interconnected but fragile web of life.

A Serious Matter

The same year that *Poison, Pests, and People* premiered, the NFB began developing another film about pollution called *River with a Problem* (1961). The documentary, written and produced by veteran NFB filmmaker David Bairstow and directed by Graham Parker, investigated water contamination, a "problem of growing concern."[46] Bairstow had just completed *Morning on the Lièvre* (1961), a visual paean to Québec's Lièvre River and photographed to the accompaniment of a narrator reading Archibald Lampman's eponymous poem. The contemplative film is an elegy to the "crystal deep" of the sublime river.[47] But Bairstow recognized that not all rivers are as splendid as the Lièvre. Other waterways in Canada carry ugly secrets deep beneath their placid surfaces. Bairstow thus elected to focus his next documentary on the Ottawa River, a "river with a burden," bringing with it "the choking refuse of civilization and industry."[48]

The pollution of the Ottawa River was a matter of public record and a source of embarrassment. In an address to Parliament in the summer of 1955, Prime Minister Louis St. Laurent called the polluted

Ottawa "a serious matter" that required an "immediate solution."[49] Six years later, Walter Gray, a reporter for the *Globe and Mail*, pointed out that the waterway had become "the shame of the nation." "The scum floating on its surface casts a repulsive effluvium over its channel as it swirls downstream," Gray wrote.[50]

In *River with a Problem*, Bairstow similarly shows how effluent from industrial activities upstream obliterates the "balance of nature." "When man dumps waste into the river," the narrator intones, a "revolution occurs in the underwater kingdom."[51] In an animated sequence, the film reveals how this "revolution" transpires. The microscopic flora in the water thrive on the excreta of creatures. When new substances are introduced into the water, the flora become preoccupied with breaking them down. The microscopic organisms feast on the dross of civilization, using up large quantities of oxygen to digest the new materials. As a result, larger entities such as fish and aquatic plants begin to suffocate. Eventually, the whole tributary perishes from a lack of oxygen. The consequences for people are severe as well. Drinking water becomes tainted. Fishing industries dry up. Marinas go bankrupt. Like the sunfish or the water lily depicted in the cartoon, the cities that rely on the river for sustenance slowly asphyxiate.

River with a Problem resembles *Poison, Pests, and People*. Like Gosnell, Bairstow identified industrial pollution as a major problem in modern society, one that would not be fixed easily. As people alter the environment, whole ecosystems suffer in unanticipated ways. Progress has a price. Yet there are important differences between the two films regarding pollution. Stylistically, Gosnell's documentary is polemical, even caustic. The agricultural industry needed to be held accountable for its irresponsible activities, Gosnell declared. Bairstow was less inflammatory. He did not take the government to task for its lax regulations, nor did he criticize the pulp industry's deplorable operational standards. In fact, Bairstow was so lukewarm in his account of who was responsible for the contamination of the Ottawa River that the Canadian Pulp and Paper Association, arguably the single biggest polluter of the waterway, praised the documentary for its even-handedness. "All have agreed that you have done a most effective job of presenting a controversial subject in a fair and impartial manner," Douglas Jones, a manager at the association, remarked.[52] In the documentary, the narrator ambiguously explains that pollution is just an unfortunate side effect of modernity. "The timeless pattern of . . . self-purification in a natural river" is disrupted by the "by-products of urban growth," the narrator says over an animated sequence of industrial expansion.[53] The film also does not mention the possibility of limiting industrial waste or penalizing the perpetrators for dumping effluent into the river.

Perhaps the most significant difference between the two films is their belief (or lack thereof) in scientific expertise and technology to restore nature. Gosnell believed that such an unwavering belief had actually led to polluted environments, whereas Bairstow believed that scientific technology was the solution to the problem. Instead of carping industry for polluting local water supplies, Bairstow optimistically focused on how Ottawa was fixing the issue of contamination. Graham Parker, the director of the film, interviews engineers, health experts, and civic officials, including the mayor of Ottawa, Charlotte Whitton, and John Pratt, a silver-haired MP for the Liberal Party, well versed in the art of folksy idioms. Each interviewee boasts about modern solutions to this environmental issue. "We have got to change our methods of thinking [and] spend a great deal more money on working with nature and not against it," Pratt explains in the film. "When this happens, the river will revert back to its natural state." The concept of "working with nature" is not entirely accurate. The individuals in the documentary prefer fixing nature than working alongside it. Nature is presented as static. Equilibrium can be restored if people add or delete the right elements. Bairstow fixates on technological solutions, such as a state-of-the-art interceptor sewer, to the issue of waste. Although the cost is high ($32 million) and the engineering complex, installing an interceptor sewer that runs two and a half miles is "worth it to restore our mighty river."[54]

Bairstow also glorifies the civil servants who use science to determine safety levels in drinking water. The Water Purification Board, which is tasked with assessing the effects of radioactive materials on fish, mussels, and other organisms, "determines the maximum quantity we can accept in our waters without any danger." According to the film, the board is a key factor in the Ottawa River's rehabilitation and, more importantly, in maintaining the health of citizens.[55]

River with a Problem reflected a larger reformist attitude toward environmental management prevalent in the 1960s. City planners in the middle of the twentieth century generally believed that they could stimulate municipal growth and create healthy living spaces through a combination of science, technology, and urban planning.[56] The policies of J. R. Menzie, chief of the Public Health Engineering Division of the Department of National Health and Welfare, embodied such technocratic thinking. Menzie was confident that his staff could "fix the Ottawa River" and thereby improve the quality of life for the residents of the nation's capital. With the aid of modern sewage systems and sophisticated water treatment technologies, city engineers could initiate "effective remedial action."[57] Menzie, who appears in *River with a Problem*, believed that the biggest challenge in cleaning a river of this magnitude was not philosophical (everyone agreed that there was a pollution problem) but financial: the city needed to find enough money to build an entirely new sewer system. The federal government was willing to provide low-interest loans to the city for remediation, but most of the costs would have to be paid by Ottawa. Thus, if remediation was to proceed, then the public had to be convinced that cleaning up the river was necessary and that their tax dollars were essential to that effort.

It was within this larger context that *River with a Problem* was produced. Indeed, the documentary seems to be more like a political leaflet than journalistic filmmaking. It certainly was perceived that way by Ottawa politicians, who saw in the documentary an opportunity to stimulate audience support for the project. In a letter to Parker, Mayor Whitton explained that the film could also be used to garner support for the cleanup of the city's "great waterways." She was confident that "everyone who saw this film" would have a "better understanding of this tremendous problem."[58] MP Pratt likewise explained to Bairstow that he was going to use the documentary to spread "the cause of anti-pollution among the communities of [his] riding." The MP did have one major criticism of the film, however. He and other MPs who saw it were "puzzled" that there was no mention of legislation that passed in 1960 that lent municipalities two-thirds of the cost of sewage disposal plants at "a very low rate of interest for a period of up to 50 years."[59] "The feeling on Parliament Hill," wrote Pratt, "is that . . . some mention might have been made of the fact that the government has made money available to any municipality wishing to eradicate this unpleasant problem."[60] No doubt his complaint was related to the concern that the public might dismiss remediation as too expensive. Despite this quibble, the film carefully tempers its environmental critiques and endorses government solutions to problems in nature.

The Enduring Wilderness

One of the most popular subjects in this period of environmental filmmaking at the NFB was wilderness. Echoing the passionate voices of nineteenth-century wilderness advocates such as John Muir and Henry David Thoreau, a small number of NFB filmmakers exclaimed that contemporary society must protect its wild spaces from the "expanding patterns of mankind."[61] The first film to celebrate wild nature as an alternative to the polluted modern world was *The Enduring Wilderness* (1963). Directed by Ernest Reid and shot by the award-winning photographer Christopher Chapman, the documentary reflected a growing anxiety about environmental issues in Canada, including public apprehensions about the preservation of wild spaces and people's alienation from the natural world. Released a year before the Wilderness Preservation Act in the United States,

Figure 4. Still from *The Enduring Wilderness* (1963). Used with permission of the National Film Board.

The Enduring Wilderness (originally titled *The Meaning of Wilderness*) argued that the value of nature cannot be measured in boards per feet or cubic volumes. Nature's true worth, the filmmakers asserted, was found in its breathtaking and sublime beauty. When people leave the city and experience nature in its primeval state, they become physically and spiritually rejuvenated.

Although the film promotes a nonutilitarian land ethic, it was sponsored by the federal government, not especially known for a radical interpretation of nature. In the spring of 1962, the National Parks Branch contacted NFB liaison Graham Crabtree and requested that the NFB produce a documentary that encouraged people to visit the country's national parks.[62] The branch saw an opportunity to boost park revenue and to support the "important work" that it was doing to protect Canada's natural heritage.[63] The NFB agreed to make the documentary and then handed the reins over to Reid and Chapman. After several preliminary discussions with the branch, the two filmmakers outlined a nonfictional film that expressed the branch's "philosophy behind the preservation and establishment of National Park areas."[64]

The filmmakers proposed a contemplative, poetic documentary, however—a style that diverged from most NFB sponsored films. (The CWS would follow a similar approach with its popular *Hinterland Who's Who* series released the same year.) *The Enduring Wilderness* employed stunning cinematography and sparse narration, displaying to viewers that wild nature was a "public good" and that wilderness spaces such as those preserved by the National Parks Branch satisfied people's "spiritual longing to contend against wind and cold, and storm and tide."[65]

The film was perhaps the first of its kind in NFB cinema, but it engaged with a much longer history of wilderness aesthetics. Most North Americans in the seventeenth through the nineteenth centuries believed that the wilderness was a savage world, antithetical to progress and an obstacle to overcome. A vocal minority in the nineteenth century opposed this war with the natural world. To quote Roderick Nash, these individuals momentarily "lowered [their] axe and gazed westward from a hardwood ridge at the wild country." What they beheld left them awestruck.[66] In these rapturous moments, they determined that society's enmity with nature was harmful, in both physical and spiritual senses. Romantics such as Ralph Waldo Emerson, Henry David Thoreau, and John Muir believed that wilderness "uncorrupted by man's artificial constructions" was ideal for intellectual and moral growth and a place for "perceiving and worshipping God."[67]

Canada's own conversion to the gospel of wilderness came a bit later. In Canada, early twentieth-century writers such as Ernest Thompson Seton, Grey Owl, and Farley Mowat similarly preached that wild nature was a place for spiritual restoration. Their musings inspired a generation of Canadians who likewise yearned to get back to nature. Vacationing in the great outdoors became so ingrained in postwar culture that historian W. L. Morton described wilderness outings as "the basic rhythm of Canadian life." Everyone went camping. "The typical Canadian," wrote Morton, "spends most of his holiday among the lakes of the Shield or the peaks of the Rockies."[68]

Most alfresco activities were based in Canada's provincial and national parks. The natural amenities of parks, advertised in glossy pamphlets and newspaper ads, were perfect for middle-class urbanites seeking a wilderness retreat. Furthermore, most parks were geographically accessible, yet they still afforded tourists a chance to breathe fresh air and experience solitude.[69] As they pitched their tents beside a lake and listened to the cry of a loon, visitors could imagine what the land was like before modern civilization complicated everything. As a National Parks Branch brochure published in 1957 boasted, wilderness parks introduced visitors to a world where nature "flourished in its *original state*." Tourists escaping the city could immerse themselves in "outstanding natural landscapes . . . as they appeared before man arrived."[70]

The expectation that national parks contained nature in its original (and therefore unspoiled) state was a product of historical and cultural factors. As historian Alan MacEachern observes, Canada's national parks were in fact established and maintained for a variety of purposes. In some cases, their raison d'être was to protect natural resources such as timber and game from subsistence hunters, rural populations, and Indigenous people. Certain parks permitted hunting within their boundaries as long as the hunter had a licence, whereas other parks provided resource industries with special access so that they could harvest valuable raw materials. Parks also functioned as ecological preserves and prohibited any kind of resource extraction within their precincts.

Many national parks served all these purposes at different points in their histories, but the most common role for a national park in the middle of the twentieth century was as a wilderness sanctuary and natural preserve. This particular use emerged at the end of the nineteenth century, when the first national parks were established. Riding the crest of wilderness sentiment in Canada and the United

States, park founders declared that certain spaces owned by the federal government would remain unaltered and henceforth be protected for the benefit of Canadians. Although restaurants, lodges, and other amenities were constructed within the parks, they were still marketed to Canadians as pristine and untrammelled.

It is on this form of land use that *The Enduring Wilderness* focuses. The filmmakers promote national parks as wilderness preserves where Canadians can experience what the country was like before Europeans arrived. They go on to say that parks are vital to the health of the nation, since they allow people to appreciate the wild splendour of the country. This kind of experience was especially important in the modern world. People needed "the tonic of wildness," the narrator explains in the documentary. Upon entering Canada's beautiful parks, visitors are immediately "refreshed by the sight of [nature's] inexhaustible vigour." There are no loud automobiles. No smoke belching from a steel mill. Just the sound of a pileated woodpecker and the smell of pine. These places contain a "secret meaning . . . that can be found only in the heart of the wilderness."[71]

Chapman uses elaborate compositions and long takes to accentuate the splendour of virginal wilderness. The documentary begins with a slow dissolve from a black screen to a panoramic shot of the Pacific coast. Dark waves heave themselves onto a rocky shore and then slide back into the ocean. Chapman lingers on the image of the elemental battle between water and earth for several beats. The rhythm of the tide is mesmerizing. The waves move back and forth, drawing the viewer into the frame. For Chapman, such displays of primal forces invite the viewer to consider nature's raw strength and eternality. "We should feel that taming the wilderness is an impossible task," he scrawled in the margin of his script.[72]

Evocative cinematography was key to communicating the awe of wilderness. During production, Chapman suggested to his director that the film should let the Canadian landscape "speak for itself." "Visuals" were far better suited than narration or voice-over to conveying "the feeling of actually being in wilderness." Excessive nondiegetic sound distracted audiences from the splendour of nature, he argued.[73] Audiences should feel like they are visiting a national park. In the end, viewers were captivated by Chapman's camerawork. His depiction of nature was "superlative," exclaimed one viewer.[74] "[Chapman] captures the feeling of solitude and grandeur that is the spirit of the wilderness," remarked another audience member.[75]

It was important to Chapman that he communicate the majesty of the wilderness to viewers because it was something that was quickly disappearing, at least outside national parks. After the opening scene, the documentary proceeds to narrate the history of civilization. Its story can be summed up thus: human avarice and industrial progress have destroyed many wild spaces. "Our history is short," the narrator says after several minutes of silence. "Only four hundred years ago the first settlers came through the surf and up the shore, seeking a home in the brooding forests of the new land." After a few shots of wilderness scenery, the camera cuts to a wide shot of a small cabin huddled against the foot of a mountain. Dark forest envelops it on every other side. The narrator continues that "for the pioneer, the fight against the wilderness was lonely and long. At first, their work made little impression on the vast stretches of mountain, forest, and plain." When "civilization spread," the narrator continues, "the pattern of nature eventually gave way to the pattern of man." The camera tilts down a mountainside to a train slicing through the landscape like a scalpel. Then the film cuts to an iron bridge hanging perilously over a once-pristine shoreline. The film jumps forward again, this time to a series of well-manicured farms, the wilderness pushed back. The history of progress flashes before our eyes. Every image contains less wilderness than the image before it. The film continues as the camera pans over a pulp mill, belching smokestacks, and finally an entanglement of highways. Settlers eliminated much of the wilderness and, in its place, created a world more conducive to a life of convenience and capitalism.[76]

Exchanging wild nature for a world of concrete was a devil's bargain, though. The synthetic cityscapes are dull and have "little

Figure 5. Still from *The Enduring Wilderness* (1963). Used with permission of the National Film Board.

variety." They "tend to look alike," the narrator bemoans.[77] Chapman's crowded and angular depictions of industrial society convey a sense of artificiality and imprisonment. Shots of polluted environs, colossal skyscrapers, and an endless stream of automobiles flicker across the screen to the tune of blaring horns and jumbo jets. Slabs of cement and iron scaffolding crowd the edges of the frame. The whole sequence depicts the Canadian metropolis as a claustrophobic nightmare.

Chapman's portrayal of urban life paralleled the forewarnings of midcentury cultural critics who argued that postwar culture was conformist and, worse, stifling. In the 1950s, American intellectuals such as C. Wright Mills and William Whyte warned that mass-produced goods, standardized workspaces, and suburban environments eroded the human soul and its desire for freedom of movement and individuality.[78] Modern society was characterized by routine and tedium. Most middle-class North Americans "left home, spiritually as well as physically, to take the vows of organization life," Whyte laments in *The Organization Man*.[79] In Canada, postwar residents similarly fell prey to what geographer Richard Harris calls "creeping conformity"— a world of sameness and banality.[80]

The Enduring Wilderness suggests that the only way to escape from the dreariness of this modern world is to visit wild spaces. Paralleling the contemporary discourses of the Sierra Club and the writings of Wallace Stegner in the United States, Reid and Chapman articulated a growing desire to escape from technology and conformity and to find personal rejuvenation and therapeutic relief in the wilderness. A "return to wilderness is tranquility regained," Chapman mused during the production of the documentary.[81] In contrast to the mundane and repetitive cityscapes of twentieth-century society, wilderness is presented as diverse and abundant, a "temple that is infinitely complex." The narrator goes on to explain that every part of this system "is interwoven with another." "From the prowling predators to the enzymes in the soil, the ecological relationships are subtle and deep yet so carefully balanced," he reports.[82]

The elegance (and mysteriousness) of this ecological web is visualized throughout the documentary. Chapman photographs herds of bison as they move across the plains and then zooms in on a bee as it pollinates a flower. Each shot is linked through colour and movement, indicating that all of nature (at least nature in its wild state) is connected in some subtle but discernible and powerful way.

Humans are not a part of this web, at least not according to the film. Most of the documentary shows national parks as free of people. There is no impression that people—not even Indigenous peoples—ever lived on the lands. People are only visitors, and nature trails are described in the film only as paths that allow people to "visit" this "natural museum" temporarily.[83] But this description of national parks as a place of untouched wilderness is illusory. National parks were not immune to the grasp of civilization. As tourists pushed into untrammelled lands to find real nature, inevitably they brought with them the types of development that they sought to escape.

W. Phillip Keller, an agrologist and a famous nature writer, lamented in 1961 that the construction of highways was destroying the country's "finest park scenery." It was not just roads that ran through national parks, for more and more tourists were visiting them. According to Keller, park traffic had increased a whopping 1,000 percent in just ten years. The Department of Northern Affairs and National Resources explained in its annual report for 1957–58 that 3.5 million people had visited parks in the previous year, 2 million more visitors than three years before. The department anticipated 7 million visitors by 1975.[84] Keller was concerned about the mounting trash that these visitors were leaving behind. More people meant more garbage and more pollution. Nevertheless, the film perpetuates the idea that parks are uncorrupted and that the world outside the confines of these spaces is somehow tainted and less natural.

The Enduring Wilderness celebrates national parks as places fundamentally distinct from human culture and therefore pure.[85] But nature is never separate from human culture—not in parks, not anywhere.[86] There is no such thing as pristine nature, as environmental historians are quick to point out. Nonhuman nature is inextricably connected to the human world. In a wilderness park, for example, people shape this protected landscape in meaningful ways just by choosing to "leave it alone." Ironically, decisions to privilege the "natural" over the "unnatural" are value judgments and cause considerable physical manipulation of the environment.[87] In the case of parks, managers and government officers preserve historical sightlines, directing the gaze of a visitor away from the manufactured landscapes of modern civilization and toward a wilderness "wed to a particular point in time"—a time when voyageurs paddled the vast stretches of rivers in their birchbark canoes.[88] Wilderness was thus *constructed* as anticivilization, a place of solitude, ruggedness, and other virtues that conveniently matched popular conceptions of Canadian identity.

The problematic depiction of wilderness as a place devoid of human culture in *The Enduring Wilderness* does not, however, negate its significance as an environmental film. Its release marked an important moment in NFB discourses on nature, which previously framed the environment merely as a site of resource exploitation.[89] The film advocates a noninstrumentalist way of thinking about land use in postwar society. National parks were vital to Canadian society because they offered a different kind of vision of the world, one in which beauty, diversity, and solitude thrived. As the narrator concludes, national parks "are museums that we visit to gain knowledge about ourselves, to weigh the value of our civilization against the ageless splendour of the wilderness."[90]

The Enduring Wilderness is a complicated film. On the one hand, the documentary supports a state vision of the nonhuman world. Ernest Reid and Christopher Chapman argue that it is the responsibility of the federal government to manage wilderness spaces through legislation and scientific foresight. "How can we use the parks without spoiling them? To preserve them unchanged for a growing population requires expert planning and management," the narrator reminds the audience. Education and expertise are also key to the preservation of natural landmarks. According to the film, park naturalists (hired by the government) are essential in teaching visitors "the meaning of wilderness."[91] On the other hand, there is a sense in which the documentary exceeds the pedagogical intent and ideological aim of the National Parks Branch. The melancholic soundtrack, the ambient noises of wildlife, and the interludes of prolonged silence in the sparse narration all invite viewers to contemplate the majesty of the wild. In many ways, then, *The Enduring Wilderness* is a deeply alluring and profound work that encourages Canadians to rethink the meaning of wilderness. Its message for a world that celebrates wildness still resonates today. Although it was sponsored by the state, the documentary exemplified the shifting sensibilities in NFB works about nature in the 1960s. The elegiac tone and the rich environmental texture of the film anticipated the works of Bill Mason and William Pettigrew. In short, *The Enduring Wilderness* was a testament to a group of NFB filmmakers who advocated an alternative vision of nature.

Bill Mason and Wildlife Preservation

NFB documentarians continued to produce films about wilderness and the role of the government in its protection. *The Enduring Wilderness* suggested that the state could help preserve wild spaces and rehabilitate society's frayed relationship with nature through legislation and scientific management. By the end of the 1960s, filmmakers began to challenge this optimistic, state-centred philosophy about wilderness preservation.

Environmentalist filmmaker Bill Mason was the most notable figure to argue that scientific management only exacerbated the problem. A closer look at his wildlife documentaries reveals a new thread in NFB films about the environment, one that countered normative ideas about the meaning of nature and people's connection to it. Mason reoriented audience perspectives by arguing that nature has a right to exist unmolested, even by the well-intentioned schemes of the state. If people respected the autonomy of the wild and let it flourish on its own, then they would discover secrets about the mysteriousness and beauty of the world and recapture within themselves the call of the wild.

Mason was a powerful advocate of wilderness in Canada. He wrote, directed, and produced twenty-six nature documentaries, seventeen of which were made for the NFB. His documentaries about canoeing and wildlife were a catalyst for the environmental movement in the 1970s. *Paddle to the Sea* (1966), arguably Mason's most famous work, an adaptation of the book by Holling C. Holling, is a beautiful film about a boy's exploration of a world outdoors. Mason's films about wolves were particularly important in the articulation of popular environmentalism in Canada. *Death of a Legend* (1971) tells the story of the wolf, which "fell afoul of predatory man and his technology," and its sequel, *Cry of the Wild* (1972), a feature-length film about the filmmaker's personal bond with wolves, argues that people must not interfere with the "rhythms and patterns" of nature.[92] Instead, they should learn to appreciate it from afar. A noninterventionist approach to wildlife preservation is the only real way to protect and honour the freedom of the wild.

Mason's conviction that wildlife should be left alone was a radical position in the mid-twentieth century even for conservationists. Historically, animals were considered resources that had to be managed by the state. For decades, the federal government defined fur-bearing animals such as deer, caribou, and beaver as public commodities like timber or uranium.[93] Predators, which did not have much economic value, were not protected by the state. In fact, carnivores were considered anathema to wildlife conservation because they destroyed more useful animals whose qualities were highly valued. Wolves, for instance, were hated by rural people and conservationists alike. Wolves hunted wild game indiscriminately and therefore killed animals with economic value. Soon wolves were "managed" in a more vicious way.

Before the state decided to intervene, residents were responsible for keeping lupine populations in check. Farmers and ranchers in the nineteenth century killed wolves because they believed that the animal was a bloodthirsty monster that feasted on easy targets such as livestock. To protect their livelihoods, they declared war against the wolves. The bounty system, established by the federal government at the beginning of the twentieth century to support farmers and ranchers, was a particularly effective way of ensuring that wolves did not kill their herds or flocks. Bounty hunters looking to earn a few extra dollars hunted and killed the animals with extreme prejudice, trading their ears and paws for financial gains.

The state began to manage these predators more actively in the 1930s and 1940s. Killing wolves, at least in national parks, was eventually outlawed in 1940 by James Harkin, the first commissioner of the Dominion Parks Branch, who claimed that "predatory animals are of great scientific, educational, recreational and economic value to society."[94] The prohibition on hunting predators in national parks and the cessation of the wolf bounty in the late 1940s were motivated by modern scientific ideas concerning the balance of ecosystems.

This ban on hunting wolves did not mean that they were free to roam as they pleased, however. Despite their importance to local ecosystems, wolves were still targeted in Canada throughout the middle part of the twentieth century. Government officers argued that though wolves needed to be protected, it was sometimes necessary to cull their numbers to maintain a harmonious balance between predator and prey. Such an ecologically sensitive task could not be entrusted to those who did not have any training in biology or wildlife management. CWS biologist Douglas Pimlott justified in *Canadian Audubon* the selective killing of wolves by the government as necessary because rural people were indiscriminate in their war against the wolf.[95]

Although the language of predator control suggested that the federal government was finally thinking along ecological lines, its schemes were more practical than biological. Wildlife conservation still had a human face. Indeed, the extermination of wolves and other predators was part of a larger state-directed plan for economic development in rural communities that relied on subsistence activities and farming. Progressive-era beliefs viewed wastefulness as an unpardonable sin. For the same reason that foresters were penalized for haphazardly cutting down timber reserves, wolves were punished for their voracious appetites. According to institutions such as the CWS, tasked with protecting wildlife, the wolf left a trail of destruction, often killing animals without eating them.

Governments in Alberta, British Columbia, and Ontario thus poisoned wolves with strychnine pellets and cyanide cartridges. The CWS also slaughtered wolves en masse.[96] In the 1950s, CWS officers slaughtered an estimated 17,500 wolves in a foolish attempt to remedy the caribou crisis plaguing the Northwest Territories.[97] (It did not occur to the CWS that decreases in caribou were the result of environmental change or human predation.) In addition to trying to protect caribou populations, state biologists killed wolves to obtain biological data. A dead wolf was valuable to scientists because it contained a wealth of information about its diet, biology, and health.

The first half of the twentieth century was not kind to wolves. First, they were ruthlessly targeted for their pelts and purported mean disposition; then government men exterminated the predators because they needed to balance nature and because wolves allegedly threatened an economic resource. However, as the century marched forward, Canadians' antipathy toward the wolf began to change. In fact, by the 1960s, it had become a popular symbol of wilderness preservation. For advocates of wilderness, the extermination of wolves by the state perfectly illustrated people's estrangement from nature. Wolves were wild and noble creatures maligned for their cruelty. Their destruction was a tragedy, for it not only slashed the population of one of Canada's most beautiful animals but also symbolized society's crumbling relationship with the natural order of things.

One of the biggest advocates for the wolf was writer-naturalist Farley Mowat. In his famous book *Never Cry Wolf*, he claimed that Canadians had typecast the animal as a murderous beast. According to Mowat, the Canadian government was responsible for this depiction, probably because it was looking for someone or something to blame for dwindling caribou populations. Mowat criticized the state and its hackneyed approach to wolf management, which relied on antiquated ideas about the cruelty of the animal. He took aim at the CWS, for which he had worked in the North. He considered the whole lot to be reprehensible, ham-fisted fools.[98] Although it claimed to act in a scientific and rational manner, the CWS killed wolves based on shaky testimony and hysterical tales about their ravenous appetite for flesh. This was tragic indeed, Mowat explained, for wolves were in fact magnificent creatures that displayed traits such as loyalty, intelligence, and even love.

The scientific community was not happy with Mowat's representation of the CWS. In the press, they disparaged *Never Cry Wolf* as a "semi-fictional" work of "fantasy."[99] They questioned his motives (Mowat was looking for publicity), his methodology (it was ill formed and unsubstantiated), and his integrity (he was flat-out dishonest). Whether Mowat was truthful or not did not much matter in the end, however. The reputation of the CWS had been tarnished. After reading *Never Cry Wolf*, concerned citizens mailed hundreds of letters to the service. They demanded that the CWS stop killing wolves. As historian Karen Jones notes, the book quickly transformed the public perception of the wolf as a "beast of waste and desolation . . . to a conservationist *cause celebre*."[100]

To rehabilitate its public image as a benevolent steward of the country's wildlife, the CWS turned to the NFB (after initial discussions with Disney fell through).[101] The CWS had a good relationship with the NFB. The same year that the NFB released *The Enduring Wilderness*, it also began airing a series of four minute-long commercials for the CWS entitled *Hinterland Who's Who*. The premise was simple: each segment described the natural habitat and behaviour of four different—but very much Canadian—animals: beaver, moose, gannet, and loon. In sixty seconds, the commercial provided key facts about the titular species through voice-over narration, courtesy of John Livingston, the executive director of the Audubon Society of Canada.

In December 1966, David Munro, director of the CWS, sent a letter to the NFB requesting that it make a documentary about the service's "commitment" to "research and management," "vital to wildlife's survival."[102] Two months later, he sent another letter specifying that the film needed to touch on three related themes: "that Canada has a wildlife heritage; that wildlife, as well as having a recreational, economic, and aesthetic value, has an important survival value to some of our peoples today; and that research and management [are] vital if the wildlife resource is to be preserved." Munro stated that he wanted the documentary to highlight the service's devotion to "properly conducted studies of wildlife" and "intelligent solutions."[103] Although the film should promote the work of the CWS, he did not want it to be overtly didactic. The documentary should be "compelling and entertaining" and "somewhat provocative," Munro explained to the NFB.[104] "It should not preach," but it should make "audiences feel something of a worry about animal preservation, perhaps have a better feeling for animals' importance."[105]

Darrell Eagles, head of the Editorial and Information Branch of the CWS, sent another letter to the NFB explaining that the documentary should be about wolves. A film about this predator would help audiences understand "the whole rationale of wise use of our renewable resources."[106] It should emphasize "without a doubt" that the survival of the wolf was due in large part to the "recent work of Wildlife Service biologists in studying this predator and communicating this information to the public." A film of this kind would "generate public support for conservation and legislation . . . [more] than any other single article or endeavor."[107]

A year later, the NFB hired Bill Mason to make the documentary for the CWS. Mason, in many ways, was the perfect man for the job. He had just finished the beloved *Paddle to the Sea* (1966), *Blake* (1969), and *Rise and Fall of the Great Lakes* (1968), and he had become known as "the unofficial in-house wilderness filmmaker at the NFB."[108] It seemed like a perfect match.

Mason, however, was not interested in making a film about CWS efforts to control nature even in the name of conservation. As a devout evangelical Christian, Mason believed that people were intent on destroying God's creation.[109] Every time they stepped in and interfered with the environment, they ruined it. In *Canoescapes*, a meditation on canoeing in the wilderness, Mason mused that "in so many of [their] activities . . . humans have to destroy something in order to create something else." "It all boils down to stupidity and greed," he declared. Civilization is a "grinding war that all of us are waging against wild things."[110]

Death of a Legend, Mason's documentary for the CWS, deviated sharply from the views of his sponsor. He did not trust that science and technology would save nature or, for that matter, humanity's soul. In fact, he claimed that human designs to manage wildlife only drove a bigger wedge between people and the natural world. Monitoring growth rates and snaring wolves for scientific research and biological data, although well intentioned, were forms of control and thus reinforced the deeply lodged belief that humans were superior to nature. The CWS approach to wildlife management was woefully short-sighted and even immoral. Animals such as the wolf should be left to roam free and undisturbed. Only then could people fully appreciate the splendour of the wild and recapture a bit of wildness in themselves.[111]

The competing perspectives of Mason and the CWS are apparent throughout *Death of a Legend*. Instead of making a film about the heroic exploits of the CWS, he made a "film that is on the side of the wolf."[112] Long-time collaborator Ken Buck exclaimed that Mason transformed a potentially "Disneyesque" film about conservation into an "iconoclastic revelation of colossal mismanagement of wilderness and the environment."[113] Specifically, the documentary argues that the "wanton killer" myth of the wolf is so deeply ingrained in Western lore that it has created a dogged cultural and legislative bias against the predator.[114] Although Mason does not mention the CWS by name, he implies that the government branch (the film's sponsor) was complicit in the persecution of the wolf and thus symptomatic of society's enmity with nature.

Death of a Legend begins by pinpointing the arrival of Europeans in North America as a pivotal moment in the history of humanity's separation from nature. "Before man came into the picture," the continent was a "community of creatures maintained by tensions and change," the narrator states. In the documentary, Mason dismisses the presence of "Indians" as having had any major ecological impact on the landscape. For him, the land was a biological Eden where wildlife flourished in beautiful harmony with one another. But then the European settlers arrived. Equipped with iron tools, a Protestant work ethic, and a religious mandate to subdue nature, New World immigrants ran roughshod over this dynamic "web." "Ecosystems did not account for the arrival of man," the narrator says as the film cuts to a montage of environmental ruin.[115] The appearance of Europeans was especially hazardous for predators such as the wolf. The film cuts to a gruesome sequence of a CWS agent shooting a wolf in the head. The animal shudders and then stiffens. A pool of blood expands under the wolf.

For Mason, humans' deep-rooted antagonism toward nature needed to change if wildlife was to thrive and humanity's soul was to be restored. In the documentary, he proposes that people can live alongside these animals, but to do so, they must first learn to appreciate them as magnificent creatures. There are three ways in which Mason depicts the wolf. First, he points out that wolves are not driven by an insatiable lust for blood but complex and noble mammals that embody the freedom of the wild. In one of the more poetic moments in the documentary, the camera lingers on a pack of wolves as they push across the backcountry, over a pack of ice, drifting from snowbank to snowbank, unhurried but purposeful. The ambient sound of the winterscape rings out as the peripatetic animals lope across the screen. Wolves kill when necessary, the narrator claims after moments of silence, but their appetites are well regulated, and they do not kill indiscriminately, as many have suggested.

Second, Mason shows that wolves are complicated social creatures that exhibit human traits such as loyalty, compassion, and generosity. In one sequence, Mason photographs wolves running through a snow-covered forest in a pack. Individual standing within the pack is carefully explained, as are their complex mating habits. Eating is even described as "a ritual as formal as a state banquet."[116] Later in the documentary, Mason focuses on the maternal instinct of the female wolf. Her gentle attention to her cub is framed in sympathetic close-ups. The cub howls as its mother licks its fur tenderly, cleaning it.

Third, Mason argues that wolves are essential to the health of ecosystems. Although many hunters claim that wolves kill game indiscriminately, the predator in fact is a valuable member of its ecological niche. It kills and consumes animals that are sick or weak, and it keeps ungulate irruptions in check. Echoing the work of American conservationist Aldo Leopold, Mason shows that the wolf is "essential to the natural scheme of things."[117] "The presence of wolves represents a healthy living wilderness, in ecological balance, and our lives are the richer for it," the filmmaker wrote in his outline of the project.[118]

By showing audiences the wolf's admirable traits and by explaining its importance to ecosystems, Mason invites the viewer to appreciate the beauty of the wilderness. In his memoirs, he reflects that the wolf is the perfect animal to "bridge the gap between ourselves and things natural."[119] Wolves are powerful and vibrant animals whose prodigious hunting ability and peripatetic lifestyle exemplify what it means to be truly free. "The wolf is a symbol of wilderness," Mason explains. "To capture [it] on film was to capture the spirit of the wild for all to share."[120]

How can humans protect something supposed to be wild and free? the film then asks. It is a question worth considering more deeply. Protection means intervention, does it not? Mason's answer to this conundrum was fundamentally different from the solutions of the CWS. The CWS believed that statistics, scientific research, and modern technologies could protect wildlife from extinction, whereas Mason argued that wildlife should be left completely alone. Only then would it truly be free. Take the wolf as an example. In *Death of a Legend*, Mason reminds audiences that the wolf can take care of itself, extraordinarily so. The predator is highly intelligent and equipped with social skills that allow it to survive in seemingly inhospitable environments without the aid of biologists or park wardens.

Despite Mason's belief that nature should be left alone, his documentaries about wolves do not always support this view. A deeper analysis of his work shows that the technocratic ideologies of the CWS are still present despite his environmentalist philosophy. During production of *Death of a Legend*, the CWS demanded that Mason include more sequences of its biologists doing fieldwork.[121] Since the CWS was financing the film, the director had little choice but to add scenes that showed government agents operating in the field.

One of the scenes that Mason filmed was of CWS biologist George Kolenoski attaching a radio collar to a female wolf. The sequence feels misplaced in a film that claims to be about the freedom and wildness of nature. The device represents the authority/superiority of the government over Canadian wildlife. Radio collars can "monitor wolves over great distances," the narrator says.[122] Instruments like the one shown in the film are essential for state biologists who study wolf movement and behaviour from afar. With the data provided by the collar, the CWS implements specific wildlife management strategies, including the manipulation and relocation of wolf populations. The film also documents the fieldwork of CWS biologist Douglas Pimlott, who watches the behaviour of the animal from a distance. According to the documentary, Canadians were becoming more cognizant of the diet of the wolf through his tireless observations. Ironically, Pimlott was one of the CWS biologists who justified the killing of wolves ten years before the release of the film.

The management ideology of the CWS was also evident in the material production of *Death of a Legend*, for Mason filmed wolves with photographic techniques used by CWS agents to survey wildlife populations, including bird's-eye shots from planes and shots taken with high-power telephoto lenses. This viewpoint allowed viewers to see clearly how wolves hunt in the Arctic. Yet the elevated perspective also implied that humans have the superior position to observe all aspects of wolf behaviour. In the context of the film, this synoptic viewpoint mimicked the objectivizing gaze of the CWS, which used aerial technology to reduce complex animal behaviour, such as migrating and hunting, to graphs and spreadsheets.

Mason's declaration that humans should embrace "nature's schemes" and not interfere with wild processes was further compromised when Mason ran up against the logistics of a difficult film shoot and a stubborn subject. Ernie Kuyt, a CWS biologist and wolf expert, warned Mason that photographing wolves in their natural habitat was prohibitive: it cost too much and was tremendously onerous.[123] Rather than tracking wolves in the wild, Kuyt recommended, the filmmaker should use an enclosure technique to photograph them. Ever the optimist, Mason was reluctant to give up on recording wolves in the wild. He could survive in the woods by himself just fine, and he was willing to be patient. However, after several failed attempts at documenting the animal in its natural habitat, he contacted the Ontario Department of Lands and Forests for help. The department had captured and domesticated a few wolves, and Mason wanted to film them.[124] Lands and Forests agreed, and he photographed the wolves in pens just outside Algonquin Park. To get more footage of the predator in action, the filmmaker then flew the wolves to Fort Smith along with several deer, which he used as bait.

The role of a wildlife filmmaker is to photograph animals behaving in ways that exhibit their behaviour and excite the audience. As Mason discovered, this was no easy task. Wolves lying beneath a spruce tree in northern Ontario were indifferent to the whims of the director, who demanded from his subjects a bit more energy. Film and television "are about movement, action, and dynamism; nature generally is not," writes film scholar Derek Bousé.[125] To get his subjects to "perform" more dynamically for the camera, Mason took a page from the playbook of the Department of Lands and Forests: he domesticated wolves on his property near Meech Lake, Québec. Sparky, a docile female, and Big Charlie, the alpha male, were tamed as pups, and the other two wolves that he brought to his property were feral. With the wolves safely enclosed on his property, Mason photographed them from many vantage points previously inaccessible. He could also coax them to play for the camera by barking out commands or tossing them delicious morsels of meat.

Keeping wolves in a kennel also allowed Mason to capture rare events, such as the birth of seven pups. He ingeniously built a den against the back of one of the fences in which he enclosed the wolves. The back of the burrow was removable so that he could poke his camera inside the pen and film the birth without disturbing the mother. Mason reasoned to himself (and his frightened neighbours) that keeping the wolves on his property was the only way that he could effectively dispel the myth that they were bloodthirsty beasts. However, in doing so, he unwittingly made the point that wolves were tameable.

Furthermore, Mason used medium-specific techniques, such as camera movements, editing, and audio tracks, to create a dynamic portrait of wolf behaviour. He used close-ups extensively. As film scholar Béla Balazs explains, good close-ups "radiate a tender human attitude in the contemplation of hidden things, a delicate solicitude, a gentle bending over the intimacies of life-in-the-miniature, a warm sensibility."[126] The shot allowed Mason to isolate an individual wolf and, with the help of some well-written narration, anthropomorphize its habits. This technique helped audiences identify with it.

The close-up also provided Mason with a plethora of editing options, including point-of-view shots and reaction shots that could be

Figure 6. Bill Mason with Charlie. Courtesy of the Mason family.

stitched together later into an exciting sequence about fighting between pack members. Exciting, perhaps, but entirely fabricated for the camera. The wolves that appear onscreen are neither as wild nor as free as Mason claims that they ought to be. They were directed in certain ways to create a sense of wildness.

The tension between his desire to leave nature alone and his practical need to manipulate it for the camera is most explicit in *Cry of the Wild*. The sequel boldly comments on and critiques his own efforts (and desire) to photograph wolves. In doing so, the filmmaker observes how people's labours to regulate nature create unintended and often deadly consequences for wildlife.

At the beginning of *Cry of the Wild*, Mason is frustrated that he is unable to record wolves in their natural habitat for *Death of a Legend*. They either run away from him or have been killed by hunters before he arrives. Mason is finally able to document Arctic wolves in their natural habitat on Baffin Island, but he does so from a considerable distance. As he watches the wolves scamper off into the tundra, he confesses that he needs to draw them closer. "I want to look into their eyes and discover the range of emotions and expressions that I know they are capable of," he says.[127] So Mason decides to raise a pack of wolves on his property near Gatineau, Québec. The experiment is mostly a success. Not only does their capture make it easy to film their behaviour; he and his family also form deep bonds with Charlie and Sparky.

The turning point of the film is profound in its own melancholic way. It dawns on Mason that domesticating wolves has led to their imprisonment and that he has become a hunter with a camera, a zookeeper with a lens. His efforts to bribe and cajole the animals for the camera are glaringly incongruous with his conviction that nature should be left alone. If he believes that nature is to be shielded from human interference, then how can he in good conscience keep wolves in a small enclosure just so that he can make a film about them?

To rectify his mistake, Mason releases Charlie and Sparky into the wild. But sadly, the wolves are unable to hunt the caribou that they require for sustenance. Their imprisonment has stripped away their ability to survive in the harsh world of fast-moving prey and savage competition. "Charlie's greatest joy in life was having his stomach rubbed," Mason observes sorrowfully as the wolves trot tentatively into the wild country. Fearing that they will starve, the filmmaker calls out to them. Hearing the voice of their benevolent master, the wolves return. In a bittersweet moment, he brings the two wolves back to the farm outside Gatineau, where they will live out their days in comfort. The damage has been done. At that moment, Mason understands that he has defiled nature by trying to possess it—even if his intentions were noble. And therein lies the environmental lesson of *Cry of the Wild* and *Death of a Legend*: people alienate themselves further from nature when they try to exert dominion over it. For nature to be truly protected, Mason concludes, he must be satisfied knowing that wolves "roam wild and free."[128]

Cry of the Wild serves as an appropriate bookend to this chapter. What makes the documentary so significant is its painful self-awareness of the challenges that people face when they try to preserve the wild. Mason's despair, in some ways, is a product of his fundamental belief that nature and people are separate and that, to remain free, the wild must remain unadulterated. This bifurcation, as many scholars have pointed out, is cultural. But words and ideas matter, and this way of thinking certainly has its consequences, as *Cry of the Wild* points out. Despite this romantic view of wild nature, Mason's recognition that our relationship with the natural world is burdened with contradictions and competing values remains poignant.

The nature documentaries produced by the NFB in the 1960s contained a variety of representations. State-centred narratives about the meaning of nature competed with "environmental" narratives that critiqued high modernism and its conviction that nature should be controlled or managed. In *Poison, Pests, and People*, Larry

Gosnell argued that humanity's efforts to boost agricultural productivity created unintended consequences for local environments and human bodies. In contrast, David Bairstow believed that though industrial pollution disturbed local environments, society could correct its mistakes if it had the proper knowledge and tools. In *River with a Problem*, he framed contamination of the Ottawa River as a technical problem that could be solved by state expertise. Ernest Reid and Christopher Chapman likewise exhibited confidence in government knowledge. Although the two filmmakers were critical of technological civilization and its conformist culture in *The Enduring Wilderness*, ultimately they believed that modern government institutions could protect pristine wilderness spaces from human uses.

The wildlife films of Bill Mason offer the most complicated example of how NFB discourses on nature evolved. As a sponsored film, *Death of a Legend* was beholden to certain views of wildlife management. However, Mason also used the documentary as a platform from which to critique the management practices of the CWS and more broadly to condemn society's efforts to control the natural world. For the first time in NFB history, a filmmaker advocated an environmental ethic arguing that nature should be left to its own "rhythms and patterns." This perspective conflicted, of course, with the high modern ideology of the film's sponsor. Agencies such as the CWS believed that it was possible, indeed essential, to manage wildlife. They argued that by tagging animals and killing pests, state experts could maintain a healthy balance in ecosystems. Despite their authority, scientists and government agents were not unchallenged in their beliefs about the value and meaning of the environment. Official voices had to share discursive space regarding the definition of nature with outspoken filmmakers and activists. *Death of a Legend* and *Cry of the Wild* were two of the first works from the NFB to demonstrate film's capacity as a medium of protest for environmentalists.

4

Challenge for Change

We are told that we own the land. But really nobody can own it, the land. For eventually everyone dies.

> —Sam Blacksmith, Cree hunter, *Cree Hunters of Mistassini*

Several hundred years before the National Film Board of Canada (NFB) was established, a large population of Cree lived in the vast boreal forests of northern Québec. They embraced the challenge of living in the North and found sustenance and meaning in its rhythms. In the seventeenth century, men with surnames such as Hudson, James, Radisson, and Des Groseilliers arrived on the continent and challenged their claim to this territory, which the Cree called Eeyou Istchee, "the land of the people." Soon, colonizers established trading posts along the riverbanks and shorelines to facilitate the export of furs and other commodities valued by the European aristocracy. For a while, the relationship between the merchants and the hunters was generally agreeable, and trade flourished. In the following centuries, however, larger European enterprises appeared at James Bay, and the mutual respect soured. Settlers coveted the timber and other natural resources found in Eeyou Istchee. Rapport between local

Indigenous peoples and European pioneers deteriorated as the latter group asserted their dominion over the landscape and the people who lived there. White colonizers quarrelled with the James Bay Cree through Confederation and into the modern age as nationalists and industry titans looked to northern Québec for profit and purpose.

The history of the Cree is often narrated as a tragic tale of cultural and ecological decline. The old ways disappeared, hunting grounds were razed, lakes were dammed, and rivers were flooded. Youth were sent to residential schools to learn how to be God-fearing citizens. White settlers, it seems, had permanently altered the social and environmental landscape of the Cree. Although there are elements of truth in this simple account, its emphasis on cultural collapse is misleading. As Hans Carlson writes in *Home Is the Hunter*, the "energy and imagination" of the Cree were challenged, not extinguished, by modern society.[1] There is a different story that needs telling, then, one that accounts for Cree resilience and adaptation. Local communities responded to the annexation of their homeland into "the rational vision and economy of North America" in creative and contradictory ways.[2]

There are many examples of Cree adaptation in the face of ecological and cultural change. For example, in the nineteenth century, Cree hunters worked alongside representatives from the Hudson's Bay Company and the federal government to protect declining beaver populations. Together the hunters created a simple but effective reserve system that shielded game stock from indiscriminate slaughter.

The Cree also adjusted to macrochanges to their homeland caused by colonization, even development projects such as La Grande, which threatened to undermine their livelihood. The hydroelectric project was disastrous for the Cree, to be sure. "With both wires and words, La Grande integrated a distant region into the technical geography of an international electrical grid and into a cultural narrative that understood the land in a way that was anathema to Cree tradition," Carlson observes.[3] Yet despite this concrete menace (and the massive effect it had on the local environment), Cree culture "continued to move like river water to find a path around the rocks," adapting yet remaining whole.[4] In the midst of radical modifications to the James Bay landscape, the residents continued to draw spiritual and physical meaning from the wilderness. To maintain their traditional livelihood, the Cree also took the fight to the province, protesting the unjust machinations of the state to the courts and to the Canadian public.

One way that the seminomadic hunters resisted the province's hydroelectric project was by exhibiting the vibrancy of their culture and showcasing the importance of the land to their people through cinema. In 1972, Cree from the village of Mistassini permitted NFB filmmakers Boyce Richardson and Tony Ianzelo to document their seasonal hunt in the bush. The hunters believed that by letting the filmmakers record their traditional life, Canadian viewers would come to appreciate the vital role of the natural world in Cree culture. In this sense, the Cree of James Bay used a different kind of technology of "wires and words" to defy the province's technocratic and nationalistic definition of nature and to replace it with a more holistic vision of human and nonhuman exchanges.

The film, called *Cree Hunters of Mistassini* (1974), was not the first NFB documentary to question the dominant narrative that humans are inherently superior to nature. Christopher Chapman, Bill Mason, and Larry Gosnell condemned society's (and specifically the government's) instrumentalist views of the environment. But the film was unique in other important respects. *Cree Hunters of Mistassini* diverged from whitecentric NFB interpretations of nature, offering an alternative vision of the environment rooted in Indigenous cosmology. In *The Enduring Wilderness*, Chapman and Reid defined wilderness as a place where humans are not. This romantic characterization unwittingly removed Indigenous peoples from the place that they had called home for centuries.[5] In contrast, Richardson and Ianzelo worked with the people of Mistassini to make a film that acknowledged the James Bay Cree's deep and enduring relationship with "empty" wilderness. For the first time in NFB history, audiences could "see the world through Indian eyes."[6] Throughout *Cree Hunters of Mistassini*, the Cree show that humans and nonhumans are connected in the world in both visible and invisible ways. Changes to the land distress the organisms, including people, that live on it and in it. To maintain the fecundity and beauty of nature, people need to be stewards of the land. This philosophy was in conflict with the vision of the state, which sought to exploit nature for economic gain.

Significantly, *Cree Hunters of Mistassini* also demonstrated the impact of environmental cinema on the extrafilmic world. Not only did the documentary provide an alternative narrative to that of high modernism; it also encouraged the Cree to seek political change on their own terms. After watching the film, many of the Cree hunters left their villages and returned to the James Bay bush despite the looming presence of the hydroelectric project.

Activism and the NFB

To understand the importance of *Cree Hunters of Mistassini* as both a political text and a new way of representing the environment in NFB cinema, we must situate the film within the larger context of Challenge for Change (CFC), a program created by the NFB to make films that spoke for the dispossessed and stimulated social activism within those groups. CFC operated from 1967 to 1980 and produced 250 films. Many still consider it to be one of the NFB's most influential and provocative contributions to nonfictional cinema.

The idea for CFC first materialized in 1965 when the Special Planning Secretariat of the Privy Council Office asked the NFB to make a film about poverty, an issue that persisted despite the government's efforts to expand social welfare services. The Privy Council's "war on poverty" intersected with the NFB's own shift to socially conscious filmmaking, and a partnership was formed. Executive producer John Kemeny was particularly excited about the idea and jumped at the opportunity to work on the pilot project. Kemeny appointed the inexperienced but talented filmmaker Tanya Ballantyne to find a Canadian family "trapped in the teeth of grinding poverty."[7] While conducting research for her film, the director was introduced to the Baileys, a family of eleven living in a derelict part of Montréal.[8] The Baileys were the ideal subject for Ballantyne and the NFB: they were miserably poor, and Mrs. Bailey was expecting her tenth child. After paying the family a measly sum of $500, Ballantyne and her crew followed them around their small apartment, dispassionately recording Mrs. Bailey's struggle to feed her ten children and Mr. Bailey's efforts to rescue his family from the city's underclass.

Canadian spectators praised *The Things I Cannot Change* (1967) for its gritty portrayal of destitution.[9] It received six awards in Canada and even won the prestigious Robert J. Flaherty Award for best feature-length documentary. The NFB was less impressed, however. Kemeny and others thought that the film was exploitative and insensitive. One of the most vocal critics of the documentary was NFB filmmaker Colin Low. He argued that *The Things I Cannot Change* revelled in the grimy desperation of the Bailey family's situation. Worse, the family did not have an opportunity to speak for themselves.

Despite being disappointed with the film, the NFB was intrigued by the political and social ideas that buoyed its production. Members of the Privy Council Office and the NFB began to discuss how they could improve the idea by using nonfictional cinema to cultivate meaningful exchanges between ordinary citizens like the Baileys and larger government institutions. In the winter of 1967, an interdepartmental committee consisting of representatives from the federal government and the NFB was formed. A month later, the committee launched a new production/distribution program to provide marginalized people with opportunities to "talk back" through filmmaking.[10] It was called Challenge for Change.

The architects of CFC had two aims for the documentary series. The first aim was to interpret social issues for people who did not have the resources or the education to understand them. According to CFC programmers, film was an ideal medium to reach disadvantaged people because of its affective qualities. "Unorthodox ideas are much more likely to be accepted if presented on emotional as well as intellectual grounds," the committee explained in its original proposal. "Many of those to whom ideas must be communicated are semi-literate. Film is the ideal way to reach them."[11]

The second aim, according to Low, Kemeny, and the other members, was to give a "voice to the voiceless."[12] By handing filmmaking technologies over to the subjects, the NFB believed that it could "cultivate debate," "disassemble hierarchies," and stimulate community empowerment through its programming.[13] CFC's founding members proclaimed optimistically that the program would be "an original and effective instrument of democracy."[14]

One of the first projects to be made for CFC was the Fogo Island experiment, a series of twenty-six short films about the inhabitants of a fishing community in Newfoundland directed by Colin Low. No longer able to fish because of resource shortages and crippling debts, the islanders were told by the federal government that they had to relocate to the mainland. They were not in favour of the government's edict, however. Fogo Island was their home. In the midst of this brewing tension, Low arrived with his camera. To help facilitate a dialogue between the disgruntled residents and the federal authorities, Low began interviewing the islanders. They were eager to share their side of the story and talked at length about their hopes and their fears as well as their generational ties to the fishing industry. During production, Low also encouraged his subjects to comment on the process of filmmaking itself. It turned out that the islanders had strong opinions about how they were being presented on film. Many were concerned that they were not being represented fairly by Low, that they were being portrayed as dumb backwater folks. During the interviews, the skeptical fishermen told the director how he should edit the footage. When the interviews were screened for the residents, Low filmed their responses, creating a series of vérité feedback loops that self-consciously documented the relationship between filmmaker and subject. After watching their interviews, the islanders began to form a more cohesive message about their livelihood and the importance of fishing as a cultural rite. When the series was completed, the community used their experience with the project to create more efficient and media savvy approaches to bringing their case to the federal government.

The "Fogo Island process" was a watershed moment for CFC. The film series demonstrated that it was possible to narrate social issues from the ground up and, more importantly, to help facilitate political representation. CFC quickly expanded its scope to include other political topics, such as sexism, racism, and environmental concerns. In 1969, CFC merged with the NFB's French program, Societé nouvelle. Together they developed "self-examination projects" with small communities around the country. The NFB lent Portapak Sony video cameras and live-sync sound equipment to local groups and taught them how to make their own movies using the lightweight technology. Unlike the cumbersome and complicated film camera, video technology was cost effective and easy to use. More importantly, it provided an instantaneous record of what was being filmed and could thus be shown anywhere at any time. Thus empowered, citizens began making videos about their discontent with the government and its disinclination to fight systemic inequalities.

The most radical films to come out of this venture were documentaries made by Indigenous people. In *These Are My People* (1969), filmmakers Willie Dunn, Roy Daniels, and Michael Kanentakeron Mitchell documented the negative impacts of white colonial settler policies on the people living at Akwesasne (St. Regis Reserve).[15] *You Are on Indian Land* (1969), directed by Mitchell, recorded the dramatic protest by the Mohawk on the International Bridge between Canada and the United States. Mitchell hoped that by filming the demonstration, he would draw attention to the political grievances of his people.[16] The film, a tremendous political and cinematic document, helped lay the groundwork for other Indigenous-authored projects at the NFB, including *Cree Hunters of Mistassini* and later the remarkable documentaries of Alanis Obomsawin.

The first five years of CFC, by most accounts, were successful. In 1971, the Departments of Agriculture, National Health and Welfare, Labour, Regional Economic Expansion, Central Mortgage and Housing, and Indian Affairs and Northern Development all contributed funding to CFC. A representative from each contributing department, as well as six representatives from the NFB, made up the committee, chaired by a member of the Privy Council Office. The budget for the program was $1.4 million, half of which was supplied by the NFB and the other half by the federal departments. By 1972, CFC had produced fifty-one films, shown on four thousand screens, to over two million viewers. In 1975, though, the program began to stagnate. The committee reluctantly extended funding to CFC in 1978 with the stipulation that the program be terminated if government representation fell below four departments. CFC limped on even though many people in the NFB thought that the program was becoming stale. After thirteen years, in 1980, budget cuts and institutional changes finally killed CFC.

Whether or not CFC was effective in inspiring social activism is up for debate. John Grierson, the cantankerous founder of the NFB and an advocate of a traditional documentary approach, considered the program to be "impractical," "juvenile," and "provincial." The ex-commissioner protested that CFC was contradictory to the NFB's founding principles because it did not promote "Canada in the making." If anything, he grumbled, it did the opposite.[17] Colin Low, in contrast, believed that the program was a crucial step in "incorporating media into the democratic process."[18] CFC filmmakers Dorothy Todd Hénaut and Bonnie Sherr Klein (mother of activist and writer Naomi Klein) agreed, claiming that the video experiment "accelerated perception and understanding and therefore accelerated action."[19] Boyce Richardson, the director of *Cree Hunters of Mistassini*, likewise argued that CFC was an effective instrument in fostering dialogue between ordinary Canadians and the government amid a "turbulent period." "Information is not just the government informing the people of what it is doing, but a loop which includes the response: the people must inform [the] government of what they think," he explained. For the journalist-turned-filmmaker, CFC helped facilitate this "loop." It was an "anomaly, but a glorious one," Richardson concluded.[20]

A number of NFB scholars also viewed the CFC experiment as a triumph. NFB historian Gary Evans argued that CFC gave the public a means to "vent their frustration and anger," an act "important to democracy's health." Furthermore, CFC allowed marginalized groups to take charge of their destinies and "aspire to an equitable social structure in a complex bureaucratic society."[21] Film scholar Jerry White concurred that CFC was "an aesthetically open-minded, socially engaged vision for Canadian cinema."[22] CFC inspired dialogue between conflicting groups and gave viewers a window into the struggles of the oppressed.

More recently, however, film scholars have questioned whether CFC fulfilled its mission to stimulate social change. In "Amateur Video and Challenge for Change," Janine Marchessault contends that the program embodied a "technological determinism" that conflated "new communication technologies with democratic participation." The NFB's social experiment was not tenable because it was established on two contradictory impulses: liberalism (which sought to preserve the common good) and CFC aims (to guarantee pluralism). This ideological confusion hindered local communities from defying the status quo. As a result, CFC instituted "access without agency."[23] In fact, the interactivity allegedly offered by video perpetuated a form of "self-surveillance." CFC "diffused action" and limited the potential for "the explosive effects of difference," Marchessault concludes.[24] The program had a lot to say about how and why people should change, but it did little to create opportunities for citizens to mobilize after the director yelled the final "cut."

Zoe Druick, who has written extensively about the NFB, also questions the progressiveness of CFC. She argues that despite its participatory ethos, CFC was the product of the Liberal mandate to manage populations and monitor political debates. As a result, its outcomes were dubious and contradictory.[25] This critique of CFC is compelling, but it overlooks several examples of filmmakers who explicitly challenged the goals of the welfare state. The strategy of the federal government to make Indigenous people full Canadian citizens was an extension of Prime Minister Pierre Trudeau's vision of a "just society." CFC films such as *The Ballad of Crowfoot* (1968), *Our Land Is Our Life* (1974), and *Cree Hunters of Mistassini*, however, loudly opposed this idea. The filmmakers and their subjects (often the same people) criticized the schemes of the state to assimilate Indigenous people into mainstream Canadian society. They also challenged the view that subsistence living was a problem that needed to be fixed through education and modernization.

It does appear that certain films created under the CFC umbrella did promote political change. By encouraging different visions of citizenship, CFC documentaries introduced the wider public to the voices and visions of the marginalized.[26] This type of representational strategy was itself a radical political act. In *Cree Hunters of Mistassini*, the conflict between the James Bay Cree and Québec epitomized the helpless position in which many Indigenous communities often found themselves. But the film does not dwell on this power dynamic; it also celebrates the Cree perspective on the world. As coauthors of the documentary, the Cree were able to guide its production in ways that emphasized the vitality and humility of their culture. Furthermore, the film invigorated the James Bay Cree to return to their homeland despite the hydroelectric project, and it helped generate sympathy for Cree sovereignty among non-Indigenous viewers. *Cree Hunters of Mistassini* also introduced a new way of thinking about the environment—an ecological imagination that challenged white definitions of the meaning and value of nature.

The James Bay Project and *Cree Hunters of Mistassini*

On 30 April 1971, Premier of Québec Robert Bourassa unveiled his plans for the "project of the century," a multibillion-dollar hydroelectric enterprise that would increase the power output of the country by a third. Standing in front of a three-panelled screen at the Colisée in Québec City, Bourassa explained to his rapt audience that the province planned to divert and dam three major rivers flowing into James Bay: La Grande, Great Whale, and Rupert. The dams would generate a whopping 10,300 megawatts of electricity for the province alone. But the project was more than just a quest for energy. According to the premier, the James Bay project was "the key to economic and social progress," "political stability," and ultimately the "future of Québec."[27] Bourassa's boast of the magnificent hydroelectric project was a savvy political move. The leader of the Liberal Party was not exactly popular in 1971. He had not made good on his promise that he would bring one hundred thousand jobs to Québec, and worse, he had looked weak during the October Crisis. To conciliate his voters, Bourassa looked to the North. As a young and competent technocrat who embraced the new Québécois policy of nationalism, he saw in the confluence of rivers and lakes at James Bay a bright future for Québec—and a way into the hearts of his voters.

Of course, the space targeted for development was far from empty, as Bourassa assumed. There were approximately ten thousand Cree and Inuit living in the James Bay region at the time of the announcement. And they were not as enthusiastic as the premier or his followers about this technocratic vision. The original inhabitants loudly protested the hydroelectric schemes of the province, which threatened to destroy their homeland and thus their way of life. Damming lakes and rivers would flood their hunting grounds. The deluge of water would also inundate the wetlands of the region and annihilate important beaver and waterfowl habitats.[28]

Led by Chief Billy Diamond, Cree representatives from Fort George, Rupert House, Eastmain, and other communities in the

James Bay area gathered at the village of Mistassini on 28 June 1971 to discuss what to do next. Although it did not gain much press at the time, the meeting was a significant one: it was the first time in modern history that the Cree met as a regional political body. The Elders from the villages decided to ask Indian Affairs to intervene on their behalf. "Only the beavers have the right to build dams in our territory," the Elders explained in a pointed letter to the then minister of Indian Affairs Jean Chrétien.[29] The Cree waited for a response from the federal government, but none came. On 18 April 1972, the Elders decided to file a permanent injunction that prohibited the Québec government from proceeding with the project, which threatened their homes. This time, the government did respond. After months of hearings and legal jockeying about who had rights and who did not, Justice Albert H. Malouf agreed to grant the injunction to the Cree. The victory was short-lived, however. The injunction was overturned a week later by the Supreme Court of Canada. Québec could have its dams. To improve relations with the Cree, the province offered to settle with the aggrieved parties for a total of $225 million. But money was not what the Cree wanted. Dejected, they returned to Mistassini to discuss the settlement. Eventually, the Cree accepted the offer in August 1974. It was officially approved in November 1975 in a contract that became known as the James Bay and Northern Québec Agreement.

The drawn-out legal battle between Québec and the James Bay Cree articulated the fundamental differences between settler and Cree culture. In particular, it highlighted the competing meanings of environment and place. It pitted a dominant society that generally viewed nature as a static object to be used to generate economic profit against a hunting culture that saw the James Bay wilderness as a complex and mysterious web of symbiotic organisms.[30] These radically different worldviews made it difficult for either side to understand the other, let alone communicate those differences. Indeed, one of the challenges that the James Bay Cree faced in the ongoing debate about "whose land?" was the court's limited knowledge of the Cree's reliance on the James Bay wilderness to provide sustenance. To determine whether the Cree had rights to the land, government lawyers pigeonholed Indigenous hunting culture into Western narratives of science, progress, and ownership. In the eyes of the court, hunting was just an occupation rather than a holistic activity that was cultural as much as it was practical. As a result, the richness of Cree life was reduced to a bland portfolio of statistics, graphs, and charts. As Boyce Richardson observes in *Strangers Devour the Land*, Bourassa and his gang of lawyers spent months trying to get the Cree to admit that they were "more white than Indian," since they used snowmobiles and "ate Kentucky Fried Chicken." They insisted on asking the wrong questions, such as "How much?" "How many?" "Where's the boundary?" "What's the address?" It was, as Richardson puts it, "a dialogue ·of the deaf."[31]

After Chrétien's failure to respond and during the frustrating court battle, the Cree began looking for other ways to demonstrate the breadth and depth of their relationship with the land. One method was documentary filmmaking. With the help of NFB filmmakers Boyce Richardson and Tony Ianzelo, the Cree hunters used the NFB and the tools of cinema to narrate their history and publicize their cause. Richardson and Ianzelo made two documentaries on behalf of the Cree in 1972 and 1974, respectively, *Cree Hunters of Mistassini* and *Our Land Is Our Life*. The first film records three Cree families as they establish a winter hunting camp near James Bay. The second film documents the final meeting of the Cree in the village of Mistassini as they ponder the government's settlement offer and reflect on the hydroelectric project's possible impact on their culture.

Although they were not Cree themselves, Richardson and Ianzelo were well suited to the task of making a documentary on Cree hunting culture. Ianzelo was one of the first filmmakers to work with Indian Film Crew trainees at the NFB in the 1960s. Richardson also had experience working with Indigenous communities across northern Québec. He was born in New Zealand and worked as a journalist in Australia, India, and England. He moved to Canada in 1957 and began writing for the *Montréal Star*. While there, Richardson penned a series of articles on Indigenous rights and the ecological effects of northern development in Quebec. His most important work in this period was on the James Bay Cree and their ongoing fight with the province and its hydroelectric project. Richardson interviewed local Cree and learned about the different ways in which they lived off the land. After talking with various Elders and hunters, the journalist eventually grasped that large-scale development would destroy their assiduous yet fragile subsistence culture. But what could the Cree do? "Never before in Canadian history had so politically powerless a group tried to stop so huge a scheme," Richardson wrote about the bleakness of the Cree's situation.[32]

In the summer of 1972, Robert Courneyer, the chairman of the CFC committee and a civil servant in the Privy Council Office, invited Richardson to make a documentary about Indigenous rights.[33] After the meeting with Courneyer, Richardson went back to visit the Cree. He quickly discovered that the James Bay Cree "felt strongly about the need for such a film." According to Richardson, a number of communities in the North wanted a documentary that presented their "arguments and feelings about the land" to "the dominant society."[34] Richardson approached the NFB to see if it would be interested in a documentary on the impact of La Grande dam on Cree culture in James Bay—a subject that kept coming up in his discussions with band leaders across the province. His pitch was simple: Philip Awashish, a young, university-educated Cree from Mistassini, would travel from community to community interviewing Cree residents about the hydroelectric project. He would then show the footage in the villages throughout James Bay.[35] Both Richardson and Awashish believed that the documentary would encourage the Cree to protest the James Bay project as a united people. Cree hunters had been in touch frequently during their hunting season, but none of this took the form of formal political gatherings. The producers of CFC were excited about Richardson's proposal. It was exactly the kind of film in which CFC was interested. Not only would a film like this generate sympathy for the Cree's tenuous political situation in predominantly white communities, but also it would provide the Cree with a platform to resist the Québec government and, more broadly, colonialism.

The federal government was lukewarm about Richardson's proposal, however. According to Gary Evans, "There were powerful forces in Ottawa (in the Prime Minister's office, some believed) who did not want the subject [of the James Bay project] broached from a political point of view."[36] Richardson was flummoxed. In a memo to the CFC committee, Richardson criticized the Privy Council Office for not supporting the film and yielding to "political pressure from the highest level."[37] Although the reasons behind the government's opposition to the proposed documentary are not revealed in any internal NFB document, one can speculate that the federal government did not want to antagonize Québec further amid the turmoil. Cree rights and Québec sovereignty were sensitive (and potentially volatile) issues.

Although the "vibrations were bad," Richardson continued to develop the film project, which he had originally titled *Assimilation Blues*.[38] This time, he took a more tactful approach, pitching a series of benign "anthropological documents" that examined Cree culture. With the help of Colin Low, Richardson outlined a series on "native people in Canadian society." The ambiguous language gave the filmmaker the latitude to make the film that he had wanted to make all along, but it also had the ring of an ethnographically impartial film that appealed to the scientific sensibilities of the federal government. Richardson believed he had managed to "outsmart the feds."[39] The government accepted the revised proposal, and he began shooting *Cree Hunters of Mistassini*.

On the surface, the documentary appeared to conform to the wishes of the federal government. It did not discuss the social impacts of colonial projects such as La Grande, nor did it reprimand the state's callousness toward the James Bay Cree and their legitimate claim to the land. Such commentary only "reinforces everybody's prejudices anyways," Richardson admitted.[40] As a result, *Cree Hunters of Mistassini* has no climax, no cut to a wide shot of a flooded forest or Bourassa bragging about the awesome power of the province's massive hydroelectric project. Instead, the documentary concludes quietly with the Cree families packing their meagre belongings for their journey south after another successful hunting season. As they trek into the wilderness, the narrator simply remarks that the James Bay hydroelectric project is under way. Then the documentary fades to black.[41]

Cree Hunters of Mistassini was far more political than its austere style let on, however. The ambiguous ending appropriately mirrored the uncertain fate of the Cree. Indeed, a closer viewing of the film and the context within which it was produced shows that the austere work was thoroughly revolutionary in its presentation of the Cree reality and ecological worldview. The documentary not only celebrated an Indigenous perspective of the natural world but also "made an immensely powerful political point" about the impact of La Grande and how the Québec government's high modern schemes threatened the traditional livelihoods of the Cree. Ironically, Richardson opined that this contemplative approach was actually more effective in persuading audiences of Cree sovereignty than the heavy-handed approach of the sequel, *Our Land Is Our Life*, "full of heavily ironic juxtapositions designed to irritate right-wingers."[42] By following three hunting families in the wilderness, *Cree Hunters of Mistassini* boldly asks, "How could anyone think of creating huge man-made lakes, or damming and diverting the ancient waters from which the Cree had received their sustenance since time immemorial?"[43]

Cree Hunters of Mistassini

The documentary begins in medias res with the filmmakers' arrival in James Bay occurring at the moment that the Cree are protesting Bourassa's plan for a mammoth hydroelectric project. An airplane circles the vast wilderness. From the window of the craft, James Bay looks impenetrable. Glassy lakes and winding tributaries surround the forest from every possible angle. Although the terrain appears to be vacant, the narrator informs viewers that both human and non-human beings have lived in this remote country for "at least three thousand years."[44] In contrast to earlier NFB documentaries, which depict wilderness as an empty object to be dominated, or as a Platonic ideal, *Cree Hunters of Mistassini* explicitly declares that these places are in fact homeland. And contested. According to the narrator, the "white man" has begun to challenge Indigenous claims to this abundant land in the form of a large hydroelectric project. The Cree "hunt as they have always done," but their traditional practices are vulnerable to the proposed damming of La Grande.[45] Confronted with the appetite of a growing province flush with nationalist fervour, the Cree must adapt if their culture is to survive.

The rest of the documentary takes place at the hunting grounds of Sam Blacksmith, an old trapper and tallyman from Mistassini.[46] After the opening aerial sequence, the film cuts to a scene introducing the Blacksmith, Jolly, and Voyageur families. The Cree look timidly at the camera as it frames them in a style reminiscent of a family portrait. The images of seminomadic hunters peering at the camera evoke the colonial aesthetics of early twentieth-century ethnography. Yet this kind of "orientalist" reading is subverted in the film. As the scene plays out, it becomes clear that it is the Cree who are scrutinizing us, the viewer, and more broadly, white colonial settlers. The longer the family members gaze at the camera, the more it becomes apparent that the filmmakers (and by extension the viewers) are interlopers, outsiders who have been summoned by the Cree to bear witness to their world.[47] The technique of having the Cree stare straight into the camera repudiates the notion that the observer is more knowledgeable and therefore superior than the subject. In fact, it is the other way around.

The sequence also signals to the viewer that the Cree are in fact coauthors of the documentary. As Richardson explains in the film, *Cree Hunters of Mistassini* could not have been made without Sam

Blacksmith and the other hunters. Blacksmith had met with the film-makers before the film shoot to see whether they could handle the rigours of bush life before filming began. After several conversations with Richardson and Ianzelo, Blacksmith finally permitted the men to visit his camp.[48] His motivation for vetting the two filmmakers was political. From the tallyman's perspective, the documentary was an important opportunity for the James Bay Cree, and he did not want some hacks from the South misrepresenting them. Blacksmith believed that one way his people could resist the James Bay hydro-electric project was to show outsiders the simplicity of their way of life. "[He] understood this film was to be seen by thousands on television," Richardson reflected after the film was released.[49] Blacksmith wanted to ensure that this "white man" communicated their beliefs accurately and respectfully.[50] So he closely monitored the production from start to finish. Blacksmith supervised what was shown in the documentary, especially moments that purported to "show the reality and quality of Indian life."[51]

Thus, what we see in *Cree Hunters of Mistassini* is a visual and narrative expression of the Cree worldview. That is not to say Richardson and Ianzelo's stamp is not on the film. Certainly, their perspective as white southerners is evident in the documentary. But as Richardson explained, the Cree families were instrumental in the aesthetic of the film. They dictated the pace of the movie by helping with the editing.[52] A rough cut of the documentary was finally shown to the families in 1973 and again in March 1974. Each time the film was shown, the Cree translated key interviews and provided Richardson with feedback on certain sequences pertaining to food preparation and hunting rituals.[53]

For the Cree, the most important aspect of their culture that they wanted to convey was their deep relationship with the James Bay environment. On a practical level, the land provided the hunters and their families with physical nourishment. It sustained them with food and other necessities even during the punishing winter months. The documentary has dozens of scenes of harvesting, hunting, and foraging activities. Each sequence is filmed up close and often without the support of a tripod. The jerky motion of the camera, the laboured breathing of the subject, and the ambient sounds of the forest interior create an unromantic portrait of living off the land. These images and the film's general visual aesthetic are the opposite of the idyllic wilderness cinematography of Bill Mason and Christopher Chapman. James Bay is not an empty landscape viewed from some overlook; it is a place where people live; it is an environment that demands of those who live there that they work hard and skilfully. Nature is a place of labour and meaning. Of closeness. Although the work is gruelling, the Cree enjoy the fruits of their labour at the end of the day in their warm lodges. A close bond is formed between the three families and the filmmakers as they eat and smoke together. Working in nature has produced a deep satisfaction that one can experience only after tracking game for a full day.

The documentary also respectfully expresses the spiritual imagination of the Cree, which sees the land as a sacred place. Activities such as hunting, trapping, and fishing are closely defined by their belief in the supernatural qualities of nature.[54] Each time Blacksmith and the other Cree hunters enter the forest, they encounter a world of spiritual beings and forces. Animals such as beaver, bear, grouse, and moose had their own personalities and temperaments. So did the wind and the trees. In one scene, Blacksmith leaves the shell-white bones of a black bear on top of a makeshift edifice. As he performs his duties, he explains that the platform is erected so that dogs cannot "violate them." Degrading the bones of the bear would make its spirit angry. Precautions must be taken "because nothing can be hidden from the bear," Blacksmith says. "If the bear knows he is not well respected," then it will be very difficult to hunt him again.[55] The smallest disturbance or spiritual misstep can have an enormous impact on the hunter's success and therefore a person's survival. Richardson explains in the narration that Blacksmith and the other hunters frequently have to contend with the capriciousness of the spirits. Any display of impertinence or carelessness can cause the spirits to be resentful and maybe even spiteful. They might not give themselves up as food.

The Cree perception of the James Bay environment as a place of mutable entities and entangled spiritual relationships is an important aspect of the documentary's ecological imagination and in particular its subversive representation of environmental care. Animals and plants are presented as dynamic entities. Recognizing that nature is an interrelated system of both human and nonhuman figures means that the Cree must be respectful as they carry out their rituals. Nature is not there just for the benefit of hunters. It exists to sustain life in all its forms. The Cree hunter kills sparingly and with gratitude and humility because he recognizes that such violent acts, though necessary, reverberate throughout the entire James Bay world. This understanding of the natural world is explained when Blacksmith kills a pregnant moose. Before they haul the carcass back to their camp, the hunters perform an important ritual over the dead animal. The moose was unable to fulfill her role as a mother, so the hunters "give a little of the life of the mother to the calf," Blacksmith explains. After cutting a piece of flesh from the dead cow, Black-smith opens the jaws of the fetus and places the meat in its mouth. The hunters honour the moose so that it might "continue to flourish." "This is always done," Blacksmith explains gravely to the camera.[56] Hunting is a sacred act, and carelessness or indifference can disrupt the delicate web of existence.

According to the Cree, responsibility for the forest was given to them by the spirits. As scions of the land, they are obligated to tend to it as a garden. They help maintain it by balancing growth and harvest in a pattern analogous to modern land management practices.[57] Ronnie Jolly, for instance, had not been to his hunting territory in several years because it needed time to replenish. Later in the film, Blacksmith tells the crew that he "may leave the ground alone for a year or two so there will be something there when we return." "The [beaver] becomes scarce if we hunt every winter," the hunter says.[58] Blacksmith's and the other families' reverent attitude toward nature is a clear counterpoint to the high modern schemes of Bourassa and the state. The hydroelectric project proposed to modify the land without restraint or spiritual sensitivity. In contrast, Blacksmith and the hunters believe that nature has its limits and that for it to endure, they need to live simply and humbly.

The point of all this in the film is to argue that the Cree are the rightful heirs to James Bay, not the provincial government. For centuries, they have been the caretakers of the land, protecting it from harm and drawing meaning from its mysterious cadences. As Blacksmith informs viewers, the area where he lives was given to him "after the old man who hunted on it died." Since then, he has toiled on the land as a trapper, a fisherman, and a hunter for thirty years. But this does not mean that he is the "master" of the land. "A man who lives by hunting cherishes the land. A man who lives by hunting truly respects the land. A man who owns the land really cannot because he dies," Blacksmith says pointedly.[59] There is something important in this Cree perspective on caretaking that transcends Western notions of ownership. In the film, it becomes clear that the Cree have a cultural and spiritual union with the wilderness that supersedes the Québec government's legal definition of property and ownership.[60]

Cree Agency and Ethnographic Cinema

Although *Cree Hunters of Mistassini* respects the ecological wisdom and humility of Cree hunting culture, it is nonetheless important to acknowledge some of the documentary's limitations. Perhaps the most conspicuous problem with the film is that the directors sometimes cultivate an image of the "ecological Indian." Richardson romanticizes the Cree community for surviving in the isolated wilderness "without accidents, illnesses, or quarrels."[61] As we saw in chapter 2, such representations were common in NFB films about Indigenous peoples and demonstrated their enduring status as "ecological Indians" in Canadian culture.

There are other issues in the film as well. According to the production notes, Richardson and Ianzelo contrived certain scenes to enhance the story's drama. To create moments of excitement, the filmmakers flew several of the Cree hunters to different parts of James Bay so that they could kill a moose for the camera. The documentarians also brought in building supplies to construct a hunting lodge that accommodated the film crew and their gear.[62] On a practical level, these decisions made filming in the bush easier, cheaper, and more engaging. But, as Graeme Wynn notes, this decision also reaffirms a colonial way of representing Indigenous peoples.[63]

But one must be careful to only see the film as a questionable piece of colonial work. If anything, the use of modern tools during production demonstrates Blacksmith's adeptness in using traditional practices and appropriating so-called modern technologies to sustain his family's long-standing ties to the land. If nails and hammers provided by Richardson and Ianzelo made building their cabins easier in the challenging wilderness, then why not take full advantage

Figure 7. Still from *Cree Hunters of Mistassini* (1974). Used with permission of the National Film Board.

of them? Cree adaptability is evident in the documentary itself. On several occasions, Blacksmith shows the cameraman that he uses the "white man's technology" to survive the winter. Snowmobiles, chainsaws, and bush radios are all common features in the hunting camp of the Cree. The difference between Cree society and modern Canadian society, however, is that the people of Eeyou Istchee use technology carefully and purposefully. A Cree hunter "always places skill above superfluous technology," anthropologist Ronald Niezen explains.[64]

Furthermore, the Cree participated in making the documentary. They demonstrate their adaptability and resiliency to colonial assimilation in the documentary by taking over the cinematic means of production. Blacksmith is cognizant that filmmaking (even its moments of artificiality) can help the Cree show outsiders their vibrant culture and thus help amplify their grievance against the Québec government. This agency exemplifies their ability to navigate both continuity and change in the extrafilmic world. Despite the remoteness of their land, the Cree were willing to engage with outsiders and share their own visions of the world. As Carlson writes, "Contact was not so much a moment in time as an ongoing process through which two culturally different peoples began to live with and speak to and about one another."[65]

Challenge for Change?

Although some scholars claim that the CFC program provided its subjects with only an illusion of political agency, the legacy of *Cree Hunters of Mistassini* hints that in certain instances, NFB cinema was in fact a springboard for political action and self-determination. For the James Bay Cree, the production and distribution of *Cree Hunters of Mistassini* and its follow-up, *Our Land Is Our Life*, was a major moment in their confrontation with the state. The film rallied local

Cree to return to the bush and encouraged them to unify against the government of Québec and protest its hydroelectric project.

Before *Cree Hunters of Mistassini* was released, programmers at CFC envisioned how it might be used by the Cree to oppose the claims of Bourassa and, more broadly, the James Bay hydroelectric project. From an educational standpoint, the documentary would inform Cree on the current state of affairs. "Clearly, there is a need for an effective means of communication so as to improve the chances of the affected Indian population to become fully aware of the effect of the project on their lives," the NFB report explained.[66] But education was not enough. The CFC model demanded that the subjects participate in the distribution of the documentary:

> Then there is a need to bring these people together to form
> a common front to defend their rights and have a voice in
> the decisions affecting their lives. The aim of the James Bay
> Communications project would be to fill those needs for com-
> munication between the Indians, and subsequently between
> Indians and Southern decision-makers. With the help of VTR
> [video tape recorder] equipment in the hands of Native social
> animators, information can be rapidly disseminated, exchanges
> of views with and between the communities aided, and aware-
> ness of problems and possible solutions can be accelerated. The
> Cree will then be in a position to communicate with the Southern
> Québec Indians, with the James Bay Corporation and the Québec
> Government, and with Ottawa and can use videotape as one
> possible means of supporting their views.[67]

Cree Hunters of Mistassini was more than an informative documen-
tary; it was a way to spark a communications network that bridged the spatial and temporal gaps that historically had confounded unity among the isolated Cree communities. Eventually, the chorus of voices and shared experiences would reverberate all the way to the halls of Québec City.

To ensure that the documentary had maximum political effect, the NFB strategically released *Cree Hunters of Mistassini* during the court case. In a 1974 memo, CFC producer Ian Ball relayed to the regional distribution coordinators that "the negotiations between James Bay residents and the PQ government [were] underway" and that they should seize the moment and "expose the film as widely as possible."[68] The NFB acted quickly. Between April and June 1974, the NFB screened *Cree Hunters of Mistassini* and its companion, *Our Land Is Our Life*, for sixty-one different Cree communities across James Bay and down into southern Québec. CFC used "animators" from major communities affected by the hydroelectric project to promote the film and facilitate postscreening discussions with Cree audiences.[69] Travelling around the province with their projection equipment, the CFC animators had three tasks: "to stimulate a reflection on the life, the culture, and the situation of the Indian; to sensitize Québecers to the problems of the Indians and to the questions surrounding the economic development of the North; and to contribute to a growth in the solidarity between Indian groups by exposing the similarities of the kind of life they lead."[70]

Mark Zanis, a distribution coordinator with the NFB, urged the distributors to learn all the details about the hydroelectric project and its potential impact on Cree culture. Many of the viewers were informed of the situation, and they were deeply concerned about its potential impact on their livelihood. Zanis warned the animators to be prepared to answer questions such as, "When did we consent to bargaining away our natural resources?" He also instructed them to remind "audiences that the Cree allowed filmmakers to participate."[71] This was not just a film about the Cree but also a film *authorized* and indeed endorsed by the Cree.

By all accounts, the James Bay Cree responded strongly to the film after it was shown. Viewers understood what Blacksmith said about life in the bush on both cultural and symbolic levels. They got the references and the metaphors. They laughed at the jokes made at Richardson's expense and nodded when the Cree hunters talked about the "old ways."[72] Screening after screening, Cree audience members approached the animators to tell them what they thought of the documentary. A travelling report from Indigenous filmmaker Michael Kanentakeron Mitchell, who toured across James Bay with the film, noted that the Cree response to the documentary was "overwhelming."[73]

After a screening on Kipawa Reserve in Québec, an animator reported that the crowd was "enthusiastic" about the film and talked extensively about it "for hours." According to the animator, spectators from the reserves recognized Sam Blacksmith and the other hunters in the film, which generated even more buzz for the documentary.[74] In a screening that took place at Chief Billy Diamond's home at Rupert House, Cree Elders were moved to tears. They were overjoyed after seeing their own people "speaking publicly about what they feel about the land." One trapper in attendance agreed with its portrayal of hunting life. "What they say is very true." "Are they planning to make more films about life in the bush?" he inquired.[75]

The full emotional resonance of the documentary could be appreciated only by the Cree. In his report, Zanis explained that the documentary "revived memories of what that life was like in the wilderness" for Cree viewers.[76] There was an exciting momentum after each screening. Over time, *Cree Hunters of Mistassini* encouraged a growing number of Cree to return to their hunting grounds and reestablish their connections with the land despite the looming hydroelectric project. Mobilized by the stirring portrait of their culture, many viewers began to think about what it would be like to return to the old ways. Several families revisited the bush after seeing the documentary. "Many of the Cree trappers announced they were going to make plans to return to the bush in the winter," Zanis explained. Cree families from the villages followed suit and "packed their belongings for the winter hunt."[77]

The documentary also directly supported the James Bay Cree in their battle against Hydro-Québec.[78] Before the announcement by Bourassa, Cree political life generally had been organized through family based hunting communities. Rarely did Cree interact with other Cree from outside their villages. Under the leadership of Chief

Billy Diamond, Cree hunters from all over James Bay began meeting to determine how they could oppose the hydroelectric project. Zanis further reported that *Cree Hunters of Mistassini* and *Our Land Is Our Life* generated interest in the court case and encouraged the Cree to attend the briefing in Fort George with their lawyers.[79] Richardson and Ianzelo similarly claimed that the documentary heartened the hunters to negotiate a small reduction in the scope of the project and to receive some financial compensation.[80] Although a settlement was not the ideal outcome for the Cree, it did allow them to determine their future in certain respects. As Diamond mentioned to the Montréal *Gazette*, the Cree were "very reluctant to sign the agreement" but realized that by settling, "the rights and the land are protected as much as possible from white man's intrusion and white man's use." "It guarantees that we can continue to live in harmony with nature," Diamond added.[81]

On a more general level, *Cree Hunters of Mistassini*'s cinéma-vérité style prompted non-Indigenous viewers to reconsider their own views of the natural world. As the camera shadows the Cree hunters, outsiders become immersed in an ecologically rich landscape and are thus invited to contemplate how people are shaped by the natural world and vice versa. According to NFB employee Rick Dale, audiences in Ontario connected the documentary to the media coverage of the Berger Inquiry into the Mackenzie Valley pipeline and the Indigenous blockade of a BC railway. The film helped raise consciousness in meaningful and productive ways. "In all these events, the lifestyle, talents, and rights of our Indians were brought to the consciousness of non-natives. The Indians are making all kinds of waves. It is in this milieu that the Challenge for Change films are at their best—audiences want to know what's going on and why," Dale reported.[82]

The Anglican Church in Québec exclaimed—based on the film—that it wanted the provincial government to halt all northern development until land claims had been settled.[83] In the *Montréal Star*, film critic Joan Irwin praised the documentary for giving her a "clear view of real life of the North American Indian." It convinced her that the government should "leave in the Cree's hand . . . the huge tracts of wilderness land they need and tend so carefully."[84] A review in *The Booklist* likewise praised the film for its visual splendour, which highlights the Cree's intimate relationship with the environment. The film "uses superbly restrained cinematography" that never forces one to be conscious of "technique." Richardson frames the narrative elements with a "minimum of visual bias, allowing one to discover each element for oneself." The documentary also "avoids the easy approach of stimulating the audience's response by placing the Indians in a pathetic context, asking for pity rather than encouraging respect."[85] In a screening in Montréal, the predominantly white audience remarked that the film was a "powerful" treatise on Cree rights. An hour-long discussion held after the screening revealed that people in the crowd asked for suggestions on what they could do to help the Cree cause.[86]

In its first two decades of documentary filmmaking, the NFB framed the environment as a resource to be managed and exploited. Its emphasis on control and order embodied a state way of seeing geographic spaces in the middle of the twentieth century. In the 1960s, discourses about nature began to evolve. Some filmmakers argued that nature was not static or uniform. Rather, it was an intricate and dynamic ecosystem, and its value was multifaceted. They also contended that efforts to control the environment tended to produce disastrous ecological problems that ruined local ecosystems and human bodies. Although these protoenvironmental works challenged normative attitudes toward nature, they were also conspicuously whitecentric. Issues such as wilderness preservation and ecological protection were generally portrayed as white, middle-class issues. There was no mention of how environmental damage disproportionately affected marginalized groups or of how nonwhite discourses could cultivate a more holistic (and therefore sustainable) way of thinking about nature. This would all change, of course, with *Cree Hunters of Mistassini*. The NFB film, directed by Boyce Richardson and coauthored by the James Bay Cree, was the first to posit an environmental ethic that embraced Indigenous viewpoints.

The ecological imagination of the CFC documentary is significant for several reasons. The documentary advanced the idea that the Cree were the stewards of the James Bay wilderness and had been for thousands of years. This long-standing connection with the natural world, which Richardson depicts as a physical, emotional, and spiritual bond, buttresses their claim to this territory, a fact disputed by Québec. Indeed, the film does a superior job of expressing the hunter's complex relationship with the land compared with that of the Cree's lawyers.

By celebrating this representation of nature, the film implicitly critiqued Québec's hydroelectric project and by extension the state's high modern vision of the land. Not only would La Grande have dreadful consequences for the James Bay environment, but also it would threaten the very basis of Cree culture. For Sam Blacksmith and the other Cree hunters, the hydroelectric project represented "a terrible and vast reduction of [their] entire world."[87] The film does a fair job of explaining why this is the case. The land is more than just a source of occupation; it is a source of their nourishment as a people. "Nothing, neither jobs nor money, meant more to [the Cree] than their land," the information sheet for the documentary states.[88] "You can't just run a road in and say, 'we'll need some gas stations along the way and the Indians can run the gas stations.' No Indian in James Bay has asked for gas stations," Richardson remarked pointedly in an interview.[89]

In this sense, the film exceeds all other NFB environmental documentaries that came before it. It skilfully challenges certain Western definitions of the meaning of nature through its cinematography and narrative arc. Furthermore, the film helped activate marginalized communities that called the wilderness home. Inspired by the documentary and its accurate portrayal of hunting in the bush, Cree from all over Québec returned to the forest and reestablished their ties with the land.

More broadly, *Cree Hunters of Mistassini* is a clarion call to viewers across Canada to meditate on the true value of nature. Its meditative approach encourages viewers to develop a more respectful and humble attitude toward the environment. Although the NFB was a way for the government to teach audiences how to think about and behave toward nature in ways that aligned with its nation-building project, *Cree Hunters of Mistassini* demonstrates that NFB cinema sometimes challenged the hegemony of the state. The CFC film objected to the high modern schemes of Québec and disavowed its reductive view of the human and nonhuman world.

Conclusion

It is an "inescapable truth," write Graeme Harper and Jonathan Rayner, that cinema contributes to the "imagining and definition" of the natural world.[1] Through moving pictures, we experience and learn to negotiate the physical environment around us.[2] In examining the documentary cinema of the National Film Board of Canada (NFB), we see the different ways that ideologies, institutions, and individuals shape how viewers think about nature.

This book has tracked the various representations of nature in NFB documentaries from early wartime films that depicted the exploitation of the country's natural resources to "environmental" documentaries of the 1970s, which challenged the notion that nature exists for the benefit of humans. My intention when I sat down to write this book was to investigate how the government co-opted the art of cinema to broadcast political views about the meaning and value of nature. Although this investigation certainly focused on that element, it became clear that filmmakers, even those sponsored by the state, oftentimes used nonfictional cinema as a stage from which to reimagine nature in alternative and sometimes radical ways.

How did the NFB represent nature? At first, it saw nature as a convenient symbol with which it could unite Canadians under a specific kind of national identity. Visualizing nature in this way was not new, of course. Geography has long been a part of the country's nationalist rhetoric, for it embodies the ideals central to Anglo-Canadian nationalism: ruggedness, industriousness, adventurousness, and so forth. Politicians and other nationalists frequently described the land as a force that shaped the history and national character of the country. The NFB was no different. Filmmakers continued to mythologize the view that nature was the defining feature of Canada.[3] Films from *Canadian Landscape* (1941) to *Canada: The Land* (1971) suggested that modern Canada was chiselled out of raw nature and that its people were moulded by the weathered contours of the landscape. NFB films such as *Song of the Mountains* (1947), *The Enduring Wilderness* (1963), and *Epilogue* (1971) likewise transported viewers to primordial wilderness spaces. Here, in these depictions of raw wilderness, spectators were reminded of their past lives as voyageurs in the impenetrable bush, forging a national destiny one beaver pelt at a time. Even filmmakers who contested official discourses on the exploitation of natural resources and industrialization advocated for a national identity that was defined by Canadians' closeness to the natural world. Bill Mason and Christopher Chapman argued in their own ways that to protect the wild was to preserve an icon of the country's heritage in its most robust and virginal state.

This popular depiction of nature had ideological baggage, of course. Although it was a convenient way of nation building, NFB representations of nature frequently excluded marginalized peoples from their framings of the environment. Natural spaces as visualized in films such as *The Enduring Wilderness* were uninhabited, a realm independent of human culture. In reality, however, a spectacularly diverse population of Indigenous peoples once inhabited these environs. Where were they, then, in NFB films about the natural environment? In some cases, Indigenous peoples were sketched into the landscape by NFB filmmakers to create a primitive mise en scène. More commonly, their presence was completely ignored. Not only did this presentation of wilderness spaces reaffirm an Anglo and emphatically white definition of nature, but also it suppressed Indigenous narratives about the meaning and value of the environment.

Nature was envisioned in other ways that supported the nation-building goals of the state. Depictions of an ordered and well-managed landscape framed nature as a national resource that united citizens from coast to coast to coast. Every Canadian could have a hand in unleashing this natural wealth through hard work and state-managed strategies. Nature transformed was a potent (and timely) symbol of national progress and postwar economic development.

NFB filmmakers relied on a consistent aesthetic and ideological schema to convey government discourses about the utility of the natural world in the 1940s and 1950s. Documentaries such as *Timber Front* (1940) and *Windbreaks on the Prairies* (1943) implied that the true worth of nature is in boards per feet and grain tonnage. Wartime films encouraged Canadians to exploit resources widely because they were needed to help the country win the war. Postwar agricultural films produced by Evelyn Cherry for the Agricultural Production Unit likewise encouraged Canadians to take advantage of the natural plenitude of the country.

Government-sponsored films about natural resources were clearly informed by the objectives of the welfare state. NFB agricultural documentaries taught farmers how to modernize their farms through science and technology. If agrarians did not approach the soil with knowledge and expertise, then they would risk ecological and economic devastation. As the narrator of *Canadian Wheat Story* (1944) explains, the modern farmer not only must "consider the effects of soil and weather conditions" when he plants his crops but also needs to consult the agricultural specialists working at the government-established plant-breeding program. Only then can the farmer be confident that his wheat harvest will meet Canada's "high export standards."[4]

The technocratic language of controlling or fixing nature was closely associated with another important state-centred theme in NFB films. They were characterized by their high modernism and its belief that "a sweeping, rational engineering of all aspects of social life" can "improve the human condition."[5] Images of modern farming technology, gleaming airstrips in the North, or crops dowsed in chemical pesticides paralleled the state's logic that nature should be rendered passive and then transformed. To quote the narrator of Roman Kroitor's *The Great Plains* (1950), "By applying his work and ingenuity to [it], the land at first thought barren has been put to man's use."[6]

Documentary filmmaking itself was a key technology in the ongoing project of the government to rationalize the environmental and social spaces of Canada. The camera collected valuable information about the geological and biological features of the landscape, visual data that tacitly justified the development and exploitation of the environment. Filmmaking assisted the government in two ways: by abridging the complexity of the natural world and by naturalizing state authority over the environment. As NFB film crews travelled through these places with their all-seeing technology, they claimed intellectual and physical authority for the federal government.

Representations of nature in NFB cinema were not monolithic, however. As Philip Rosen writes, "The concept of national cinema is always implicated in a dialectic of nation and anti-nation."[7] Although there was a strong current of state discipline in NFB discourses on nature, there were surprising moments of ideological conflict between filmmakers and their government sponsors. Filmmakers began countering state-authorized perspectives on the symbolic and economic value of the environment. The work of Larry Gosnell epitomized this new wave of environmental filmmaking. Despite political pressure from the Department of Agriculture, Gosnell made a film that challenged society's reliance on technocratic solutions to improve nature. In *Poison, Pests, and People* (1960), he argued that humans' efforts to reshape the landscape through the use of pesticides were both myopic and destructive. People's exertions to stimulate agricultural productivity and transform the land resulted in unintended consequences—namely, the poisoning of local ecosystems and human bodies.

Bill Mason's *Death of a Legend* (1971) and *Cry of the Wild* (1972) similarly castigated the management practices of state institutions. According to Mason, the conservation goals of the Canadian Wildlife Service embodied a blind faith in the technocratic and the modern.

Its efforts to control nature were flawed because they were based on the view that humans are superior to nature. Mason pleaded for a more ecologically conscious understanding of human and nonhuman relationships, one characterized by humility and an appreciation of the freedom of the wild.

In the late 1960s and throughout the 1970s, NFB filmmakers used programs such as Challenge for Change (CFC) to ask more provocative questions about the relationship between humans and nature. Society's desire for industrial growth and technological solutions to problems related to environmental contamination and resource scarcity was problematic and harmful. The most significant documentary to make this claim was *Cree Hunters of Mistassini* (1974). Unlike earlier films about Indigenous peoples and nature, the documentary privileged their environmental cosmology. In the film, the Cree demonstrate that wilderness is more than an economic resource or a beautiful place where people are only visitors; it is a home where human and nonhuman beings live together in harmony. The James Bay landscape provided the Cree and all other living things with physical strength and spiritual purpose. This representation of nature was further noteworthy because it directly countered Québec's high modern assessment of the land. Under Robert Bourassa, Québec envisioned a modern and productive landscape in which massive dams would generate millions of watts in hydroelectric power. This scheme, however, had terrible consequences for the James Bay Cree, who called this wilderness home. *Cree Hunters of Mistassini*, more than any other film up to that point, protested the state's vision of nature.

We must be careful, however, not to label all NFB environmental films post-1960s as radical departures from earlier works about nature. Government discourses were still present in NFB documentaries throughout this period. State influence persisted through the 1970s and into the 1980s in the form of sponsored films. Conservation films such as *This Is an Emergency* (1979), *Protection for Our Renewable Resources* (1979), and *The Future Is Now* (1979) were all prompted by the federal government during the energy crisis. The state was also instrumental in the creation of Studio E, a short-lived film unit devoted to making environmental pictures. Studio E produced a series of environmental advocacy films, including the antinuclear film *No Act of God* (1978) and Martin DeFalco's *Class Project: The Garbage Movie* (1980). In spite of its seemingly radical aesthetic, the films of Studio E were fairly benign and supported state efforts to intervene in environmental education. Along with the feminist production unit Studio D, Studio E films were an important aspect of the NFB's efforts to "reflect the cultural maturity" of Canada in the 1980s while maintaining the view that the state was ultimately a benevolent institution.[8] In the case of Studio E, the state was still the main arbiter of human-ecological relationships.

Our journey began in 1939 and ended in 1974 with the production of the CFC film *Cree Hunters of Mistassini*. Boyce Richardson's documentary struck me as a good place to finish because it articulates so many of the themes discussed in the book. First, it reveals that NFB films were negotiated texts that competed with and sometimes confounded the official attitude and policy of the government. Despite the ongoing presence of the state in the process of production, filmmakers were able to use their cameras to depict the contradictions of local social and ecological environments. Traditional Cree hunting culture was fundamentally different from the colonial experiences of the state, which saw nature as a frontier to be subdued and transformed.

Second, *Cree Hunters of Mistassini* illustrates the different ways in which filmmakers used the technology and grammar of cinema to construct a certain kind of picture of nature. The cinéma-vérité aesthetic of Tony Ianzelo and Boyce Richardson effectively places the viewer within the cultural and ecological reality of Cree life. Contrast this aesthetic with the works of Christopher Chapman, who used a combination of contrast lighting and wide frames to represent the sublimity of Canadian wilderness spaces, or Evelyn Cherry, who relied on expository filmmaking to teach Canadian farmers how to modernize their farms. In each case, the form of the film—its aesthetics and narrative devices—supported its content.

Third, *Cree Hunters of Mistassini* demonstrates the political impact of NFB films on the extrafilmic world. For Cree audiences, the film was one of the catalysts in their confrontation with Québec. The film reminded many Cree of their traditional homeland and their spiritual relationship with the James Bay environment. The documentary inspired many Cree hunters to unite and return to the bush despite the looming threat of the hydroelectric project.

Where my project ends, hopefully new investigations will begin. There is still an interesting story to be told about the environmental documentaries produced by the NFB in the 1980s and 1990s. The construction of nature in this period was influenced in remarkable ways by developments in media technologies and the emergence of new funding sources and distribution channels. By the early 1980s, private film and television industries had exceeded the production output of the NFB. Moreover, the creation of Telefilm (1984) and smaller programs such as the Ontario Development Film Corporation helped finance the projects of young, independent filmmakers. These new avenues provided directors with creative licence and radical filmmaking opportunities previously unavailable to them. Film scholar Peter Stevens observed in 1993 that this independent documentary cinema opposed mainstream media and "differ[ed] entirely from the prescriptive plans to develop better informed citizens, as set out by John Grierson at the National Film Board."[9] Inspired by the rise of identity politics, documentarians began exploring new ways to express subjectivity and difference. For some independent filmmakers, the NFB represented everything that was wrong with the mainstream. Still, a number of indie filmmakers saw the NFB as a platform from which to contest the status quo from within. In the 1980s and 1990s, the NFB increasingly promoted a style of nonfictional cinema that was individualistic and autobiographical.[10] The NFB mandate to improve diversity and representation emboldened women and Indigenous filmmakers to make documentaries about their real-life experiences in ways that many spectators had never witnessed. This kind of subjectivity prompts interesting questions about the nature of cinema and, indeed, the cinema of nature. An ecocritical/historical investigation of this period of nonfictional filmmaking can reveal new perspectives on the complex ways that cinema, nature, and government institutions intersect.

In 2012, the governing Conservative Party slashed the NFB's funding by $6.7 million and eliminated seventy-three jobs.[11] The cuts crippled the ability of the institution to maintain its extensive archive, which contains films, photographs, and thousands of pages of production notes. Thanks to the outstanding work of André D'Ulisse, head archivist at the NFB, I was able to dig through piles of film material and related documents without too much difficulty. But there were still gaps. Despite the best efforts of the NFB to preserve its past, production notes and other historical clues were sometimes missing or misfiled. It occurred to me while I was sifting through boxes of film scripts and shot lists that it is crucial to preserve these filmic records. The production notes, memos, scripts, and budget sheets contain important details about the filmmaking process; they shed light on how filmmakers thought about and interacted with their subjects.

Generally, the films of the NFB, most of which are available online now, reveal much about Canada's past, including how the country narrated its history. *Screening Nature and Nation* is just one example of the stories that we can tell using NFB historical documents. I have used them in three different ways: to provide a new historical perspective on Canadian environmental history by showing how the state was an active participant in the cultural construction of nature, to posit a new way of thinking about the NFB by demonstrating the extent to which nature and environmental issues were parts of its cinema, and to give historical context to emerging environmental attitudes in Canada by suggesting that NFB representations helped precipitate and simultaneously reflect ideas about the environment. There are a number of other ways that NFB films can be used within scholarly and popular contexts. For new stories about the NFB to be told, it is essential that we protect our archives and cultural institutions.

Notes

Introduction

1 John Grierson, quoted in D. B. Jones, *Movies and Memoranda: An Interpretive History of the National Film Board of Canada* (Ottawa: Canadian Film Institute, 1981), 30.

2 Quoted in Katherine Balpataky, "Call of the Wild," excerpted from *Canadian Wildlife*, Winter 2004, *Hinterland Who's Who: 50 Years*, https://www.hww.ca/en/about-us/50th/history.html.

3 Brian J. Low, *NFB Kids: Portrayals of Children by the National Film Board of Canada, 1939–1989* (Waterloo, ON: Wilfrid Laurier University Press, 2002).

4 National Film Act, s. 9(a), cited in Canada, *Report of the Royal Commission on National Development in the Arts, Letters and Sciences* (Ottawa: King's Printer, 1951), 51. The original legislation in 1939 stipulated that it was to "make and distribute films designed to help Canadians in all parts of Canada to understand the ways of living and the problems of Canadians in other parts" (Canada, *An Act to Create a National Film Board*, Statutes of Canada, 1939, 103). The wording changed in 1950 after the NFB underwent a government review.

5 Zoe Druick argues convincingly that the NFB was a social technology of liberal democracy. See Zoe Druick, *Projecting Canada: Government Policy and Documentary Film at the National Film Board* (Montréal and Kingston: McGill-Queen's University Press, 2007), 3, 23. NFB documentaries were "privileged sites of production," providing viewers with "a way of seeing the nation," Druick writes (9).

6 Ibid., 11.

7 Ibid., 23. See also Christopher E. Gittings, *Canadian National Cinema: Ideology, Difference, and Representation* (New York: Routledge, 2002), 88–89.

8 Federal and provincial bodies mediated the ecological behaviours of Canadians throughout the twentieth century. Education and law-making were the two most effective methods for communicating and enforcing state objectives regarding the environment. Sometimes government institutions used nontraditional approaches, such as publishing comic books, to educate Canadians on how to think about and behave toward nature. See Mark McLaughlin, "Rise of the Eco-Comics: The State, Environmental Education

and Canadian Comic Books, 1971–1975," *Material Culture Review* 77 (2013): 3–23.

9 National Film Board, *Canada: A Year of the Land* (Ottawa: Queen's Printer, 1967), 1.

10 Ibid.

11 Benedict Anderson, *Imagined Communities: Reflections on the Spread of Nationalism* (1983; repr., New York: Verso, 1991).

12 NFB filmmaking activities can also be seen as an extension of a new liberal vision to manage social and environmental spaces. See James Murton, *Creating a Modern Countryside: Liberalism and Land Resettlement in British Columbia* (Vancouver: UBC Press, 2007), 6.

13 See Tina Loo, *States of Nature: Conserving Canada's Wildlife in the Twentieth Century* (Vancouver: UBC Press, 2007); H. V. Nelles, *The Politics of Development: Forests, Mines, and Hydro-Electric Power in Ontario, 1849–1941* (Toronto: Macmillan, 1974); Graeme Wynn, *Canada and Arctic North America* (Vancouver: UBC Press, 2007); and Melissa Clark-Jones, *A Staple State: Canadian Industrial Resources in Cold War* (Toronto: University of Toronto Press, 1987).

14 James C. Scott, *Seeing like a State: How Certain Schemes to Improve the Human Condition Have Failed* (New Haven, CT: Yale University Press, 1998), 4.

15 Daniel Macfarlane, *Negotiating a River: Canada, the US, and the Creation of the St. Lawrence Seaway* (Vancouver: UBC Press, 2014); Douglas R. Francis, *The Technological Imperative in Canada: An Intellectual History* (Vancouver: UBC Press, 2009); Matthew Farish and P. Whitney Lackenbauer, "High Modernism in the Arctic: Planning Frobisher Bay and Inuvik," *Journal of Historical Geography* 35, no. 3 (2009): 517–44; Caroline Desbiens, *Power from the North: Territory, Identity, and the Culture of Hydroelectricity in Québec* (Vancouver: UBC Press, 2013).

16 Tina Loo, "High Modernism, Conflict, and the Nature of Change in Canada: A Look at *Seeing like a State*," *Canadian Historical Review* 97, no. 1 (2016): 42.

17 This high modernism is also evident in the magical realism of the fictional *Ti-Jean* series produced by the NFB. For a superb essay on the films of *Ti-Jean* and its high modern values, see Matt Dyce and Jonathan Peyton, "Magical Realism: Canadian Geography on Screen in the 1950s," *NiCHE*, 21 February 2018, https://niche-canada.org/2018/02/21/magical-regionalism-canadian-geography-on-screen-in-the-1950s/#_edn29.

18 Loo, "High Modernism," 42–43.

19 Jeanne Haffner, *The View from Above: The Science of Social Space* (Cambridge, MA: MIT Press, 2013), 112–13.

20 Adrian Ivakhiv, "An Ecophilosophy of the Moving Image," in *Ecocinema Theory and Practice*, ed. Stephen Rust, Salma Monani, and Sean Cubitt (New York: Routledge, 2013), 88.

21 Several environmental historians have examined the relationship between nature and film. See, for example, Gregg Mitman, *Reel Nature: America's Romance with Wildlife on Film* (Cambridge, MA: Harvard University Press, 1999); and Finis Dunaway, *Natural Visions: The Power of Images in American Environmental Reform* (Chicago: University of Chicago Press, 2005).

22 See Pat Brereton, *Hollywood Utopia: Ecology in Contemporary American Cinema* (Bristol: Intellect, 2005); Jonathan Burt, *Animals in Film* (London: Reaktion, 2002); Cynthia Chris, *Watching Wildlife* (Minneapolis: University of Minnesota Press, 2007); Sean Cubitt, *EcoMedia: Key Issues* (New York: Rodopi, 2005); Jhan Hochman, *Green Cultural Studies: Nature in Film, Novel, and Theory* (Moscow: University of Idaho Press, 1998); David Ingram, *Green Screen: Environmentalism and Hollywood Cinema* (1998; repr., Exeter: University of Exeter Press, 2004); Scott MacDonald, *The Garden in the Machine: A Field Guide to Independent Films About Place* (Berkeley: University of California Press, 2001); and Anat Pick and Guinevere Narraway, eds., *Screening Nature: Cinema Beyond the Human* (New York: Berghahn, 2013).

23 Siegfried Kracauer, *Theory of Film: The Redemption of Physical Reality* (Oxford: Oxford University Press, 1960), li.

Chapter 1: Filming like a State

1   National Film Board Archives (hereafter NFBA), minutes of NFB meeting of 14 September 1943, 3.

2   Ibid.

3   Ibid., 4.

4   Ibid., 3.

5   Advisory Committee on Post-War Reconstruction, *Final Report of the Subcommittee* (Ottawa: Edmond Cloutier, 1944), 21.

6   An Act to Create a National Film Board, R.S.C. 1939, 2 Geo. VI, c. 20, p. 103.

7   Quoted in D. B. Jones, *Movies and Memoranda: An Interpretive History of the National Film Board of Canada* (Ottawa: Canadian Film Institute, 1981), 41.

8   John Grierson, "The Documentary Idea," *Complete Photographer* 4, no. 92 (1942): 83.

9   Edgar Antsey, quoted in Jones, *Movies and Memoranda*, 42.

10 William Goetz, "The Canadian Wartime Documentary: *Canada Carries On* and *The World in Action*," *Cinema Journal* 16, no. 2 (Spring 1977): 65.

11 Although Grierson wanted his films to appear impartial, there was a considerable amount of prestidigitation in the films that he produced. To broadcast government views clearly, NFB directors abstracted images and sounds from specific places and assembled them into sequences. Short films and newsreels about the Second World War frequently utilized Eisensteinian editing techniques, such as jump-cuts and baroque movie scores, to give the films and newsreels emotional subtexts.

12 John Grierson, "A Film Policy for Canada," *Canadian Affairs* 1 (1944): 3.

13 NFBA, minutes of NFB meeting of 14 September 1943, 4.

14 NFBA, *Coal Face Canada* file, "Moving Picture: Coal Production in Canada," n.d.

15 *Coal Face Canada*, prod. Robert Edmonds, NFB, 1944.

16 *The Strategy of Metals*, prod. Stuart Legg, NFB, 1941; *Battle for Oil*, prod. Stuart Spottiswoode, NFB, 1942.

17 *Food—Weapons of Conquest*, prod. Stuart Legg, NFB, 1941.

18 *Hands for the Harvest*, prod. James Beveridge, NFB, 1943.

19 *Timber Front*, prod. Stanley Hawes and Frank Badgley, NFB, 1940.

20 Ibid.

21 Ibid.

22 See Bruce Hodgins and Jamie Benidickson, *The Temagami Experience: Recreation, Resources and Aboriginal Rights in the Northern Ontario Wilderness* (Toronto: University of Toronto Press, 1989); and R. Peter Gillis and Thomas Roach, *Lost Initiatives: Canada's Forest Industries, Forest Policy, and Forest Conservation* (New York: Greenwood, 1986).

23 Canada, *Lands, Parks and Forests Branch: Report for the Fiscal Year Ended March 31, 1939* (Ottawa: Department of Mines and Resources, 1939), 138, http://cfs.nrcan.gc.ca/pubwarehouse/pdfs/30918.pdf.

24 *Timber Front*.

25 Ibid.

26 NFBA, *According to Need* file, John Grierson to Donald Gordon, chairman of Wartime Prices and Trade Board, 29 May 1944.

27 NFBA, *According to Need* file, "Information Sheet," November 1944.

28 *According to Need*, prod. Dallas Jones, NFB, 1944.

29 Ibid.

30 Ibid.

31 NFBA, *According to Need* file, "Memorandum to the National Film Board," 13 October 1944.

32 Ibid.

33 John Grierson, CBC Radio, 30 November 1940.

34 *New Home in the West*, prod. Dallas Jones, NFB, 1943.

35 Ibid.

36 *Canadian Wheat Story*, prod. Crawley Films, NFB, 1944.

37 *New Home in the West*.

38 *Canadian Wheat Story*.

39 *Battle of the Harvests*, prod. Stanley Jackson, NFB, 1942.

40 *Look to the North*, prod. James Beveridge, NFB, 1944.

41 *Land in Trust*, prod. Lawrence Cherry and Evelyn Cherry, NFB, 1949.

42 *Red Runs the Fraser*, prod. Sydney Newman, NFB, 1949.

43 Ibid.

44 Carol Payne, *The Official Picture: The National Film Board of Canada's Still Photography Division and the Image of Canada, 1941–1971* (Montréal and Kingston: McGill-Queen's University Press, 2013), 107.

45 Grierson, "Film Policy for Canada," 4.

46 Olga Denisko, "Working in the Private Film Industry," *Interlock* 4–5 (1976): 15.

47 "They Make Movies," *Free Press Weekly Prairie Farmer*, 22 May 1946.

48 Denisko, "Working," 20.

49 NFBA, minutes of NFB meeting of 14 September 1943, 3.

50 NFBA, *Windbreaks on the Prairies* file, John Grierson to L. W. Brockington, 1 November 1939.

51 *Windbreaks on the Prairies*, prod. Evelyn Cherry, NFB, 1943.

52 Historian Finis Dunaway has shown that American filmmaker Pare Lorentz was one of the first to criticize the ecological mismanagement of farmers. His film *The Plow That Broke the Plains* criticizes agrarians' haphazard exploitation of the West. Although there is no mention of Lorentz's work in Cherry's notes, the director appears to have been a major influence on her work. See Finis Dunaway, *Natural Visions: The Power of Images in American Environmental Reform* (Chicago: University of Chicago Press, 2005).

53 *Windbreaks on the Prairies.*

54 Ibid.

55 NFBA, *Windbreaks on the Prairies* file, Allan Beaven to John Grierson, 16 October 1940.

56 NFBA, *Five Steps to Better Farm Living* file, "Condensed Guide for Film Utilization," n.d.

57 NFBA, *Five Steps to Better Farm Living* file, "Fact Sheet," n.d.

58 H. R. Hare, *Little Chats on Farm Management* (Ottawa: Economics Division— Marketing Service, Dominion Department of Agriculture, 1943), 2.

59 Ibid., 4.

60 Ibid., 22.

61 NFBA, *Five Steps to Better Farm Living* file, Evelyn Cherry to "Sol," 16 September 1944.

62 Hare, *Little Chats*, 2.

63 Joshua Nygren, "The Bulldozer in the Watershed: Conservation, Water, and Technological Optimism in the Post–World War II United States," *Environmental History* 21 (2016): 127.

64 NFBA, *Five Steps to Better Farm Living* file, Evelyn Cherry to Lawrence Cherry, 9 July 1944.

65 Olga Denisko, "Pot Pourri," *NFB Newsletter*, Summer 1975, 11.

66 NFBA, *Five Steps to Better Farm Living* file, Evelyn Cherry to "Sol," 16 September 1944.

67 NFBA, *Land in Trust* file, Evelyn Cherry to Roger Morin, 4 March 1950, 1.

68 Quoted in ibid.

69 Ibid., 2.

70 Zoe Druick, *Projecting Canada: Government Policy and Documentary Film at the National Film Board* (Montréal and Kingston: McGill-Queen's University Press, 2007), 82.

71 Donald Buchanan, "The Projection of Canada," *University of Toronto Quarterly* 13, no. 4 (1944): 305.

72 *Let's Look at Water*, prod. Harold Randall, NFB, 1947.

73 Clinton Evans, *War on Weeds in the Prairie West: An Environmental History* (Calgary: University of Calgary Press, 2002), 160.

74 *The World at Your Feet*, prod. Michael Spencer, NFB, 1953.

75 Ibid.

76 NFBA, *The World at Your Feet* file, "Background Information," May 1953.

77 NFBA, *The World at Your Feet* file, James Gordon Taggart, memo to staff, 8 June 1953.

78 *Chemical Conquest*, prod. Michael Spencer, NFB, 1956.

79 NFBA, *Chemical Conquest* file, "Research Summary," n.d., 1.

80   Ibid., 5.

81   See Edmund Russell, *War and Nature: Fighting Humans and Insects with Chemicals from WW1 to Silent Spring* (Cambridge: Cambridge University Press, 2001).

82   *Chemical Conquest.*

83   NFBA, *Chemical Conquest* file, "Draft Outline Chemical Film," n.d., 1.

84   NFBA, *Chemical Conquest* file, "Research Summary," n.d., 9.

85   Ibid., 10.

86   NFBA, *Chemical Conquest* file, "Draft Outline Chemical Film," n.d., 2.

87   *Chemical Conquest.*

Chapter 2: Visions of the North

1   Martin Lefebvre, introduction to *Landscape and Film*, ed. Martin Lefebvre (London: Routledge, 2006), xxviii.

2   Sherrill Grace, *Canada and the Idea of the North* (Montréal and Kingston: McGill-Queen's University Press, 2001), 51.

3   Margaret Atwood, *Strange Things: The Malevolent North in Canadian Literature* (Oxford: Clarendon, 1995), 8.

4   Quoted in Grace, *Canada*, 14.

5   See Rob Shields, *Places on the Margin: Alternative Geographies of Modernity* (London: Routledge, 1991), 31; Renée Hulan, *Northern Experience and Myths of Canadian Culture* (Montréal and Kingston: McGill-Queen's University Press, 2002); David Heinimann, "Latitude Rising: Historical Continuity in Canadian Nordicity," *Journal of Canadian Studies* 28, no. 2 (1993): 134–39; and John Moss, "The Cartography of Dreams," *Journal of Canadian Studies* 28, no. 2 (1993): 140–58.

6   Louis-Edmond Hamelin, *Canadian Nordicity: It's Your North Too* (Montréal: Harvest House, 1979), 17.

7   Pierre Berton, *The Mysterious North* (Toronto: McClelland & Stewart, 1956).

8   Shelagh Grant, "Myths of North in Canadian Ethos," *Northern Review* 3, no. 4 (1989): 16.

9   See Russell Potter, *Arctic Spectacles: The Frozen North in Visual Culture, 1818–1875* (Montréal and Kingston: McGill-Queen's University Press, 2007); and Janice Cavell, *Tracing the Connected Narrative: Arctic Exploration in British Print Culture, 1818–1860* (Toronto: University of Toronto Press, 2008).

10   The term *Arctic sublime* was coined by Chauncey Loomis in "The Arctic Sublime," in *Nature and the Victorian Imagination*, ed. U. C. Knoepflmacher and G. B. Tennyson (Berkeley: University of California Press, 1977), 95–112.

11   Lawren Harris, "Revelation of Art in Canada," *Canadian Theosophist* 7, no. 5 (1926): 86.

12   Harris, quoted in Christine Sowiak, "Contemporary Canadian Art: Locating Identity," in *A Passion for Identity: Canadian Studies for the 21st Century*, ed. Beverly Jean Rasporich and David Taras (Scarborough, ON: Nelson Thomson Learning, 2001), 256.

13   Peter Davidson, *The Idea of the North* (London: Reaktion, 2005), 194.

14 *Canadian Landscape*, prod. Radford Crawley, NFB, 1941.

15 Graeme Harper and Jonathan Rayner, introduction to *Cinema and Land-scape*, ed. Graeme Harper and Jonathan Rayner (Bristol: Intellect, 2010), 23.

16 Bruce Braun, *The Intemperate Rainforest: Nature, Culture, and Power on Can-ada's West Coast* (Minneapolis: University of Minnesota Press, 2002), 129.

17 Barbara Wade Rose, *"Budge": What Happened to Canada's King of Film?* (Toronto: ECW Press, 1998), 55.

18 W. J. T. Mitchell, *Landscape and Power* (1994; repr., Chicago: University of Chicago Press, 2002), 262.

19 *Canadian Landscape.*

20 R. G. Haliburton, *The Men of the North and Their Place in History: A Lecture Delivered Before the Montréal Literary Club* (Montréal: John Lovell, 1869).

21 George R. Parkin, *Imperial Federalism: The Problem of National Unity* (Lon-don: Macmillan, 1892), 115–19. See also Brian Osborne, "The Iconography of Nationhood in Canadian Art," in *The Iconography of Landscape*, ed. Denis Cosgrove and Stephen Daniels (Cambridge: Cambridge University Press, 1988), 171.

22 Arthur Irwin, "The Canadian," *Maclean's*, 1 February 1950, 20.

23 National Film Board, *Canada: A Year of the Land* (Ottawa: Queen's Printer, 1967), 1.

24 Harold Innis, *The Fur Trade in Canada: An Introduction to Canadian Economic History* (1930; repr., Toronto: University of Toronto Press, 1999); Donald Creighton, *The Commercial Empire of the St. Lawrence 1760–1850* (New Haven, CT: Yale University Press, 1937).

25 Northrop Frye, *The Bush Garden: Essays on the Canadian Imagination* (Toronto: Anansi, 1971), 29.

26 Claire Campbell, "'It Was Canadian, Then Typically Canadian': Revisiting Wilderness at Historic Sites," *British Journal of Canadian Studies* 21, no. 1 (2008): 8.

27 Benedict Anderson, *Imagined Communities: Reflections on the Spread of Nationalism* (1983; repr., New York: Verso, 1991).

28 NFBA, *Canadian Landscape* file, Ross Mclean to H. O. McCurry, National Gallery, 24 January 1942.

29 Quoted in Carol Payne, *The Official Picture: The National Film Board of Can-ada's Still Photography Division and the Image of Canada, 1941–1971* (Montréal and Kingston: McGill-Queen's University Press, 2013), 168.

30 This was a popular trope in twentieth century Canada. See Joan Sangster, "The Beaver as Ideology: Constructing Images of Inuit and Native LIfe in Post-World War II Canada," *Anthropologica*, 49, no. 2 (2007), 192. See also Ann Fienup-Riordan, *Freeze Frame: Alaska Eskimos in the Movies* (Seattle: University of Washington Press, 1995).

31 Robert McMillan, "Ethnology and the NFB: The Laura Boulton Mysteries," *Canadian Journal of Film Studies* 1, no. 2 (1991): 70.

32 Ibid.

33 E. Ann Kaplan, *Looking for the Other: Feminism, Film, and the Imperial Gaze* (London: Routledge, 1997).

34 *Eskimo Arts and Crafts*, prod. Laura Boulton, NFB, 1943.

35 Doug Wilkinson, *Land of the Long Day* (Toronto: Clarke, Irwin, 1955), 18.

36 Greg Burliuk, "Son of Idlout," *Whig Standard* (Kingston, ON), 7 March 1992, 5.

37 NFBA, *Land of the Long Day* file, "Information Sheet," n.d.

38 NFBA, *Land of the Long Day* file, "Toronto Film Society—Member Evaluation Form," n.d.

39 NFBA, *Land of the Long Day* file, "Baffin Island Script Commentary," 17 March 1952.

40 NFBA, *Land of the Long Day* file, "Shot List," reel 4, 7 March 1952, 2.

41 Ibid.

42 Wilkinson was not the first filmmaker, of course, to conjure up a sense of spatial and temporal exoticness through behind-the-scenes trickery. In Robert Flaherty's documentary *Nanook of the North* (1922), the director famously stages the sequence of Nanook taking a bite out of a gramophone record. The scene is meant to be amusing, but it also expresses the perceived crudeness of Inuit culture.

43 Wilkinson, *Land of the Long Day*, 11.

44 Shari Huhndorf, "Nanook and His Contemporaries: Imagining Eskimos in American Culture, 1897–1922," *Critical Inquiry* 20, no. 1 (2000): 134.

45 Shepard Krech III, *The Ecological Indian* (New York: Norton, 1999).

46 Neil Evernden, *The Social Creation of Nature* (Baltimore: Johns Hopkins University Press, 1992), 25.

47 Doug Wilkinson, "A Vanishing Canadian," *Beaver*, Spring 1959, 28.

48 Ibid., 25.

49 Adrian Ivakhiv, "An Ecophilosophy of the Moving Image," in *Ecocinema Theory and Practice*, ed. Stephen Rust, Salma Monani, and Sean Cubitt (New York: Routledge, 2013), 148.

50 Ibid.

51 See Frank Tester and Peter Kulchyski, *Tammarniit (Mistakes): Inuit Relocations in the Eastern Arctic, 1939–63* (Vancouver: UBC Press, 1994).

52 Frances Abele, "Canadian Contradictions: Forty Years of Northern Political Development," *Arctic* 40, no. 4 (1987): 315.

53 It is important to remember that "films stand still, but their subjects move on. . . . Even as a film is being shot, its subjects are in transition, moving toward a future that the film cannot contain." David MacDougall, *Transcultural Cinema* (Princeton, NJ: Princeton University Press, 1998), 33. This is particularly salient in the story of Joseph Idlout. The NFB film *Between Two Worlds* (1990), directed by Barry Greenwald and produced by Arctic activist Peter Raymont, documents Idlout's life after the filming of *Land of the Long Day*. Idlout eventually became a trapper and guide for the government. Trying to improve his family's fortunes, he gets caught up in the "white world." Idlout does not know who he is or where he belongs. He is caught "between two worlds."

54 *The Annanacks*, prod. René Bonnière, NFB, 1964.

55 Ibid.

56 Matthew Farish and P. Whitney Lackenbauer, "High Modernism in the Arctic: Planning Frobisher Bay and Inuvik," *Journal of Historical Geography* 35, no. 3 (2009): 517–44.

57 *Annanacks.*
58 *Across Arctic Ungava*, prod. Michael Spencer, NFB, 1949.
59 NFBA, *Across Arctic Ungava* file, official information sheet, n.d.
60 Jacques Rousseau, "Northern Research Reports: Botany: By Canoe Across the Ungava Peninsula via the Kogaluk and Payne Rivers," *Arctic* 1, no. 2 (1948): 134.
61 Ibid.
62 NFBA, *Across Arctic Ungava* file, Michael Spencer to Chester Kissick, "Re: 'Ungava,'" 15 June 1949.
63 NFBA, *Across Arctic Ungava* file, Michael Spencer to P. J. Alcock, 3 July 1949.
64 NFBA, *Across Arctic Ungava* file, official information sheet, n.d.
65 *Across Arctic Ungava.*
66 Jacques Rousseau, "The Vegetation and Life Zones of George River, Eastern Ungava and the Welfare of the Natives," *Arctic* 1, no. 2 (1948): 93.
67 NFBA, *Across Arctic Ungava* file, "Jean Michéa Notes," n.d.
68 J. P. Michéa, *Annual Report of the National Museum for the Fiscal Year 1948–1949* (Ottawa: Edmond Cloutier, 1949), 54–55.
69 Jacques Rousseau, "À travers l'Ungava," *Actualité économique* 25 (1949): 83–120.
70 Rousseau, "Vegetation and Life Zones," 96.
71 For the historical roots of this kind of representation, see Janice Cavell, "Arctic Exploration in Canadian Print Culture, 1890–1930," *Papers of the Bibliographical Society of Canada* 44, no. 2 (2006): 7–43.
72 NFBA, *High Arctic: Life on the Land* file, R. D. Muir, "Statement of Intent," n.d.
73 NFBA, *High Arctic: Life on the Land* file, Strowan Robertson to Tom Daly, re "Film Proposal," n.d., 1.
74 Tom Daly, interviewed in Peter Harcourt, "The Innocent Eye: An Aspect of the Work of the National Film Board of Canada," *Sight and Sound* 34, no. 1 (1965): 21. See also Gary Evans, *In the National Interest: A Chronicle of the National Film Board of Canada from 1949 to 1989* (Toronto: University of Toronto Press, 1991), 68–70.
75 NFBA, *High Arctic: Life on the Land* file, "A Teacher's Guide to the Film," n.d., 1.
76 Ibid., 3.
77 *High Arctic: Life on the Land*, prod. Strowan Robertson and Hugh O'Connor, NFB, 1958.
78 Ibid.
79 NFBA, *High Arctic: Life on the Land* file, R. D. Muir, "Statement of Intent," n.d.
80 Ibid.
81 Stephen Bocking, "Science and Spaces in the Northern Environment," *Environmental History* 12 (2007): 869.
82 Gordon Smith, "Weather Stations in the Canadian North and Arctic Sovereignty," *Journal of Military and Strategic Studies* 11, no. 3 (2009): 1–63.
83 Edward Jones-Imhotep, "Communicating the North: Scientific Practice and Canadian Postwar Identity," *Osiris* 24, no. 1 (2009): 146–47.
84 *Arctic IV*, prod. Colin Low, NFB, 1974.

85 Ibid.

86 NFBA, *Across Arctic Ungava* file, Jacques Rousseau to Michael Spencer, 27 June 1949, 1.

87 Ibid., 2.

88 Bruno Latour, *Science in Action: How to Follow Scientists and Engineers through Society* (Cambridge, MA: Harvard University Press, 1987), 220.

89 Ibid.

90 Ibid., 223.

91 Ibid., 227.

92 Bill Nichols, *Representing Reality: Issues and Concepts in Documentary* (Bloomington: Indiana University Press, 1991), 31. See also John Tagg, *The Burden of Representations: Essays on Photographies and Histories* (London: Macmillan, 1988). Tagg looks at how photographic documentation contributed to the rise of bureaucratic forms of state power since the late nineteenth century.

93 *Highways North*, prod. Canada in Action Series, NFB, 1944.

94 *Northwest by Air*, prod. James Beveridge and Margaret Parry, NFB, 1944.

95 *Northwest Frontier*, prod. James Beveridge, NFB, 1942.

96 David Nye, *American Technological Sublime* (Cambridge, MA: MIT Press, 1994).

97 *Northwest Frontier*.

98 *A Northern Challenge*, prod. Bill Roozeboom, NFB, 1973.

99 NFBA, *Down North* file, "Information Sheet," 1959.

100 *Down North*, prod. John Howe, NFB, 1958.

101 NFBA, *The Accessible North* file, "Commentary—The Accessible Arctic," November 1967.

102 *The Accessible North*, prod. David Bairstow, NFB, 1967.

103 NFBA, *North* file, "Film Poster," n.d.

104 NFBA, *North* file, T. V. Adams to Frank Spiller, 6 March 1967.

105 NFBA, *North* file, William Canning to Jon Evans, 3 May 1967.

106 Ibid.

107 NFBA, *North* file, T. V. Adams to Jon Evans, 14 April 1967.

108 NFBA, *North* file, William Canning to Jon Evans, 3 May 1967.

109 NFBA, *North* file, "Distribution Proposal for Film Entitled *North*," 2 October 1972.

110 NFBA, *North* file, J. Soutendum to Lorne Mitchell, 13 September 1971.

111 NFBA, *North* file, "Film Poster," n.d.

112 Vilhjalmur Stefansson, *The Friendly Arctic: The Story of Five Years in Polar Regions* (New York: Macmillan, 1922), 314.

113 Ibid., 687.

114 See Richard Finnie's *In the Shadow of the Pole* (1928), *The Arctic Patrol* (1929), and *Patrol to the Northwest Passage* (1931) for early filmic examples that documented the opening of the North.

115 P. Whitney Lackenbauer and Matthew Farish, "The Cold War on Canadian Soil: Militarizing a Northern Environment," *Environmental History* 12 (2007): 920–50.

116 Lester B. Pearson, "Canada Looks 'Down North,'" *Foreign Affairs: An American Quarterly Review* 24, no. 4 (1946): 639.

117 Ibid., 642.

118 Ibid., 646.

119 John Sandlos and Arn Keeling, "Claiming the New North: Development Colonialism at the Pine Point Mine, Northwest Territories," *Environment and History* 2 (2012): 7–18.

120 John Diefenbaker, "A New Vision," opening campaign speech, Winnipeg, 12 February 1958.

121 *Northern Challenge.*

122 Ibid.

123 William Guynn, *A Cinema of Nonfiction* (Cranbury: Fairleigh Dickinson University Press, 1990), 14.

124 For a good resource on the relationship among the North, nationalism, and cinema, see Scott Mackenzie, ed., *Films on Ice: Cinemas of the Arctic* (Edinburgh: Edinburgh University Press, 2014).

125 Harold Innis, *Changing Concepts of Time* (Toronto: Rowman & Littlefield, 1952), 18–19.

126 NFBA, "1962 NFB Activities in the North," 11 February 1963.

127 Ibid.

128 Vincent Massey Archives, B1987-0082/34I, file 4, Vincent Massey, "His Excellency's Remarks at the National Film Board," 27 January 1956.

129 Hamelin, *Canadian Nordicity*, 92.

130 Although I do not examine in this chapter the voices of northern people who produced their own images and stories of the North, there are a few examples worth mentioning. NFB films such as *Between Two Worlds* (1990), *If the Weather Permits* (2003), *Inuuvunga: I Am Inuk, I Am Alive* (2004), *Qallunaat! Why White People Are Funny* (2006), and the *Nunavut Animation Lab* series have responded to the dominant discourse that constructed the North as a homogeneous space outside history. Films in the 1990s and 2000s also included ecological critiques of the South's insatiable appetite in the North and the issues of climate change. *People of the Ice* (2003), *Climate on the Edge* (2003), and *Never Lose Sight* (2009) are but a few examples. This is all to say that the North is continually being reformulated and remapped and that NFB cinema is part of its ongoing construction.

Chapter 3: Cry of the Wild

1 An Act to Create a National Film Board, R.S.C. 1939, 2 Geo. VI, c. 20, pp. 101–5. This mandate was slightly modified in 1950 but retained its core objective to present Canada to the world. An Act Respecting the National Film Board, R.S.C. 1950, pp. 1, 567–74.

2 Jim Leach, "Dark Satanic Mills: Denys Arcand's *On est au coton*," in *Candid Eyes: Essays on Canadian Documentaries*, ed. Jim Leach and Jeannette Sloniowski (Toronto: University of Toronto Press, 2003), 87.

3 *Poison, Pests, and People*, prod. Don Mulholland, NFB, 1960.

4 *River with a Problem*, prod. David Bairstow, NFB, 1961.

5   *The Enduring Wilderness*, prod. Ernest Reid, NFB, 1963.

6   *Death of a Legend*, prod. Bill Mason, NFB, 1971.

7   Éric Rohmer and Louis Marcorelles, "Entretien avec Jean Rouch," *Cahiers du cinéma* 144 (June 1963): 1–22.

8   Kirwan Cox, "Canada," in *Encyclopedia of Documentary Film*, ed. Ian Aitken (New York: Routledge, 2006), 128.

9   Peter Harcourt, "Images and Information: The Dialogic Structure of *Bûcherons de la Manouane* by Arthur Lamothe," in Leach and Sloniowski, *Candid Eyes*, 62.

10 Jim Leach and Jeannette Sloniowski, introduction to Leach and Sloniowski, *Candid Eyes*, 7.

11 NFBA, *Annual Report*, 1965–66, 7.

12 Ibid.

13 Samuel P. Hays, *Explorations in Environmental History: Essays* (Pittsburgh: University of Pittsburgh Press, 1998), 380.

14 John McCormick, *Reclaiming Paradise: The Global Environmental Movement* (Bloomington: Indiana University Press, 1989), 47–48.

15 See Adam Rome, "'Give Earth a Chance': The Environmental Movement and the 1960s," *Journal of American History* 90, no. 2 (2003): 525–54.

16 Samuel P. Hays, *Beauty, Health, and Permanence: Environmental Politics in the United States, 1955–1985* (New York: Cambridge University Press, 1987), 3. See also Adam Rome, *The Bulldozer in the Countryside: Suburban Sprawl and the Rise of American Environmentalism* (New York: Cambridge University Press, 2001); and Robert Gottlieb, *Forcing the Spring: The Transformation of the Environmental Movement* (Washington, DC: Island Press, 1993).

17 Mark Dowie, *Losing Ground: American Environmentalism at the Close of the Twentieth Century* (Cambridge, MA: MIT Press, 1995), 23.

18 Mark McLaughlin, "Green Shoots: Aerial Insecticide Spraying and the Growth of Environmental Consciousness in New Brunswick," *Acadiensis* 40, no. 1 (2011): 4.

19 Jennifer Read, "'Let Us Heed the Voice of Youth': Laundry Detergents, Phosphates and the Emergence of the Environmental Movement in Ontario," *Journal of the Canadian Historical Association* 7 (1996): 230.

20 Ryan O'Connor, *The First Green Wave: Pollution Probe and the Origins of Environmental Activism in Ontario* (Vancouver: UBC Press, 2015).

21 NFBA, *Chemical Conquest* file, "Draft Outline Chemical Film," n.d., 1.

22 NFBA, *Poison, Pests, and People* file, "Chemicals in Agriculture Notes," 17 April 1958, 1.

23 Ibid.

24 Ibid.

25 Ibid., 3.

26 Ibid., 2.

27 Ibid.

28 Cyanamid of Canada, *Your Farm and How to Keep It Productive* (Montréal: Cyanamid, 1959), 6, 7.

29 NFBA, *Poison, Pests, and People* file, Julian Biggs, memo to Don Mulholland, 10 August 1959.

30 NFBA, *Poison, Pests, and People* file, Don Mulholland to Larry Gosnell, 3 July 1959, 1.

31 NFBA, *Poison, Pests, and People* file, Larry Gosnell to Don Mulholland, 17 July 1959.

32 NFBA, *Poison, Pests, and People* file, "Chemicals in Agriculture Notes," n.d., 4.

33 Ibid.

34 Ibid.

35 *Poison, Pests, and People*, prod. David Bairstow, NFB, 1960.

36 Ibid.

37 NFBA, *Poison, Pests, and People* file, "Script," by Larry Gosnell, 1.

38 "Insecticide Film Shelved: Pressure Put on NFB Former Producer Says," *Globe and Mail*, 1 February 1963, 4.

39 NFBA, *Deadly Dilemma* file, Peter Jones to Michael Spencer, "Re: *Deadly Dilemma* Revision," 23 May 1962.

40 Ibid.

41 Ryan O'Connor, "An Ecological Call to Arms: *The Air of Death* and the Origins of Environmentalism in Ontario," *Ontario History* 105, no. 1 (2013): 19–46.

42 Ontario Advisory Committee on Pollution, *Report of the Committee Appointed to Inquire into and Report upon the Pollution of Air, Soil, and Water in the Townships of Dunnville, Moulton, and Sherbrooke, Haldimand County* (Toronto: Queen's Printer, 1968), 346.

43 Ibid., 285.

44 NFBA, *Poison, Pests, and People* file, promotional poster, 1960.

45 Rachel Carson, *Silent Spring* (Greenwich: Fawcett, 1962), 297.

46 NFBA, *River with a Problem* file, "Info Sheet," 1961.

47 *Morning on the Lièvre*, prod. David Bairstow, NFB, 1961.

48 NFBA, *River with a Problem* file, "Info Sheet," 1961.

49 "River Pollution a Serious Matter," *Globe and Mail*, 15 July 1955, 8.

50 Walter Gray, "A Perfect Example of Pollution," *Globe and Mail*, 1 June 1961, 7.

51 *River with a Problem*.

52 NFBA, *River with a Problem* file, R. A. Jones, assistant executive secretary, to David Bairstow, 24 July 1961.

53 *River with a Problem*.

54 Ibid.

55 Ibid.

56 See Matthew Gandy, *Concrete and Clay: Reworking Nature in New York City* (Cambridge, MA: MIT Press, 2003); and Christopher Fullerton, "A Changing of the Guard: Regional Planning in Ottawa, 1945–1974," *Urban History Review* 34, no. 1 (2005): 100–112.

57 Gray, "Perfect Example," 7.

58 NFBA, *River with a Problem* file, Charlotte Whitton to Graham Parker, 12 February 1962.

59 Ibid.

60 NFBA, *River with a Problem* file, John Pratt to David Bairstow, 13 February 1962.

61 *The Enduring Wilderness*, prod. Ernest Reid, NFB, 1963.

62 NFBA, *The Enduring Wilderness* file, Sid Roberts, National Parks Branch, to Graham Crabtree, liaison officer, NFB, 15 May 1962.

63 Ibid.

64 NFBA, *The Enduring Wilderness* file, Christopher Chapman, "The Meaning of Wilderness," 12 June 1962.

65 NFBA, *The Enduring Wilderness* file, "Script Notes," n.d.

66 Roderick Nash, *Wilderness and the American Mind* (New Haven, CT: Yale University Press, 1982), 68.

67 Roderick Nash, "The American Wilderness in Historical Perspective," *American Society for Environmental History* 6, no. 4 (1963): 4.

68 W. L. Morton, *The Canadian Identity* (Toronto: University of Toronto Press, 1961), 5.

69 The history of national parks shows us that the meaning and value attributed to these places were multifaceted and constantly changing. In Canada, national parks were first established at the end of the nineteenth century to accommodate middle-class fantasies about the sublime and to protect natural resources from abuse. Seventy years later they were regulated and perceived primarily as ecological preserves. The best book on the subject is Alan MacEachern, *Natural Selections: National Parks in Atlantic Canada, 1935–1970* (Montréal and Kingston: McGill-Queen's University Press, 2001).

70 Canada, *Wisdom's Heritage: The National Parks of Canada* (Ottawa: Department of Northern Affairs and National Resources, 1957), 1.

71 NFBA, *The Enduring Wilderness* file, Christopher Chapman, "Wilderness" (script), n.d., 4.

72 NFBA, *The Enduring Wilderness* file, Christopher Chapman, "The Meaning of Wilderness" (script), 12 June 1962, 2.

73 Ibid., 1.

74 John Hepworth, "Cinema 65," *Loyola News*, 26 March 1965, 1.

75 "Canadian Films Win Awards," *St. Catharines Standard*, 24 April 1965, 3.

76 *Enduring Wilderness*.

77 Ibid.

78 William Whyte, *The Organization Man* (New York: Simon and Schuster, 1956); C. Wright Mills, *White Collar: The American Middle Classes* (Oxford: Oxford University Press, 1951).

79 Whyte, *Organization Man*, 3.

80 Richard Harris, *Creeping Conformity: How Canada Became Suburban* (Toronto: University of Toronto Press, 2004).

81 NFBA, *The Enduring Wilderness* file, "Look to the Wilderness Review," n.d., 6.

82 Ibid., 4.

83 *Enduring Wilderness*.

84 W. Phillip Keller, *Canada's Wild Glory* (Toronto: Nelson, Foster, and Scott, 1961), 4.

85 J. Keri Cronin, *Manufacturing National Park Nature: Photography, Ecology, and the Wilderness Industry of Jasper* (Vancouver: UBC Press, 2012).

86 William Cronon, ed., *Uncommon Ground: Rethinking the Human Place in Nature* (New York: W. W. Norton, 1995).

87   MacEachern, *Natural Selections*, 9.

88   Claire Campbell, "'It Was Canadian, Then Typically Canadian': Revisiting Wilderness at Historic Sites," *British Journal of Canadian Studies* 21, no. 1 (2008): 6.

89   For scholarship on the origins of the wilderness preservation movement, see Kevin Marsh, *Drawing Lines in the Forest: Creating Wilderness Areas in the Pacific Northwest* (Seattle: University of Washington Press, 2010); Paul Sutter, *Driven Wild: How the Fight Against Automobiles Launched the Modern Wilderness Movement* (Seattle: University of Washington Press, 2002); and James Turner, *The Promise of Wilderness: American Environmental Politics since 1964* (Seattle: University of Washington Press, 2012).

90   *Enduring Wilderness*.

91   Ibid.

92   *Cry of the Wild*, prod. Bill Mason, NFB, 1972.

93   Tina Loo, *States of Nature: Conserving Canada's Wildlife in the Twentieth Century* (Vancouver: UBC Press, 2007), 152.

94   Quoted in ibid., 158.

95   Ibid., 161.

96   Ibid, 158, 159. See also Alexander J. Burnett, *A Passion for Wildlife: The History of the Canadian Wildlife Service* (Vancouver: UBC Press, 2003).

97   Barry Lopez, *Of Wolves and Men* (New York: Simon and Schuster, 1978), 175.

98   Farley Mowat, *Never Cry Wolf* (1963; repr., New York: Little, Brown, 1999), vi.

99   A. W. F. Banfield, "Review of *Never Cry Wolf*," *Canadian Field Naturalist* 78, no. 1 (1964): 52–53.

100 Karen Jones, "'Never Cry Wolf': Science, Sentiment, and the Literary Rehabilitation of *Canis Lupus*," *Canadian Historical Review* 84 (2001): 71–72.

101 At first, the CWS approached Disney to make the film, but the project never went into production because the two parties could not settle on a viable budget.

102 Library and Archives Canada, RG 84, A-2-a, vol. 2134, file U266, pt. 4, David A. Munro, director, Canadian Wildlife Service, memo to Department of Indian Affairs and Northern Development, 15 December 1967.

103 NFBA, *Death of a Legend* file, "General Guidelines to Be Used in Developing a Theme for a Canadian Wild Life Film," 16 February 1966, 1.

104 Ibid., 3.

105 Ibid., 2.

106 NFBA, *Death of a Legend* file, Darrell Eagles to David Bairstow, 22 July 1966.

107 NFBA, *Death of a Legend* file, "Wildlife Film Project," n.d.

108 Ken Buck, *Bill Mason: Wilderness Artist from Heart to Hand* (Calgary: Rocky Mountain Books, 2005), 163.

109 For more on the intersection between his faith and his environmentalism, see Bill Mason, *Path of the Paddle* (Toronto: Van Nostrand Reinhold, 1980); Bill Mason, "Perspectives on Wilderness and Creativity," *Park News* 19, no. 2 (1982): 9–11; Bill Mason, *Song of the Paddle* (Toronto: Key Porter Books, 1988); and James Raffan, *Fire in the Bones: Bill Mason and the Canadian Canoeing Tradition* (Toronto: HarperCollins, 1996).

110 Bill Mason, *Canoescapes* (Toronto: Stoddart, 1995), 156.

111 Tina Loo was the first to identify Mason as a vital voice in the history of wildlife preservation in Canada. Loo, *States of Nature*, 176–81.

112 NFBA, *Death of a Legend* file, film information sheet, n.d.

113 Buck, *Bill Mason*, 166.

114 Ibid.

115 *Death of a Legend.*

116 Ibid.

117 NFBA, *Death of a Legend* file, film information sheet, n.d.

118 NFBA, *Death of a Legend* file, Bill Mason, "Outline for 'The Wolf,'" 3 October 1967, 4.

119 Quoted in Raffan, *Fire in the Bones*, 188.

120 *Cry of the Wild.*

121 NFBA, *Death of a Legend* file, "Notes of a Meeting Held to Discuss Production Plans for the Wolf Film," 21 September 1967.

122 *Death of a Legend.*

123 NFBA, *Death of a Legend* file, Bernard Devlin to David Bairstow, "Wildlife Project Feasibility," 27 June 1966, 2.

124 NFBA, *Death of a Legend* file, Ernie Kuyt to Bernard Devlin, 8 November 1966.

125 Derek Bousé, *Wildlife Films* (Philadelphia: University of Philadelphia Press, 2000), 4.

126 Béla Balazs, "Theory of the Film," in *Film Theory and Criticism: Introductory Reading*, 3rd ed., ed. Gerald Mast and Marshall Cohen (Oxford: Oxford University Press, 1985), 256.

127 *Cry of the Wild.*

128 Ibid.

Chapter 4: Challenge for Change

1 Hans Carlson, *Home Is the Hunter* (Vancouver: UBC Press, 2009), 5.

2 Ibid.

3 Ibid., 204.

4 Ibid., 257.

5 Carolyn Merchant, "Shades of Darkness: Race and Environmental History," *Environmental History* 8, no. 3 (2003): 381.

6 Richardson, quoted in Gary Evans, *In the National Interest: A Chronicle of the National Film Board of Canada from 1949 to 1989* (Toronto: University of Toronto Press, 1991), 170.

7 Ibid., 158.

8 NFBA, *The Things I Cannot Change* file, "The Bailey Family: Eleven Going on Twelve: Proposal for a Half Hour 16mm Black and White Film to Be Produced for the Privy Council," n.d.

9 *The Things I Cannot Change*, prod. John Kemeny, NFB, 1967.

10 NFBA, Challenge for Change (CFC) file, "Challenge for Change: Proposal for an Action-Program of Film Activities in the Area of Poverty," 16 January 1967, 1.

11 NFBA, CFC file, "Proposal for a Program of Film Activities in the Area of Poverty and Change," 16 February 1967, 1.

12   Ibid.
13   NFBA, CFC file, "Challenge for Change Program: A Report Prepared by the National Film Board of Canada," 11 December 1967, 1.
14   NFBA, CFC file, "Challenge for Change," 18 December 1973, 2.
15   Noel Starblanket, "A Voice for Indians: An Indian Film Crew," *CFC/SN Newsletter* 2 (1968): 2.
16   *You Are on Indian Land*, prod. George C. Stoney, NFB, 1969.
17   John Grierson, "Memo to Michelle About Decentralizing the Means of Production," *CFC/SN Newsletter* 8 (1972): 4.
18   Colin Low, "Grierson and Challenge for Change," in *Challenge for Change: Activist Documentary at the National Film Board of Canada*, ed. Thomas Waugh, Michael Brendan Baker, and Ezra Winton (Montréal and Kingston: McGill-Queen's University Press, 2010), 17.
19   Dorothy Todd Hénaut and Bonnie Sherr Klein, "In the Hands of Citizens: A Video Report," *CFC/SN Newsletter* 4 (1969): 5.
20   NFBA, CFC file, Boyce Richardson, "Film in the Service of the People," n.d., 1.
21   Evans, *In the National Interest*, 175.
22   Jerry White, "The Winds of Fogo," in *The Cinema of Canada*, ed. Jerry White (New York: Wallflower, 2006), 79.
23   Janine Marchessault, "Amateur Video and Challenge for Change," in Waugh, Baker, and Winton, *Challenge for Change*, 365.
24   Ibid., 360.
25   Zoe Druick, "Meeting at the Poverty Line: Government Policy, Social Work, and Media Activism in the Challenge for Change Program," in Waugh, Baker, and Winton, *Challenge for Change*, 344.
26   CFC also affected documentary cinema. Although the program ended in 1980, CFC filmmakers such as Bonnie Sherr Klein went on to New York to preach the "media to the people" movement. Other filmmakers used the ideas and resources of CFC to form the short-lived Studio E (Environment) of the NFB in 1974.
27   Quoted in Carlson, *Home Is the Hunter*, 207.
28   Ronald Niezen, "Power and Dignity: The Social Consequences of Hydro-Electric Development for the James Bay Cree," *Canadian Review of Sociology and Anthropology* 30, no. 4 (1993): 512.
29   Quoted in Boyce Richardson, *Strangers Devour the Land* (Vancouver: Douglas & McIntyre, 1991), 84.
30   Harvey A. Feit, "Hunting and the Quest for Power: The James Bay Cree and the Whitemen in the 20th Century," in *Native Peoples: The Canadian Experience*, ed. R. Bruce Morrison and C. Roderick Wilson (Toronto: McClelland & Stewart, 1995), 4.
31   Richardson, *Strangers Devour the Land*, 23.
32   Ibid.
33   Before he made *Cree Hunters of Mistassini*, Richardson directed *Job's Garden* (1973), a documentary about Job Bearskin and his wife, Mary. For the journalist-turned-filmmaker, the Bearskins' lives exemplified the Cree's profound understanding of humans' role in taking care of nature.

34 NFBA, *Cree Hunters of Mistassini* file, "Boyce Richardson to Interdepartmental Committee, Challenge for Change" (memo), 2 December 1973, 4.

35 Boyce Richardson, "Doctorate for Philip Awashish," *Nation*, 11 September 2009, http://www.nationnewsarchives.ca/article/doctorate-for-philip-awashish/.

36 Evans, *In the National Interest*, 170.

37 NFBA, *Cree Hunters of Mistassini* file, "Boyce Richardson to Interdepartmental Committee, Challenge for Change" (memo), 2 December 1973, 1.

38 NFBA, *Cree Hunters of Mistassini* file, Boyce Richardson, *"Assimilation Blues* Film Notes," n.d.

39 Quoted in Michelle Stewart, *"Cree Hunters of Mistassini*: CFC and Aboriginal Rights," in Waugh, Baker, and Winton, *Challenge for Change*, 182.

40 NFBA, *Cree Hunters of Mistassini* file, "Notes from a Conversation with the Filmmakers," n.d., 1.

41 Stewart, *"Cree Hunters of Mistassini,"* 183.

42 Quoted in Stewart, *"Cree Hunters of Mistassini,"* 183.

43 Richardson, "Doctorate for Philip Awashish."

44 *Cree Hunters of Mistassini*, prod. Colin Low, NFB, 1974.

45 Ibid.

46 Mistassini is a small settlement originally established as a meeting place where the Cree gathered during the warm months of summer to catch fish, hunt caribou, and trade furs. Even in the 1960s, the village was little more than a collection of tents and huts congregated around the Hudson's Bay Company trading post and the Anglican church. In an effort to put Indigenous people in villages, the provincial government built roads and power grids across the James Bay region. Despite these changes, the majority of the Cree preferred to dwell in the forested region outside Mistassini. Blacksmith, for example, had been hunting on his 1,200 square acres of territory for approximately thirty years.

47 Stewart, *"Cree Hunters of Mistassini,"* 185.

48 Richardson, *Strangers Devour the Land*, 201.

49 NFBA, *Cree Hunters of Mistassini* file, "Notes from a Conversation with the Filmmakers," n.d., 2.

50 NFBA, Cree Hunters of Mistassini file, Boyce Richardson, *"Assimilation Blues* Film Notes," n.d., 2.

51 *Cree Hunters of Mistassini*.

52 Richardson, *Strangers Devour the Land*, 288.

53 Ibid.

54 Claude Peloquin and Fikrit Berkes, "Local Knowledge, Subsistence Harvests and Social-Ecological Complexity in James Bay," *Human Ecology* 37 (2009): 535.

55 *Cree Hunters of Mistassini*.

56 Ibid.

57 Feit, "Hunting and the Quest for Power," 4.

58 *Cree Hunters of Mistassini*.

59 Ibid.

60 Stewart, *Cree Hunters of Mistassini*, 186.

61 Ibid.
62 Richardson, *Strangers Devour the Land*, 273.
63 Graeme Wynn, "Foreword: Dignity and Power," *Home Is the Hunter*, xvii.
64 Niezen, "Power and Dignity," 515.
65 Carlson, *Home Is the Hunter*, 17.
66 NFBA, *Cree Hunters of Mistassini* file, "The James Bay Communications Project" (memo), n.d.
67 Ibid.
68 NFBA, *Cree Hunters of Mistassini* file, Ian Ball to Lynne Williams and Regional Distribution Coordinators, 17 March 1974.
69 NFBA, *Cree Hunters of Mistassini* file, L. Renaud-Roberts, memo to Regional Distribution Coordinators, 1 October 1974.
70 NFBA, *Cree Hunters of Mistassini* file, Mark Zanis, "NFB Distribution Plan," 24 September 1974.
71 NFBA, *Cree Hunters of Mistassini* file, "Distribution Kit for *Cree Hunters*," n.d., 2.
72 NFBA, *Cree Hunters of Mistassini* file, B. Petawabano, "Report on the Screening of *Our Land Is Our Life* and *Cree Hunters of Mistassini* at Rupert's House and Eastmain in Québec," 1975.
73 NFBA, *Cree Hunters of Mistassini* file, Michael Mitchell, "North American Indian Travelling College—Report of Screening of National Film Board's Films," n.d., 2.
74 NFBA, *Cree Hunters of Mistassini* file, "Kipawa Reserve (Québec) Report," 22 December 1974, 1.
75 B. Petawabano, "Report on the Screening at the Rupert's House and Eastmain in Québec," 1975, 1.
76 NFBA, *Cree Hunters of Mistassini* file, Mark Zanis, "Animator's Report," 1974, 1.
77 Ibid.
78 Rick Moore, "Canada's Challenge for Change: Documentary Film and Video as an Exercise of Power through the Production of Cultural Reality" (PhD diss., University of Oregon, 1988).
79 NFBA, CFC file, "Challenge for Change Report on *Cree Hunters*," 29 November 1974, 1.
80 NFBA, *Cree Hunters of Mistassini* file, Boyce Richardson and Tony Ianzelo, "Report on *Cree Hunters*," 24 September 1974.
81 Quoted in Linda Diebel, "The Aftermath: Natives Settle for 150 Million," *Gazette* (Montréal), 16 November 1974, 1.
82 NFBA, *Cree Hunters of Mistassini* file, Rick Dale, "National Film Board, Challenge for Change, Animator's Report, Ontario Region," 27 June 1975, 1.
83 Ibid.
84 Joan Irwin, "Film Explains Life of Cree," *Montréal Star*, 2 July 1974, 4.
85 "*Cree Hunters of Mistassini* Film Review," *Booklist*, November 1975, 1.
86 NFBA, *Cree Hunters of Mistassini* file, "Notes from a Film Showing in Montréal," 20 November 1974.
87 Matthew Coon Come, quoted in Graeme Wynn, "Northern Exposures," *Environmental History* 12, no. 2 (2007): 389.

88   NFBA, *Cree Hunters of Mistassini* file, "Information Sheet," n.d., 1.

89   NFBA, *Cree Hunters of Mistassini* file, "Notes from a Conversation with the Filmmakers," n.d., 2.

Conclusion

1   Graeme Harper and Jonathan Rayner, introduction to *Cinema and Landscape*, ed. Graeme Harper and Jonathan Rayner (Bristol: Intellect, 2010), 24.

2   Stephen Rust and Salma Monani, "Introduction: Cuts to Dissolves—Defining and Situating Ecocinema Studies," in *Ecocinema Theory and Practice*, ed. Stephen Rust, Salma Monani, and Sean Cubitt (New York: Routledge, 2013), 1.

3   Despite the NFB's decision to move the headquarters to Montréal in 1956 and despite its efforts to establish regional studios in the 1970s, francophone, Indigenous, and local voices on the homeland were generally overshadowed by an emphatically Anglo-Canadian idea of nationhood.

4   *Canadian Wheat Story*, prod. J. Stanley Moore, NFB, 1944.

5   James C. Scott, *Seeing like a State: How Certain Schemes to Improve the Human Condition Have Failed* (New Haven, CT: Yale University Press, 1998), 88.

6   *The Great Plains*, prod. Tom Daly, NFB, 1950.

7   Philip Rosen, "Nation and Anti-Nation: Concepts of National Cinema in the 'New' Media Era," *Diaspora* 5, no. 3 (1996): 391.

8   NFBA, "Government Film Commissioner's Report," in *Annual Report*, 1979–80, 6.

9   Peter Stevens, *Brink of Reality: New Canadian Documentary Film and Video* (Toronto: Between the Lines, 1993), 8.

10   Zoe Druick, *Projecting Canada: Government Policy and Documentary Film at the National Film Board* (Montréal and Kingston: McGill-Queen's University Press, 2007), 164.

11   Guy Dixon, "Budget Cuts? The National Film Board Is Not Afraid," *Globe and Mail*, 16 April 2012, https://www.theglobeandmail.com/arts/film/budget-cuts-national-film-board-is-not-afraid/article4100642/.

Selected Bibliography

Archival and Library Sources

National Film Board Archives (NFBA), Montréal

According to Need file
Across Arctic Ungava file
Annual reports, 1939–80
Canadian Landscape file
Challenge for Change file
Chemical Conquest file
Coal Face Canada file
Cree Hunters of Mistassini file
Deadly Dilemma file
Death of a Legend file
Down North file
The Enduring Wilderness file
Five Steps to Better Farm Living file
High Arctic: Life on the Land file
Land in Trust file
Land of the Long Day file
Netsilik Series file
NFB minutes, 1939–75
Poison, Pests, and People file
River with a Problem file
Timber Front file
Windbreaks on the Prairies file
World at Your Feet file

Library and Archives Canada (LAC), Ottawa

Canadian Parks Service, RG 84

Montréal Botanical Gardens (MBC), Montréal, Québec

Jacques Rousseau fonds

Vincent Massey Archives (VMA), Toronto

Vincent Massey papers

Films

The Accessible North. Produced by David Bairstow, NFB, 1967.

According to Need. Produced by Dallas Jones, NFB, 1944.

Across Arctic Ungava. Produced by Michael Spencer, NFB, 1949.

The Air of Death. Produced by Larry Gosnell, CBC, 1967.

Alexander Mackenzie: Lord of the North. Produced by David Bairstow, NFB, 1964.

Angotee: Story of an Eskimo Boy. Produced by Doug Wilkinson, NFB, 1953.

The Annanacks. Produced by René Bonnière, NFB, 1964.

Arctic Hunters. Produced by Laura Boulton, NFB, 1944.

Arctic IV. Produced by Colin Low, NFB, 1974.

The Ballad of Crowfoot. Produced by Willie Dunn, NFB, 1968.

Battle for Oil. Produced by Stuart Spottiswoode, NFB, 1942.

Battle of the Harvests. Produced by Stanley Jackson, NFB, 1942.

Between Two Worlds. Produced by Peter Raymont, NFB, 1990.

Blake. Produced by Douglas Jackson, NFB, 1969.

Canada: The Land. Produced by Gerald Potterton, NFB, 1971.

Canadian Landscape. Produced by Radford Crawley, NFB, 1941.

Canadian Wheat Story. Produced by J. Stanley Moore, NFB, 1944.

Chemical Conquest. Produced by Michael Spencer, NFB, 1956.

Class Project: The Garbage Movie. Directed by Martin DeFalco, NFB, 1980.

Climate on the Edge. Produced by Jean Lemire, NFB, 2003.

Coal Face Canada. Produced by Robert Edmonds, NFB, 1944.

Cree Hunters of Mistassini. Produced by Colin Low, NFB, 1974.

Cry of the Wild. Produced by Bill Mason, NFB, 1972.

Deadly Dilemma. Produced by Don Mulholland, NFB, 1961.

Death of a Legend. Produced by Bill Mason, NFB, 1971.

Down North. Produced by John Howe, NFB, 1958.

The Enduring Wilderness. Produced by Ernest Reid, NFB, 1963.

Epilogue. Produced by William Pettigrew, NFB, 1971.

Eskimo Arts and Crafts. Produced by Laura Boulton, NFB, 1943.

Eskimo Summer. Produced by Laura Boulton, NFB, 1944.

Exercise Muskox. Produced by Robert Anderson and E. W. Scythes, NFB, 1946.

Farm Electrification. Produced by Evelyn Cherry, NFB, 1946.

Five Steps to Better Farm Living. Produced by Evelyn Cherry, NFB, 1945.

Hands for the Harvest. Produced by James Beveridge, NFB, 1943.

High Arctic: Life on the Land. Produced by Strowan Robertson and Hugh
    O'Connor, NFB, 1958.

Highways North. Produced by Canada in Action Series, NFB, 1944.

How to Build an Igloo. Produced by Doug Wilkinson, NFB, 1949.

If the Weather Permits. Produced by Elisapie Isaac, NFB, 2003.

In Search of the Bowhead Whale. Produced by William Brind, NFB, 1974.

Inuuvunga: I Am Inuk, I Am Alive. Produced by Pierre Lapointe, NFB, 2004.

Land in Trust. Produced by Lawrence Cherry and Evelyn Cherry, NFB, 1949.

Land of Pioneers. Produced by James Beveridge and Margaret Perry, NFB, 1944.

Land of the Long Day. Produced by Michael Spencer, NFB, 1952.

The Last Voyage of Henry Hudson. Produced by Richard Gilbert, NFB, 1964.

Let's Look at Water. Produced by Harold Randall, NFB, 1947.

Look to the Forest. Produced by Donald Fraser, NFB, 1950.

Look to the North. Produced by James Beveridge, NFB, 1944.

Morning on the Lièvre. Produced by David Bairstow, NFB, 1961.

Nanook of the North. Produced by Robert Flaherty, 1922.

New Home in the West. Produced by Dallas Jones NFB, 1943.

North. Produced by Bill Canning, NFB, 1969.

A Northern Challenge. Produced by Bill Roozeboom, NFB, 1973.

Northwest by Air. Produced by James Beveridge and Margaret Parry, NFB, 1944.

Northwest Frontier. Produced by James Beveridge, NFB, 1942.

Our Land Is Our Life. Produced by Boyce Richardson, NFB, 1974.

Our Northern Citizen. Produced by Grant McLean, NFB, 1956.

Paddle to the Sea. Produced by Bill Mason, NFB, 1966.

Paul Tomkowicz: Street-Railway Switchman. Produced by Romon Kroitor and
    Tom Daly, NFB, 1953.

People of the Ice. Produced by Jean Lemire, NFB, 2003.

Poison, Pests, and People. Produced by Don Mulholland, NFB, 1960.

Pour la suite du monde. Produced by Pierre Perrault and Michel Brault, NFB, 1963.

Qallunaat! Why White People Are Funny. Produced by Mark Sandiford, NFB, 2006.

Red Runs the Fraser. Produced by Sydney Newman, NFB, 1949.

Rise and Fall of the Great Lakes. Produced by Bill Mason, NFB, 1968.

River with a Problem. Produced by David Bairstow, NFB, 1961.

Soils for Tomorrow. Produced by Alvin Armstrong, NFB, 1945.

Song of the Mountains. Produced by NFB, 1947.

Stefansson: The Arctic Prophet. Produced by John Kemeny, NFB, 1965.

The Strategy of Metals. Produced by Stuart Legg, NFB, 1941.

The Things I Cannot Change. Produced by John Kemeny, NFB, 1967.

Timber Front. Produced by Stanley Hawes and Frank Badgley, NFB, 1940.

Tomorrow Is Too Late. Produced by David Bairstow, NFB, 1974.

Trees Are a Crop. Produced by Evelyn Cherry, NFB, 1950.

Water for Prairies. Produced by Lawrence Cherry, NFB, 1950.

Windbreaks on the Prairies. Produced by Evelyn Cherry, NFB, 1943.

The World at Your Feet. Produced by Michael Spencer, NFB, 1953.

You Are on Indian Land. Produced by George C. Stoney, NFB, 1969.

Primary Sources

Cyanamid of Canada. *Your Farm and How to Keep It Productive*. Montréal: Cyanamid, 1959.

Grierson, John. "The Documentary Idea." *Complete Photographer* 4, no. 92 (1942): 83–86.

———. "A Film Policy for Canada." *Canadian Affairs* 1 (1944): 3–15.

———. "Memo to Michelle About Decentralizing the Means of Production." *CFC/SN Newsletter* 8 (1972): 4–7.

Mason, Bill. *Canoescapes*. Toronto: Stoddart, 1995.

———. *Path of the Paddle*. Toronto: Van Nostrand Reinhold, 1980.

———. "Perspectives on Wilderness and Creativity." *Park News* 19, no. 2 (1982): 9–11.

———. *Song of the Paddle*. Toronto: Key Porter Books, 1988.

Richardson, Boyce. *Strangers Devour the Land*. Vancouver: Douglas & McIntyre, 1991.

Rousseau, Jacques. "Northern Research Reports: Botany: By Canoe Across the Ungava Peninsula via the Kogaluk and Payne Rivers." *Arctic* 1, no. 2 (1948): 133–35.

———. "Toundra." *Extrait de liaison*, January 1950, 31–35.

———. "À travers l'Ungava." *Actualité économique* 25 (1949): 83–120.

———. "The Vegetation and Life Zones of George River, Eastern Ungava and the Welfare of the Natives." *Arctic* 1, no. 2 (1948): 93–96.

Wilkinson, Doug. *Land of the Long Day*. Toronto: Clarke, Irwin, 1955.

Government Publications and Documents

An Act Respecting the National Film Board. R.S.C. 1950.

An Act to Create a National Film Board. R.S.C. 1939.

Advisory Committee on Post-War Reconstruction. *Final Report of the Subcommittee*. Ottawa: Edmond Cloutier, 1944.

Canada. *Lands, Parks and Forests Branch: Report for the Fiscal Year Ended March 31, 1939*. Ottawa: Department of Mines and Resources, 1939.

———. *Report of the Royal Commission on National Development in the Arts, Letters and Sciences*. Ottawa: King's Printer, 1951.

———. *Wisdom's Heritage: The National Parks of Canada*. Ottawa: Department of Northern Affairs and National Resources, 1957.

Hare, H. R. *Little Chats on Farm Management*. Ottawa: Economics Division—Marketing Service, Dominion Department of Agriculture, 1943.

National Film Board. *Canada: A Year of the Land*. Ottawa: Queen's Printer, 1967.

Ontario Advisory Committee on Pollution. *Report of the Committee Appointed to Inquire into and Report upon the Pollution of Air, Soil, and Water in the Townships of Dunnville, Moulton, and Sherbrooke, Haldimand County*. Toronto: Queen's Printer, 1968.

Secondary Sources

Abele, Frances. "Canadian Contradictions: Forty Years of Northern Political Development." *Arctic* 40, no. 4 (1987): 310–20.

Anderson, Benedict. *Imagined Communities: Reflections on the Spread of Nationalism*. 1983. Reprint, New York: Verso, 1991.

Atwood, Margaret. *Strange Things: The Malevolent North in Canadian Literature*. Oxford: Clarendon, 1995.

Balazs, Béla. "Theory of the Film." In *Film Theory and Criticism: Introductory Reading*, 3rd ed., edited by Gerald Mast and Marshall Cohen, 255–64. Oxford: Oxford University Press, 1985.

Balpataky, Katherine. "Call of the Wild." Excerpted from *Canadian Wildlife*, Winter 2004. *Hinterland Who's Who: 50 Years*. https://www.hww.ca/en/about-us/50th/history.html.

Banfield, A. W. F. "Review of *Never Cry Wolf*." *Canadian Field Naturalist* 78, no. 1 (1964): 52–53.

Berton, Pierre. *The Mysterious North*. Toronto: McClelland & Stewart, 1956.

Bocking, Stephen. "Science and Spaces in the Northern Environment." *Environmental History* 12 (2007): 867–94.

Booklist. "*Cree Hunters of Mistassini* Film Review." November 1975.

Bousé, Derek. *Wildlife Films*. Philadelphia: University of Philadelphia Press, 2000.

Braun, Bruce. *The Intemperate Rainforest: Nature, Culture, and Power on Canada's West Coast*. Minneapolis: University of Minnesota Press, 2002.

Brereton, Pat. *Hollywood Utopia: Ecology in Contemporary American Cinema*. Bristol: Intellect, 2005.

Buchanan, Donald. "The Projection of Canada." *University of Toronto Quarterly* 13, no. 4 (1944): 298–305.

Buck, Ken. *Bill Mason: Wilderness Artist from Heart to Hand*. Calgary: Rocky Mountain Books, 2005.

Burnett, Alexander J. *A Passion for Wildlife: The History of the Canadian Wildlife Service*. Vancouver: UBC Press, 2003.

Burt, Jonathan. *Animals in Film*. London: Reaktion, 2002.

Campbell, Claire. "'It Was Canadian, Then Typically Canadian': Revisiting Wilderness at Historic Sites." *British Journal of Canadian Studies* 21, no. 1 (2008): 5–34.

Carlson, Hans. *Home Is the Hunter*. Vancouver: UBC Press, 2009.

Carson, Rachel. *Silent Spring*. New York: Houghton Mifflin Harcourt, 1962.

Cavell, Janice. "Arctic Exploration in Canadian Print Culture, 1890–1930." *Papers of the Bibliographical Society of Canada* 44, no. 2 (2006): 7–43.

———. *Tracing the Connected Narrative: Arctic Exploration in British Print Culture, 1818–1860*. Toronto: University of Toronto Press, 2008.

Chris, Cynthia. *Watching Wildlife*. Minneapolis: University of Minnesota Press, 2007.

Clark-Jones, Melissa. *A Staple State: Canadian Industrial Resources in Cold War*. Toronto: University of Toronto Press, 1987.

Cox, Kirwan. "Canada." In *Encyclopedia of Documentary Film*, edited by Ian Aitken, 125–36. New York: Routledge, 2006.

Creighton, Donald. *The Commercial Empire of the St. Lawrence 1760–1850*. New Haven, CT: Yale University Press, 1937.

Cronin, J. Keri. *Manufacturing National Park Nature: Photography, Ecology, and the Wilderness Industry of Jasper*. Vancouver: UBC Press, 2012.

Cronon, William, ed. *Uncommon Ground: Rethinking the Human Place in Nature*. New York: W. W. Norton, 1995.

Cubitt, Sean. *EcoMedia: Key Issues*. New York: Rodopi, 2005.

Davidson, Peter. *The Idea of the North*. London: Reaktion, 2005.

Denisko, Olga. "Pot Pourri." *NFB Newsletter*, Summer 1975.

———. "Working in the Private Film Industry." *Interlock* 4–5 (1976): 15–20.

Desbiens, Caroline. *Power from the North: Territory, Identity, and the Culture of Hydroelectricity in Québec*. Vancouver: UBC Press, 2013.

Diebel, Linda. "The Aftermath: Natives Settle for 150 Million." *Gazette* (Montréal), 16 November 1974.

Dixon, Guy. "Budget Cuts? The National Film Board Is Not Afraid." *Globe and Mail*, 16 April 2012. https://www.theglobeandmail.com/arts/film/budget -cuts-national-film-board-is-not-afraid/article4100642/.

Dowie, Mark. *Losing Ground: American Environmentalism at the Close of the Twentieth Century*. Cambridge, MA: MIT Press, 1995.

Druick, Zoe. "Meeting at the Poverty Line: Government Policy, Social Work, and Media Activism in the Challenge for Change Program." In *Challenge for Change: Activist Documentary at the National Film Board of Canada*, edited by Thomas Waugh, Michael Brendan Baker, and Ezra Winton, 337–53. Montréal and Kingston: McGill-Queen's University Press, 2010.

———. *Projecting Canada: Government Policy and Documentary Film at the National Film Board*. Montréal and Kingston: McGill-Queen's University Press, 2007.

Dunaway, Finis. *Natural Visions: The Power of Images in American Environmental Reform*. Chicago: University of Chicago Press, 2005.

Dyce, Matt, and Jonathan Peyton. "Magical Realism: Canadian Geography on Screen in the 1950s." *NiCHE*, 21 February 2018. https://niche-canada.org/ 2018/02/21/magical-regionalism-canadian-geography-on-screen-in-the -1950s/#_edn29.

Evans, Clinton. *War on Weeds in the Prairie West: An Environmental History*. Calgary: University of Calgary Press, 2002.

Evans, Gary. *In the National Interest: A Chronicle of the National Film Board of Canada from 1949 to 1989*. Toronto: University of Toronto Press, 1991.

Evernden, Neil. *The Social Creation of Nature*. Baltimore: Johns Hopkins University Press, 1992.

Farish, Matthew, and P. Whitney Lackenbauer. "High Modernism in the Arctic: Planning Frobisher Bay and Inuvik." *Journal of Historical Geography* 35, no. 3 (2009): 517–44.

Feit, Harvey A. "Hunting and the Quest for Power: The James Bay Cree and the Whitemen in the 20th Century." In *Native Peoples: The Canadian Experience*, edited by R. Bruce Morrison and C. Roderick Wilson, 181–223. Toronto: McClelland & Stewart, 1995.

Fienup-Riordan, Ann. *Freeze Frame: Alaska Eskimos in the Movies*. Seattle: University of Washington Press, 1995.

Francis, Douglas R. *The Technological Imperative in Canada: An Intellectual History*. Vancouver: UBC Press, 2009.

Frye, Northrop. *The Bush Garden: Essays on the Canadian Imagination*. Toronto: Anansi, 1971.

Fullerton, Christopher. "A Changing of the Guard: Regional Planning in Ottawa, 1945–1974." *Urban History Review* 34, no. 1 (2005): 100–112.

Gandy, Matthew. *Concrete and Clay: Reworking Nature in New York City*. Cambridge, MA: MIT Press, 2003.

Gillis, R. Peter, and Thomas Roach. *Lost Initiatives: Canada's Forest Industries, Forest Policy, and Forest Conservation*. New York: Greenwood, 1986.

Gittings, Christopher E. *Canadian National Cinema: Ideology, Difference, and Representation*. New York: Routledge, 2002.

Globe and Mail. "Insecticide Film Shelved: Pressure Put on NFB Former Producer Says." 1 February 1963.

———. "River Pollution a Serious Matter." 15 July 1955.

Goetz, William. "The Canadian Wartime Documentary: *Canada Carries On* and *The World in Action*." *Cinema Journal* 16, no. 2 (Spring 1977): 59–80.

Gottlieb, Robert. *Forcing the Spring: The Transformation of the Environmental Movement*. Washington, DC: Island Press, 1993.

Grace, Sherrill. *Canada and the Idea of the North*. Montréal and Kingston: McGill-Queen's University Press, 2001.

Grant, Shelagh. "Myths of North in Canadian Ethos." *Northern Review* 3, no. 4 (1989): 15–41.

Gray, Walter. "A Perfect Example of Pollution." *Globe and Mail*, 1 June 1961.

Guynn, William. *A Cinema of Nonfiction*. Cranbury: Fairleigh Dickinson University Press, 1990.

Haffner, Jeanne. *The View from Above: The Science of Social Space*. Cambridge, MA: MIT Press, 2013.

Haliburton, R. G. *The Men of the North and Their Place in History: A Lecture Delivered Before the Montréal Literary Club*. Montréal: John Lovell, 1869.

Hamelin, Louis-Edmond. *Canadian Nordicity: It's Your North Too*. Montréal: Harvest House, 1979.

Harcourt, Peter. "Images and Information: The Dialogic Structure of *Bûcherons de la Manouane* by Arthur Lamothe." In *Candid Eyes: Essays on Canadian Documentaries*, edited by Jim Leach and Jeannette Sloniowski, 61–74. Toronto: University of Toronto Press, 2003.

———. "The Innocent Eye: An Aspect of the Work of the National Film Board of Canada." *Sight and Sound* 34, no. 1 (1965): 19–23.

Harper, Graeme, and Jonathan Rayner, eds. *Cinema and Landscape*. Bristol: Intellect, 2010.

Harris, Lawren. "Revelation of Art in Canada." *Canadian Theosophist* 7, no. 5 (1926): 86–88.

Harris, Richard. *Creeping Conformity: How Canada Became Suburban*. Toronto: University of Toronto Press, 2004.

Hays, Samuel P. *Beauty, Health, and Permanence: Environmental Politics in the United States, 1955–1985*. New York: Cambridge University Press, 1987.

———. *Explorations in Environmental History: Essays*. Pittsburgh: University of Pittsburgh Press, 1998.

Heinimann, David. "Latitude Rising: Historical Continuity in Canadian Nordicity." *Journal of Canadian Studies* 28, no. 2 (1993): 134–39.

Hénaut, Dorothy Todd, and Bonnie Sherr Klein. "In the Hands of Citizens: A Video Report." *CFC/SN Newsletter* 4 (1969): 2–5.

Hepworth, John. "Cinema 65." *Loyola News*, 26 March 1965.

Hochman, Jhan. *Green Cultural Studies: Nature in Film, Novel, and Theory*. Moscow: University of Idaho Press, 1998.

Hodgins, Bruce, and Jamie Benidickson. *The Temagami Experience: Recreation, Resources and Aboriginal Rights in the Northern Ontario Wilderness*. Toronto: University of Toronto Press, 1989.

Huhndorf, Shari. "Nanook and His Contemporaries: Imagining Eskimos in American Culture, 1897–1922." *Critical Inquiry* 20, no. 1 (2000): 122–48.

Hulan, Renée. *Northern Experience and Myths of Canadian Culture*. Montréal and Kingston: McGill-Queen's University Press, 2002.

Ingram, David. *Green Screen: Environmentalism and Hollywood Cinema*. 1998. Reprint, Exeter: University of Exeter Press, 2004.

Innis, Harold. *Changing Concepts of Time*. Toronto: Rowman & Littlefield, 1952.

———. *The Fur Trade in Canada: An Introduction to Canadian Economic History*. 1930. Reprint, Toronto: University of Toronto Press, 1999.

Irwin, Arthur. "The Canadian." *Maclean's*, 1 February 1950.

Irwin, Joan. "Film Explains Life of Cree." *Montréal Star*, 2 July 1974.

Ivakhiv, Adrian. *Ecologies of the Moving Image: Cinema, Affect, Nature*. Waterloo, ON: Wilfrid Laurier University Press, 2013.

Jones, D. B. *Movies and Memoranda: An Interpretive History of the National Film Board of Canada*. Ottawa: Canadian Film Institute, 1981.

Jones, Karen. "'Never Cry Wolf': Science, Sentiment, and the Literary Rehabilitation of *Canis Lupus*." *Canadian Historical Review* 84 (2001): 65–94.

Jones-Imhotep, Edward. "Communicating the North: Scientific Practice and Canadian Postwar Identity." *Osiris* 24, no. 1 (2009): 146–47.

Kaplan, E. Ann. *Looking for the Other: Feminism, Film, and the Imperial Gaze*. London: Routledge, 1997.

Keller, W. Phillip. *Canada's Wild Glory*. Toronto: Nelson, Foster, and Scott, 1961.

Kracauer, Siegfried. *Theory of Film: The Redemption of Physical Reality*. Oxford: Oxford University Press, 1960.

Krech, Shepard, III. *The Ecological Indian*. New York: Norton, 1999.

Lackenbauer, P. Whitney, and Matthew Farish. "The Cold War on Canadian Soil: Militarizing a Northern Environment." *Environmental History* 12 (2007): 920–50.

Latour, Bruno. *Science in Action: How to Follow Scientists and Engineers through Society*. Cambridge, MA: Harvard University Press, 1987.

Leach, Jim, and Jeannette Sloniowski, eds. *Candid Eyes: Essays on Canadian Documentaries*. Toronto: University of Toronto Press, 2003.

Lefebvre, Martin, ed. *Landscape and Film*. London: Routledge, 2006.

Loo, Tina. "High Modernism, Conflict, and the Nature of Change in Canada: A Look at *Seeing like a State*." *Canadian Historical Review* 97, no. 1 (2016): 34–58.

———. *States of Nature: Conserving Canada's Wildlife in the Twentieth Century*. Vancouver: UBC Press, 2007.

Loomis, Chauncey. "The Arctic Sublime." In *Nature and the Victorian Imagination*, edited by U. C. Knoepflmacher and G. B. Tennyson, 95–112. Berkeley: University of California Press, 1977.

Lopez, Barry. *Of Wolves and Men*. New York: Simon and Schuster, 1978.

Low, Brian J. *NFB Kids: Portrayals of Children by the National Film Board of Canada, 1939–1989*. Waterloo, ON: Wilfrid Laurier University Press, 2002.

Low, Colin. "Grierson and Challenge for Change." In *Challenge for Change: Activist Documentary at the National Film Board of Canada*, edited by Thomas Waugh, Michael Brendan Baker, and Ezra Winton, 16–23. Montréal and Kingston: McGill-Queen's University Press, 2010.

MacDonald, Scott. *The Garden in the Machine: A Field Guide to Independent Films About Place*. Berkeley: University of California Press, 2001.

MacDougall, David. *Transcultural Cinema*. Princeton, NJ: Princeton University Press, 1998.

MacEachern, Alan. *Natural Selections: National Parks in Atlantic Canada, 1935–1970*. Montréal and Kingston: McGill-Queen's University Press, 2001.

Macfarlane, Daniel. *Negotiating a River: Canada, the US, and the Creation of the St. Lawrence Seaway*. Vancouver: UBC Press, 2014.

MacKay, Bruce. "Theme Song." In *Cry of the Wild*, NFB, 1972.

Mackenzie, Scott, ed. *Films on Ice: Cinemas of the Arctic*. Edinburgh: Edinburgh University Press, 2014.

Marchessault, Janine. "Amateur Video and Challenge for Change." In *Challenge for Change: Activist Documentary at the National Film Board of Canada*, edited by Thomas Waugh, Michael Brendan Baker, and Ezra Winton, 354–65. Montréal and Kingston: McGill-Queen's University Press, 2010.

Marsh, Kevin. *Drawing Lines in the Forest: Creating Wilderness Areas in the Pacific Northwest*. Seattle: University of Washington Press, 2010.

McCormick, John. *Reclaiming Paradise: The Global Environmental Movement*. Bloomington: Indiana University Press, 1989.

McLaughlin, Mark. "Green Shoots: Aerial Insecticide Spraying and the Growth of Environmental Consciousness in New Brunswick." *Acadiensis* 40, no. 1 (2011): 3–23.

———. "Rise of the Eco-Comics: The State, Environmental Education and Canadian Comic Books, 1971–1975." *Material Culture Review* 77 (2013): 3–23.

McMillan, Robert. "Ethnology and the NFB: The Laura Boulton Mysteries." *Canadian Journal of Film Studies* 1, no. 2 (1991): 67–82.

Merchant, Carolyn. "Shades of Darkness: Race and Environmental History." *Environmental History* 8, no. 3 (2003): 380–94.

Michéa, J. P. *Annual Report of the National Museum for the Fiscal Year 1948–1949*. Ottawa: Edmond Cloutier, 1949.

Mills, C. Wright. *White Collar: The American Middle Classes*. Oxford: Oxford University Press, 1951.

Mitchell, W. J. T. *Landscape and Power*. 1994. Reprint, Chicago: University of Chicago Press, 2002.

Mitman, Gregg. *Reel Nature: America's Romance with Wildlife on Film.* Cambridge, MA: Harvard University Press, 1999.

Moore, Rick. "Canada's Challenge for Change: Documentary Film and Video as an Exercise of Power through the Production of Cultural Reality." PhD diss., University of Oregon, 1988.

Morton, W. L. *The Canadian Identity.* Toronto: University of Toronto Press, 1961.

Moss, John. "The Cartography of Dreams." *Journal of Canadian Studies* 28, no. 2 (1993): 140–58.

Mowat, Farley. *Never Cry Wolf.* 1963. Reprint, New York: Little, Brown, 1999.

Murton, James. *Creating a Modern Countryside: Liberalism and Land Resettlement in British Columbia.* Vancouver: UBC Press, 2007.

Nash, Roderick. "The American Wilderness in Historical Perspective." *American Society for Environmental History* 6, no. 4 (1963): 2–13.

———. *Wilderness and the American Mind.* New Haven, CT: Yale University Press, 1982.

Nelles, H. V. *The Politics of Development: Forests, Mines, and Hydro-Electric Power in Ontario, 1849–1941.* Toronto: Macmillan, 1974.

Nichols, Bill. *Representing Reality: Issues and Concepts in Documentary.* Bloomington: Indiana University Press, 1991.

Niezen, Ronald. "Power and Dignity: The Social Consequences of Hydro-Electric Development for the James Bay Cree." *Canadian Review of Sociology and Anthropology* 30, no. 4 (1993): 510–29.

Nye, David. *American Technological Sublime.* Cambridge, MA: MIT Press, 1994.

Nygren, Joshua. "The Bulldozer in the Watershed: Conservation, Water, and Technological Optimism in the Post–World War II United States." *Environmental History* 21 (2016): 126–36.

O'Connor, Ryan. "An Ecological Call to Arms: *The Air of Death* and the Origins of Environmentalism in Ontario." *Ontario History* 105, no. 1 (2013): 19–46.

———. *The First Green Wave: Pollution Probe and the Origins of Environmental Activism in Ontario.* Vancouver: UBC Press, 2015.

Parkin, George R. *Imperial Federalism: The Problem of National Unity.* London: Macmillan, 1892.

Payne, Carol. *The Official Picture: The National Film Board of Canada's Still Photography Division and the Image of Canada, 1941–1971.* Montréal and Kingston: McGill-Queen's University Press, 2013.

Pearson, Lester B. "Canada Looks 'Down North.'" *Foreign Affairs: An American Quarterly Review* 24, no. 4 (1946): 639–48.

Peloquin, Claude, and Fikrit Berkes. "Local Knowledge, Subsistence Harvests and Social-Ecological Complexity in James Bay." *Human Ecology* 37 (2009): 533–45.

Pick, Anat, and Guinevere Narraway, eds. *Screening Nature: Cinema Beyond the Human.* New York: Berghahn, 2013.

Potter, Russell. *Arctic Spectacles: The Frozen North in Visual Culture, 1818–1875.* Montréal and Kingston: McGill-Queen's University Press, 2007.

Raffan, James. *Fire in the Bones: Bill Mason and the Canadian Canoeing Tradition.* Toronto: HarperCollins, 1996.

Read, Jennifer. "'Let Us Heed the Voice of Youth': Laundry Detergents, Phosphates and the Emergence of the Environmental Movement in Ontario." *Journal of the Canadian Historical Association* 7 (1996): 227–50.

Richardson, Boyce. "Doctorate for Philip Awashish." *Nation*, 11 September 2009. http://www.nationnewsarchives.ca/article/doctorate-for-philip -awashish/.

Rohmer, Éric, and Louis Marcorelles. "Entretien avec Jean Rouch." *Cahiers du cinéma* 144 (June 1963): 1–22.

Rome, Adam. *The Bulldozer in the Countryside: Suburban Sprawl and the Rise of American Environmentalism.* New York: Cambridge University Press, 2001.
———. "'Give Earth a Chance': The Environmental Movement and the 1960s." *Journal of American History* 90, no. 2 (2003): 525–54.

Rose, Barbara Wade. *"Budge": What Happened to Canada's King of Film?* Toronto: ECW Press, 1998.

Rosen, Philip. "Nation and Anti-Nation: Concepts of National Cinema in the 'New' Media Era." *Diaspora* 5, no. 3 (1996): 375–402.

Russell, Edmund. *War and Nature: Fighting Humans and Insects with Chemicals from WW1 to Silent Spring.* Cambridge: Cambridge University Press, 2001.

Rust, Stephen, and Salma Monani. "Introduction: Cuts to Dissolves—Defining and Situating Ecocinema Studies." In *Ecocinema Theory and Practice*, edited by Stephen Rust, Salma Monani, and Sean Cubitt, 1–14. New York: Routledge, 2013.

Sandlos, John, and Arn Keeling. "Claiming the New North: Development Colonialism at the Pine Point Mine, Northwest Territories." *Environment and History* 2 (2012): 7–18.

Scott, James C. *Seeing like a State: How Certain Schemes to Improve the Human Condition Have Failed.* New Haven, CT: Yale University Press, 1998.

Shields, Rob. *Places on the Margin: Alternative Geographies of Modernity.* London: Routledge, 1991.

Smith, Gordon. "Weather Stations in the Canadian North and Arctic Sovereignty." *Journal of Military and Strategic Studies* 11, no. 3 (2009): 1–63.

Sowiak, Christine. "Contemporary Canadian Art: Locating Identity." In *A Passion for Identity: Canadian Studies for the 21st Century*, edited by Beverly Jean Rasporich and David Taras, 251–73. Scarborough, ON: Nelson Thomson Learning, 2001.

Starblanket, Noel. "A Voice for Indians: An Indian Film Crew." *CFC/SN Newsletter* 2 (1968): 11.

Stefansson, Vilhjalmur. *The Friendly Arctic: The Story of Five Years in Polar Regions*. New York: Macmillan, 1922.

Stevens, Peter. *Brink of Reality: New Canadian Documentary Film and Video*. Toronto: Between the Lines, 1993.

Stewart, Michelle. "*Cree Hunters of Mistassini*: CFC and Aboriginal Rights." In *Challenge for Change: Activist Documentary at the National Film Board of Canada*, edited by Thomas Waugh, Michael Brendan Baker, and Ezra Winton, 180–89. Montréal and Kingston: McGill-Queen's University Press, 2010.

Sutter, Paul. *Driven Wild: How the Fight Against Automobiles Launched the Modern Wilderness Movement*. Seattle: University of Washington Press, 2002.

Tagg, John. *The Burden of Representations: Essays on Photographies and Histories*. London: Macmillan, 1988.

Tester, Frank, and Peter Kulchyski. *Tammarniit (Mistakes): Inuit Relocations in the Eastern Arctic, 1939–63*. Vancouver: UBC Press, 1994.

Turner, James. *The Promise of Wilderness: American Environmental Politics since 1964*. Seattle: University of Washington Press, 2012.

Watson, Patrick. "Challenge for Change." In *Canadian Film Reader*, edited by S. Feldman and J. Nelson, 112–19. Toronto: Peter Martin Associates, 1977.

Waugh, Thomas, Michael Brendan Baker, and Ezra Winton, eds. *Challenge for Change: Activist Documentary at the National Film Board of Canada*. Montréal and Kingston: McGill-Queen's University Press, 2010.

White, Jerry, ed. *The Cinema of Canada*. New York: Wallflower, 2006.

Whyte, William. *The Organization Man*. New York: Simon and Schuster, 1956.

Wilkinson, Doug. "A Vanishing Canadian." *Beaver*, Spring 1959.

Wynn, Graeme. *Canada and Arctic North America*. Vancouver: UBC Press, 2007.

———. "Foreword: Dignity and Power." In *Home Is the Hunter*, by Hans Carlson, xi–xxi. Vancouver: UBC Press, 2009.

———. *North America and Arctic: An Environmental History*. Santa Barbara, CA: ABC Clio, 2007.

———. "Northern Exposures." *Environmental History* 12, no. 2 (2007): 388–90.

Index

Canada, Government of (*continued*)
cuts to NFB in 2012, 180; and
deforestation, 18; founding of
NFB and its role, 3; and James Bay
project, 154; methods of communicating about environment, 183n8;
and NFB funding, 96; and *North*,
87–88; and northern development,
81, 89–91; opposed to idea of documentary on James Bay, 157; and
Ottawa River pollution, 114–15, 117,
118; programs to support farmers,
37; and report on *The Air of Death*,
113; represented in *Windbreaks on
the Prairies*, 35–36; role in creating
Challenge for Change, 146, 147, 150;
role in relocation of Fogo Islanders,
148; sponsorship of *The Enduring
Wilderness*, 119; use of documentary
filmmaking to, 176; and use of NFB
to explain welfare state, 31–32; use of
NFB to further agricultural aims, 43;
wage and price controls during war,
21; and wolf policy, 129–31. *See also*
Canadian Wildlife Service (CWS);
Department of Agriculture (DOA);
government/statist view
Canada: A Year of the Land, 4, 59
Canada Carries On, 14
Canada's New Northwest (government
report), 90
Canada: The Land, 174
Canadian Broadcasting Corporation
(CBC), 112–13
Canadian Landscape, 56–58, 59, 60, 174
Canadian Pulp and Paper Association,
115–16
Canadian Radio-Television and
Telecommunications Commission
(CRTC), 113
Canadian Wheat Story, 26–27, 175
Canadian Wildlife Service (CWS):
contracts NFB to refurbish its
image, 132–33; criticized in *Never Cry
Wolf*, 131–32; and *Hinterland Who's
Who*, 120; Mason's film technique
compared to, 99; role in *Death of a
Legend*, 134, 136–38; and slaughter of
wolves, 130; view of wildlife, 142

candid eye filmmaking, 101–2
Canning, Bill, 88
Canoescapes, 133
caribou, 72, 91, 130, 131
Carlson, Hans, 144, 165
Carson, Rachel, 113–14
Challenge for Change (CFC): assess-
ments of its success, 150–52;
creation of, 146, 147–48; *Cree
Hunters of the Mistassini*, 152; Fogo
Island films, 148–49; funding of, 150;
impact on documentary cinema,
199n26; and lead up to *Cree Hunters*,
156–57; and legacy of *Cree Hunters of
the Mistassini*, 171–72; and political
effect of *Cree Hunters of the Mistassini*, 165–70, 177; radical films of,
149–50, 177; and self-examination
projects, 149–50
Chapman, Christopher: *The Enduring
Wilderness*, 118, 122–24, 125, 127, 142;
technique of, 178; view of wilderness, 9, 98
Chapman, R. A., 110–11
Chemical Conquest, 46–47, 48–49, 105, 106
Cherry, Evelyn: career of, 32–34; film
techniques used to portray farming,
39–41; and *Five Steps to Better Farm
Living*, 37–38, 39–40; hired by NFB,
34–35; how her films reflected a
state view of farming, 32, 33, 36–37,
41–42, 43, 50; leaves NFB, 43; praise
for NFB nature films, 13; technique
of, 178–79; and *Windbreaks on the
Prairies*, 34–36, 38, 39, 175
Chrétien, Jean, 154
cinephotomicrography, 45, 50
Class Project: The Garbage Movie, 178
Coal Face Canada, 15–16
Cold War, 81–82, 89, 90, 103
colonialism: and filming of *Cree Hunters of Mistassini*, 164–65; of Inuit
films, 62, 63, 72; of James Bay Cree,
143–45; and *Land of the Long Day*, 67;
and Northern films, 7–8, 83, 86–87;
and salvage ethnography, 70; and
view of Indigenous peoples, 30
conservation: and Mason's *Death of
a Legend*, 133, 134, 176; and more

recent NFB films, 177–78; and shift to environmentalist point of view, 97–98, 102–3; and war time films, 16–19, 24, 25; and wolves, 129, 130
Constantine, Brother, 26
Corral, 100
Coupon Value, 34
Courneyer, Robert, 156
Crabtree, Graham, 119
Crawley, Radford, 56–58, 60, 61, 74
Cree Hunters of the Mistassini: Cree perspective in, 9, 152, 158–63, 178; criticizes assimilation of Indigenous people, 152; as departure from typical NFB nature film, 145–46; development of, 155–57; as example of virtuoso filmmaking, 178–79; importance and legacy of, 171–72; limitations of, 163–65; political message of, 157–58, 177; release and political effect of, 165–70, 179
Cree of James Bay: adapts modern technology to cause, 164–65; and colonialism, 143–45; and development of idea for *Cree Hunters*, 145–46, 152, 155–57; fighting James Bay project, 153–55; and Mistassini settlement, 200n45; and *Our Land Is Our Life*, 152, 155,
Cree of James Bay (*continued*) 158, 167; perspective of seen in *Cree Hunters of Mistassini*, 158–63; political effect of *Cree Hunters* on, 165–70, 177; spirituality of, 161–62; view of environment, 154–55
Creighton, Donald, 60
Cry of the Wild, 98–99, 128, 140–41
Cyanamid of Canada, 108

Dale, Rick, 169
Daly, Tom, 100
Daniels, Roy, 149
DDT, 48, 104, 105, 109, 110
Deadly Dilemma, 111–12
Death of a Legend, 98–99, 128, 133–40
De Aubert de la Rue, Edgar, 74
Department of Agriculture (DOA): and *Chemical Conquest*, 48; and NFB films on agriculture, 11–12; and *Poisons*,

Pests and People, 108, 109, 112; use of Cherry's films, 42; view of science, 44; and *The World at Your Feet*, 45–46
Department of Indian Affairs and Northern Development (DIAND), 87–88
Department of Lands and Forests (Ontario), 138
Department of Mines and Resources, 90
Department of National Defence, 91
Depression, Great, 32
Diamond, Billy, 153, 168–69
Diefenbaker, John, 90
Domville, James de B., 82–83
Down North, 86–87
Drainie, John, 64
Druick, Zoe, 151–52, 183n5
D'Ulisse, André, 180
Dunn, Willie, 149

Eagles, Darrell, 133
ecological Indian myth, 68, 163
Edmonds, Robert, 15
Enduring Wilderness, The: described, 118–20, 122–25, 126–27; as expression of Canadian identity, 174; occupies middle ground in philosophy of environmental films, 98; state friendly message of, 128, 142; view of wilderness in, 145
environment: belief that Canada is shaped by its, 60–61; D. Bairstow's view of, 115–16; government view of, 7, 13, 43–44, 49–50; history of pesticide use, 107–8; Indigenous v. settler view of, 154–55; L. Gosnell's views on, 9, 115; NFBs help defining, 51–52
environmental films: *Across Arctic Ungava*, 74–76, 78, 79; *The Air of Death*, 112–13; *The Annanacks*, 72–73; and change of philosophy at NFB, 2, 96–97, 102, 170–72; *Cry of the Wild*, 140–41; *Death of a Legend*, 98–99, 128, 133–40; *The Enduring Wilderness*, 118–20, 122–25, 126–27; as factor in environmental movement, 104–5; legacy of later, 141–42; of Mason, 128–29; *Poison, Pests and People*, 105,

Harris, Lawren, 55–56
Hawes, Stanley, 24
Hays, Samuel P., 103
Hazelton, L. W., 110
Heinz (company), 109
Hénaut, Dorothy T., 150
High Arctic: Life on the Land, 79–82
high modernism: explained, 5–6; films
    offering alternative to, 146; of NFB
    films in 1940s-50s, 13, 175–76; of
    NFB films in 1960s, 141; of Ti-Jean
    series, 184n17
Highways North, 85
Hinterland Who's Who, 1, 120, 132
Hodgins, Eric, 47
Holling, Holling C., 128
How to Build an Igloo, 63–64
Huhndorf, Shari, 67
Hutchinson, Bruce, 4, 59

Ianzelo, Tony, 145, 155, 160, 164, 169
Idlout, Joseph, 64–67, 68, 190n53
Indigenous peoples: absent from *Can-
    adian Landscape*, 58; and film work
    for Challenge for Change, 149–50,
    152; and idealized view of ecological
    Indian, 68, 163; ignored in early
    NFB films, 174; and later change in
    NFB environmental films, 170–72;
    mentioned in *Death of a Legend*, 134;
    mentioned in *Down North*, 86, 87;
    political effect of *Cree Hunters of the
    Mistassini* on, 165–70; portrayal of in
    early films, 7–8, 30; view of environ-
    ment, 154–55. *See also* colonialism;
    Cree Hunters of the Mistassini; Cree of
    James Bay; Inuit
Innis, Harold, 60, 93
Inuit: *Across Arctic Ungava*, 77, 78; *The
    Annanacks*, 72–73; *Arctic Hunters*, 62;
    colonialism in films, 62, 63, 72; D.
    Wilkinson's view of, 70, 74; *Eskimo
    Arts and Crafts*, 62; films produced
    by, 193n130; *How to Build an Igloo*,
    63–64; *Land of the Long Day*, 64–67;
    and *Nanook of the North*, 190n42;
    A Northern Challenge, 91; post-war
    changes for, 70–71; romanticized
    lifestyle of, 67–68; and salvage

ethnography, 69–70; seen as time-
    less, 70
Irwin, Arthur, 59
Irwin, Joan, 169–70
Ivakhiv, Adrian, 9–10, 70

Jackson, A. Y., 56–57
Jackson, Stanley, 27
James Bay and Northern Québec
    Agreement, 154
James Bay hydroelectric project,
    153–55, 158–59, 163, 165–70, 177
Job's Garden, 199n33
Jolly, Ronnie, 162
Jones, Dallas, 23, 24, 25, 26, 27
Jones, Douglas, 116
Jones, Karen, 132
Jones-Imhotep, Edward, 82

Kadloo (Inuit hunter), 65
Kaplan, E. Ann, 63
Keller, W. Phillip, 126
Kemeny, John, 146–47, 148
Klein, Bonnie S., 150, 199n26
Kolenoski, George, 137
Kracauer, Siegfried, 10
Krech III, Shepard, 68
Kunuk, Zacharias, 3
Kuyt, Ernie, 137–38

La Grande hydroelectric project,
    144–45, 157, 158, 159
Lampman, Archibald, 114
Land in Trust, 28, 40
Land of Pioneers, 85
Land of the Long Day, 64–67
Landseer, Edwin, 55
Last Voyage of Henry Hudson, The, 74
Latour, Bruno, 83–84
Leacock, Stephen, 54
Lefebvre, Martin, 52
Lemieux, Hector, 86
Leopold, Aldo, 135
Let's Look at Water, 44
Livingston, John, 132
Look to the Forests, 28
Look to the North, 28
Lorentz, Pare, 187n52
Low, Colin, 147, 148–49, 150, 157